Praise for *Persian Girls*

"[A] lyrical and disturbing memoir." —*Publishers Weekly*

"[A] poignant, beautifully written memoir . . . a fine, profound book . . . Each scene has the shapely aura of a memory, hauled back from the deep by one telling detail. . . . [A] haunting and moving story." — JOHN FREEMAN, *Times Union*, Albany, New York

"Iran again looms large on the world stage. Rhetoric conjures fear of radical Islam and flashbacks to the Ayatollah Khomeini—images that obscure Iran's rich cultural history as Persia and ignore ordinary people torn between old and new, secular and sacred. Nahid Rachlin fills in the blanks."

—KATHLEEN MCCLAIN, *The Charlotte Observer*

"Through the touching, tragic story of two sisters, *Persian Girls* unfolds the entire drama of modern Iran. It's a beautiful, harrowing memoir of the cruelty of men toward women, and it paints the exotic scents and traditions of Tehran with the delicacy of a great novel. If you want to understand Iran, read Nahid Rachlin."

—MATT BEYNON REES, author of *The Collaborator of Bethlehem* and contributing editor, *Time*

"In elegant, beguiling, supple prose, Nahid Rachlin has chronicled the traumas and triumphs of a Persian girl, fashioning for herself a persona that is at once global and quintessentially Persian."

—ABBAS MILANI, director, Hamid & Christina Moghadam Program
    in Iranian Studies, Stanford University

"In *Persian Girls*, Nahid Rachlin tells her own story with sincerity—speaking for countless lives in many lands where survival is as exceptional as being buried under the dead weight of tradition is not."

—SALAR ABDOH, author of *Opium* and *The Poet Game*

Also by Nahid Rachlin

NOVELS

Jumping Over Fire

Foreigner

Married to a Stranger

The Heart's Desire

SHORT STORIES

Veils

Persian Girls

· A MEMOIR ·

NAHID RACHLIN

JEREMY P. TARCHER/PENGUIN

a member of Penguin Group (USA) Inc.

New York

JEREMY P. TARCHER/PENGUIN
Published by the Penguin Group
Penguin Group (USA) Inc., 375 Hudson Street, New York, New York 10014, USA •
Penguin Group (Canada), 90 Eglinton Avenue East, Suite 700, Toronto, Ontario M4P 2Y3, Canada
(a division of Pearson Penguin Canada Inc.) • Penguin Books Ltd, 80 Strand, London WC2R 0RL,
England • Penguin Ireland, 25 St Stephen's Green, Dublin 2, Ireland (a division of Penguin Books Ltd) •
Penguin Group (Australia), 250 Camberwell Road, Camberwell, Victoria 3124, Australia
(a division of Pearson Australia Group Pty Ltd) • Penguin Books India Pvt Ltd, 11 Community Centre,
Panchsheel Park, New Delhi–110 017, India • Penguin Group (NZ), 67 Apollo Drive, Rosedale,
North Shore 0632, New Zealand (a division of Pearson New Zealand Ltd) • Penguin Books
(South Africa) (Pty) Ltd, 24 Sturdee Avenue, Rosebank, Johannesburg 2196, South Africa

Penguin Books Ltd, Registered Offices: 80 Strand, London WC2R 0RL, England

First trade paperback edition 2007

All photographs are courtesy of the author.

Most Tarcher/Penguin books are available at special quantity discounts for bulk purchase for sales
promotions, premiums, fund-raising, and educational needs. Special books or book excerpts also
can be created to fit specific needs. For details, write Penguin Group (USA) Inc. Special Markets,
375 Hudson Street, New York, NY 10014.

The Library of Congress catalogued the hardcover edition as follows:

Rachlin, Nahid.
Persian girls: a memoir / by Nahid Rachlin
p.   cm.
ISBN 1-58542-520-6
1. Rachlin, Nahid.   2. Iranian American authors—Biography.   3. Iranian American
women—Biography.   4. Women—Iran—Social conditions—20th century.
5. Iran—Politics and government—1941–1979.   I. Title.
PS3568.A244Z46   2006   2006044649
813'.54—dc22
[B]

ISBN 978-1-58542-623-2 (paperback edition)

Printed in the United States of America
3   5   7   9   10   8   6   4   2

Book design by Meighan Cavanaugh

For

Pari, Manijeh, Farzaneh, Farzin,
Maryam, and Mohtaram

with love

ACKNOWLEDGMENTS

I want to express my gratitude to Ashley Shelby, whose astute comments and amazing insights into this memoir made a great difference to the outcome. I thank Gary Morris for believing in the memoir. I thank Kat Kimball and Laura Ingman at Penguin for all their help and enthusiasm. I am grateful to my family and all my friends for allowing me to be open in writing it. Special thanks to my brother, Parviz, who was of great help at crucial times of my life.

AUTHOR'S NOTE

This is a book of my memories, as I recall them, and what I was told when I was old enough to understand. I haven't interviewed family members and friends to get their impressions of certain incidents in our lives. I have changed the names of a few people, institutions, and places for the sake of privacy. I have also made minor changes and compressed certain events and dates, whenever doing so did not compromise the essence of the truth of what happened. In order to tell the story as economically as possible, I have left out or glossed over some people whom I love, their kindness, their importance in my life. My apologies to all of them.

PART ONE

Persian Girls

"You're a perfect creation of God, my dear girl. It was your destiny to be my child. As soon as a baby comes into the world an angel writes its destiny on the baby's forehead."

"I don't see any writing on my forehead," I said.

"It's written with a special invisible ink."

"Does what the angel writes stay there forever?"

"Sometimes if a person pleads with God, he might decide to tell the angel to change the writing. But no one is praying to change your destiny. I want you with me forever."

One

I have images of Maryam doing her nightly rituals in her room adjacent to mine, the door open. She kneels by her prayer rug to touch her forehead to the *mohr*. The scent of rose water she sprayed on the prayer rug and on her chador fills the air. A large, illuminated Koran stands on a wooden table on one side of the living room. She combs her hair and weaves it into a thick braid. Then she extinguishes the burgundy paraffin lamp on the mantel and comes into my room. She lies next to me and sings a lullaby, in her soft, melodious voice.

Lullaby, lullaby, my dear little child
Sparrow is sleeping
Once again the moon is high in the sky
Lullaby, lullaby, my dear lovely child
The flower went to sleep early again
Frog is silent
The pond has gone to sleep
The flower went to sleep early again
Lullaby, lullaby, my little beautiful mint flower
The pond is sleeping . . .

On summer nights we sleep under a mosquito net on the roof and she tells me stories while I look at the bright stars and the moon above. In one story a golden ladder descends from the sky and you can climb on it and go to the moon. I wait for that to happen. Every night I expect it. When nothing happens she says, "Maybe at least you will dream about it." Then I dream about it, more than once. In the dreams, I climb up the ladder until I reach the moon, touch it, then I wake.

In the morning, after her prayers, she feeds me breakfast in the living room where rays of colored light, filtering through stained-glass panes in the transom over the French doors, shine on the intricate designs of the rug. She cooks the eggs laid by chickens she keeps in a coop in the courtyard. We have bread that is delivered to the door every morning and is still warm.

I was a gift to Maryam from her younger sister, Mohtaram. I was Mohtaram's seventh baby, her fifth living child (two had died). Maryam hadn't been able to get pregnant when she was married. Then she became a widow. She had begged Mohtaram to let her adopt one of her children. Mohtaram promised her sister she could have her next child. I was that next child.

Maryam lived in the ancient neighborhood in Tehran where she and my mother grew up. The neighborhood was more or less untouched by the Shah's attempts at modernizing Iran. Little had changed there since Maryam was a child. Her neighbors were mostly working-class people, strongly observant Shia Muslims. Maryam's house was a hundred years old and, like most of the houses in the area, conformed to the standard Islamic architecture. It was set inside a courtyard with high brick walls, with no openings to the streets so that women would not have to worry about being seen unveiled by male passersby. Instead, tall French doors with stained-glass transoms opened from each room onto the courtyard and to other rooms. In the courtyard, there were three sets of staircases, one leading to the roof, one to a kitchen, one to a basement.

Maryam shared the courtyard with two other widows. Our rooms lined one side, and the porch, which extended from our rooms, was adorned with six columns engraved with animals and fruit. The communal kitchen was set off in a corner; in the center was a pool of cool, clear water used for ablutions. The courtyard was shaded by large plane and plum and pear and apple trees. The plane tree had a hollow in its trunk. Maryam had covered the floor of the hole with plastic so that I could sit inside it and play with dolls.

In autumn, Maryam and the widows filled the flower beds with roses, asters, and geraniums. Blue snapdragons crawled up the walls. A trellis against one of the brick walls supported an old grapevine with a twisted, gnarled trunk, on which Maryam lavished attention when she gardened.

"God is merciful," Maryam told me repeatedly. "He answered my prayers and sent you to me."

Alas, God wasn't merciful that day when our lives, hers and mine, underwent a sudden and irrevocable change.

❋

It was 1955. I was nine years old. The Treaty of Amity between Iran and the United States had just been signed and Iranian women were eight years away from getting the right to vote. The young Shah, who had replaced his father on the throne in 1941, was set on modernizing Iran. He had attended primary school in Switzerland and he wished to make Iran the Switzerland of the Middle East.

School was about to start for the year and Maryam was taking me shopping to buy fabric to have dresses made for me.

At the bazaar we wove in and out of narrow lanes sheltered by vaulted ceilings. Sunlight poured through little windows carved high into the walls. Donkeys, heavily laden with merchandise, made their way laboriously through the crowds. After we left the bazaar we stopped at a store where Maryam bought me a double-decker ice cream sandwich, fragrant with rose water and full of pieces of hardened cream, pressed between three thin wafers.

That evening she took me to the seamstress's house for a fitting.

"She's reached that age. Would you like me to make a chador for her?" the woman said as we were leaving. Islam required women to begin wearing chadors, or head scarves, around the age of nine. Nine was also the age when Iranian girls could legally marry.

Maryam blushed and shook her head. Aware of her embarrassment, I felt blood racing to my face, too.

"Sooner or later I need to get a chador for you," Maryam said, outside.

"We don't wear it at school," I said.

The Shah had made it optional for girls to wear a chador. Maryam chose to wear one. My school's principal, with his progressive ideas, shared the Shah's inclinations and didn't require that students cover up.

The next day began like any other day. I woke to the voice of the muezzin calling people to prayers, *Allah o Akbar*. After Maryam finished praying we had our usual breakfast—*sangag* bread still warm from the stone oven it was baked in, jam that Maryam made herself with pears and plums, mint-scented tea. On the way to school I stopped at my friend Batul's house to pick her up. Batul was my best friend and lived in the same alley as I did. We passed the public baths and the mosques, sights visible on practically every street in the Khanat Abad neighborhood.

It was a crisp, cool autumn day. The red fruit on persimmon trees on sidewalks were glistening like jewels in sunlight. Water gurgled in *joob*s running alongside the streets. The tall Alborz Mountains surrounding Tehran were clearly delineated in the distance. We paused at a stall to buy sliced hot beets and ate them as we walked.

Tehrani School for Girls was on a narrow street off Khanat Abad Avenue, about ten blocks from home. It had the same Muslim architecture as all the houses around it and was surrounded by an expansive courtyard.

At a class recess, as I stood with Batul and a few other girls under a large maple tree in the courtyard, waiting for the next class to start, I noticed a man approaching us. He was thin and short, with a pockmarked face and a brush mustache. He was wearing a suit and a tie. Even from a distance, he seemed powerful.

"Don't you recognize your father?" he asked as he came closer.

In a flash I recognized him, the man I had met only once when he came to Maryam's house with my birth mother on one of her visits. He was there for an hour or so, then left to stay with his brother who lived in midtown Tehran.

I was afraid of my father, a fear I had learned from Maryam. Having adopted me informally, Maryam didn't have legal rights to me; even if she did, my father would be able to claim me. In Iran fathers were given full control of their children, no matter the circumstance. There was no way to fight if he wanted me back. To make matters worse, my father was also a judge.

So often Maryam had said to me, "Be careful, don't go away with a stranger." Was Father the stranger she had been warning me against? Our worst fears were coming true.

"Let's go," he said. "I'm taking you to Ahvaz." He took my hand and led me forcefully toward the outside door.

"Nahid, Nahid," Batul and my other classmates called after me. I turned around and saw they were frozen in place, too stunned to do anything but call my name.

"Does my mother know about this?" I asked once we were on the street. My heart beat violently.

"You mean your aunt," he said. "I just sent a message to her. By the time she knows, we'll be on the airplane."

"I want my mother," I pleaded.

"We're going to your mother. I spoke to your principal; you aren't going to this school anymore. You'll be going to a better one, a private school in Ahvaz."

I tried to free myself but he held my arm firmly and pulled me toward Khanat Abad Avenue. Still holding me with one hand, he hailed a taxi with the other. One stopped and my father lifted me into the backseat and got in next to me, pinning my legs down with his arm.

"Let me go! Let me go!" I screamed. Through the window I saw a white chador with a polka-dot design in the distance. It was Maryam. "Mother, Mother!" As the car approached, I realized the woman wasn't Maryam.

"Don't put up a fight," my father said as the cab zigzagged through the hectic Tehran traffic. "It won't do you any good."

Before I knew it we were in the airport and then on the plane. The stewardess brought trays of food and put them in front of us. I picked up a fork and played with the pieces of rice and stew on my plate, taking reluctant bites. Nausea rose from my stomach in waves.

"I have to go to the bathroom."

"Go ahead," my father replied.

"The toilet is in the back," the stewardess said.

I must hold it until I get to the toilet, I said to myself, but my stomach tightened sharply and I began to throw up in the aisle. The stewardess gave me a bag and I turned toward the bathroom with it pressed against my lips.

When I returned, the stewardess had cleaned up the aisle.

"How do you feel?" Father asked me. "Better?"

I didn't answer.

"You'll be fine when we get home, your real home," Father said, caressing my arm. "Your mother, sisters, and brothers are all waiting for you. And I'll look after you."

Finally I fell asleep; when I awoke we were in the Ahvaz airport. I was groggy and disoriented as we rode in a taxi. Flames erupted from a tall tower, burning excess gas from the Ahvaz petroleum fields. A faint smell of petroleum filled the air.

We passed narrow streets lined with mud and straw houses and tall date and coconut palms. We entered Pahlavi Avenue, full of glittering luxury shops and modern, two-story houses and apartment buildings. Most of the women walking about were not wearing chadors and were dressed in fashionable, imported clothes. The modern avenue reminded me of the sections in north Tehran where I had ventured a few times.

At its center was a square, dominated by a large statue of the Shah.

"Stop right here," Father said to the driver, pointing to a house on a street that branched off Pahlavi Avenue just beyond the square.

The taxi came to a halt in front of the large, modern two-story house, with a wraparound balcony and two entrances.

"We're home," Father announced. A group of boys were playing hopscotch on the cement sidewalk. I felt an urge to bolt, but Father, as if aware of that urge, took hold of my hand. Grasping it firmly, he led me into the house.

A woman was sitting in a shady corner of the courtyard, holding a glass of lemonade with ice jingling in it. She wore bright red lipstick and her hair in a permanent wave. She looked so different from Maryam, who wore no makeup and let her naturally wavy hair grow long.

"Here is Nahid, Mohtaram *joon*. We have our daughter back with us," my father said to her.

Mohtaram, my birth mother.

She nodded vaguely and walked over to where we were standing. She took me in her arms, but her embrace was tentative, hesitant. I missed Maryam's firm, loving arms around me.

"Ali, show her to her room," Mohtaram said to the live-in servant, who came out of a room in the corner.

"Go ahead," Father said to me. "You can rest for a while."

Ali led me up a steep stone stairway and to a room. He left for a moment and returned with a nightgown, a bathrobe, slippers, and underwear. He told me where the bathrooms were, if I wanted to wash up. He left again and I closed the door behind him.

I lay down on the bed. I ran my hands over the folds of my dress, one Maryam had made for me. The soft springs of the bed felt strange; I was used to sleeping on a mattress rolled out on the floor of my room or under the mosquito net set up on the roof.

There was a knock on the door. "Please come to dinner, miss," Ali said from the other side.

I kept silent. He knocked again and when I didn't answer he walked away.

Gradually everything around me blurred and I plunged into a deep, dark sleep.

When I awoke, it was the middle of the night. I felt dehydrated and reached for the earthen pitcher of water Maryam always kept beside my bed. Instead my hand hit a vacuum. *I have been taken away from Maryam,* I thought in a panic. When Maryam got the message Father sent that he was taking me away, she must have started crying. Then she must have calmed herself by thinking she would come to Ahvaz as soon as possible and plead with Father to let me go back to her. *How soon will she be here? Will she be able to take me back?* A tangle of disturbing thoughts clogged my head.

The next time I woke it was dawn. *Maryam is waking up with the voice of the muezzin. She is performing ablutions at the pool's faucet. She is spreading her prayer rug on the living room floor and praying. In her prayers she pleads with God to put it in Father's heart to let me go back to her. Then she will get ready to come to Ahvaz and take me back. No, she must be already on the way.*

I sat up, breathing with difficulty. My arm, on the spot that my father had held so tightly at school, was throbbing with pain and my eyes burned with tears that wouldn't come out.

The unfamiliar room pressed in on me. It was furnished with a wooden bed, a painted white-and-pink chest, and a matching fluffy pink rug. The curtains were white with pink flowers on them. It was a comfortable, pretty room, but I missed my own room—the colorful light filling it during the day, the mantel on which I kept story magazines and hand-painted clay animals, the rug with floral and animal designs, the embroidered cushions and bolsters against the wall.

I went to the window. Outside, the square was already filled with people gathering around carts carrying a variety of merchandise—produce, clothes, household gadgets. A row of Arab women, balancing pots on their heads, passed by in a line. It was all strange.

Two

During their years growing up in Tehran, Maryam and Mohtaram had been the closest among their siblings, four sisters and two brothers. Maryam, five years older than Mohtaram, helped her little sister get dressed in the morning and combed her hair. When Mohtaram was ill, Maryam sat by her side day and night, putting cold compresses on her forehead, bathing her, and telling her stories until she got well. And it was Maryam who taught her sister how to knit, embroider, and cook.

The two sisters remained close, even though their marriages took them in different directions, on roads laid down for them by their husbands: Maryam remained a practicing Muslim, while Mohtaram became "modern."

Mohtaram was always pregnant. Maryam visited her younger sister during the pregnancies and childbirth, ostensibly to help out, but more likely just to bask in the presence of children. But it was Aziz (my grandmother) who was there when I was born, not Maryam. When Mohtaram was pregnant with me, the promised child, Maryam was caring for their older sister, Roghieh, who was seriously ill, bleeding internally. While Maryam nursed Roghieh back to health, Aziz watched over Mohtaram. It was Aziz who sent for the midwife.

That year, from the beginning of Mohtaram's pregnancy, my father was traveling all the time because of his work as a circuit judge. He was often stationed in small, unsanitary villages and didn't want to take his family along. He rarely came home, even for short visits, his work was so demanding and consuming. He left his wife and children in care of a live-in maid and Aziz. His absence had made it easier for Mohtaram to carry out her promise to her sister. She knew her husband would strongly object once he discovered I was gone, but hoped he would not go so far as to take me back.

It took fourteen hours by train to get from Ahvaz to Tehran. Aziz waited until I was six months old to make the trip, so that it would be easier to travel so many miles with me. This gift from one daughter to another had to be protected and delivered in good health.

On the day Aziz was taking me away, my father was still absent. But Mohtaram had a sudden attack of fear and anxiety. Was she wrong to believe that her husband would understand that she was helping her childless sister by giving her one of their numerous children? Aziz had to calm her down. "Don't worry, I know he's a kind man and he likes Maryam. I will speak to him, if necessary."

"I hope you're right. I don't want to disappoint my dear sister," Mohtaram said. Before putting me into my grandmother's arms to be taken away, she gave me a cool bath and dressed me in a pink cotton outfit. She squeezed milk from her breasts into a bottle and gave it to my grandmother to take along.

I was sleepless during the long, uncomfortable ride on the old train. After I finished the bottle of my mother's milk, Aziz bought goat's milk at a station stop. Other families in the compartment asked questions about me; they approved of her bringing me from a fertile married sister to a childless widow. Sisterhood, family ties, and a woman's elemental desire for a child to make her feel feminine, whole, were concepts comprehensible to everyone. They listened sympathetically as Aziz told them of Maryam's years of

Mohtaram holding infant Nahid

trying, unsuccessfully, to get pregnant. Now she was a widow, having lost her much older husband three years ago. He died of a heart attack while working at his desk. His job as owner and manager of several bakeries in Tehran had been stressful.

The women helped my grandmother by taking turns holding me, so that she could sleep a little. When we reached Tehran, Aziz hired a horse cart to take us to Maryam's house. It was November; the temperature in Tehran, surrounded by the Alborz Mountains, was at least twenty degrees cooler than in Ahvaz. Aziz put a heavy sweater she had knit herself on me and covered me with part of her chador. The horse cart went slowly—the traffic was hectic in the congested city of about two million inhabitants (now more than ten million).

At the beginning of a long cobblestoned alley, my grandmother stopped the driver. She stepped off the cart and, walking with me in her arms, approached a house. She sped up as she saw Maryam squatting by the door of her house. Maryam jumped up as we approached, and my grandmother put me into her arms.

"This is the happiest day of my life," Maryam said as she held me.

Maryam had prepared a room for me, which was separated by French doors from her own. She had put a wooden cradle there, with toys on the mantel and around the crib, and she had filled a chest in the corner with clothes. Friends, relatives, and neighbors came to Maryam's house daily, bringing presents and congratulating her for finally having the child she yearned for. After a few months, Aziz returned to Kashan, where she lived with her son and his wife. It was Maryam and me now.

As soon as I could speak I began to call Maryam "Mother," as other children called their mothers. My birth mother was "Aunt Mohtaram." When I was about five, Maryam and Aziz, who visited a few times a year, told me I had been adopted from Mohtaram. The news had no particular impact on me then.

On each of her visits Aziz brought me a different regional doll—a gypsy, a Turk, a Chinese girl—distinguished by their costumes and colorings.

"You have a special place in my heart, Nahid *joonam*, because you make Maryam so happy." Aziz was a small-boned woman, with a delicate face, almond-shaped brown eyes, and wavy dark brown hair pulled back and held in place with golden bobby pins. She was as observant a Muslim as Maryam, and as embedded in superstitious beliefs.

"You should never provoke animals," she told me. "Some of them are *div*s, with a little devil in them. You should watch out for *jin*s, too. Allah made man out of clay and the *jins* out of flames. If you ever notice *jins* hovering around, you should throw water at them and they'll go back underground." Owls were bad omens, she said, and if they came to the house we had to watch out for what might shortly unfold.

Every food was either "cold" or "hot." Yogurt, green vegetables, and citrus fruit were "cold"; fried food and nuts were "hot." She said food had to be balanced between the two, and Maryam went along with that. If one of us got sick, they tried to correct the balance.

When Maryam couldn't get pregnant, Aziz had taken her to a fortune-teller, an herbalist, and finally even consulted a male gynecologist, a last resort since it was a sin for a woman to be examined by a man (there was a shortage of female doctors). The gynecologist gave Maryam tests and said he couldn't find anything wrong with her. He added, "Not everything is known to us." It was possible it was her husband who was the cause of her not getting pregnant, but in the male-dominated society people never questioned the husbands.

Sometimes it was Aziz who put me to sleep at night. She lay next to me and told me stories from *One Thousand and One Nights*, with their intricate, interwoven plots. Whether the story revolved around a flying horse, a bird that could carry off elephants, doors that opened at the sound of a voice, or a *jin* who granted wishes, Aziz made them sound as if they were true.

❋

Maryam, like others in the neighborhood, structured her days around the rituals of religion, following its cardinal rules: prayer three times a day, *hejab* (covering hair and skin in men's presence), fasting for one month, pilgrimage, giving alms. Voices of muezzins streamed out of the surrounding mosques three times a day. Women prayed at home rather than in mosques, where men went for their prayers. Women went to mosques only on special occasions—to ask God to fulfill a wish or to listen to sermons given by different *aghounds* (Muslim priests). For alms Maryam gave so generously to the poor that she rarely had money left over at the end of the month. Her income was the rent she collected from the tenants on the other side of the courtyard, and from the profits of five bakeries she had inherited from her late husband.

It was almost a refrain with Maryam and others around her to say, "It's the life beyond that matters."

Once, arriving home from school when I was about seven years old, I found Maryam and her two tenants, Hamideh and Ezat Sadaat, both widowed, in the living room, sitting by white cloths spread on the floor. They were cutting them in a certain way.

"We're making shrouds," Maryam explained to me. "It's good to prepare for the life beyond. It's nothing to be afraid of if you're good on this earth. Death isn't final; you'll be brought back to life on the Day of Judgment. Angels will come to you and question you the moment you are in your grave. If your answers reflect that you conducted your life in the right way, the angels will lift you and deliver you to paradise. If badness comes through you'll be sent to hell where burning fires await you."

The sound of traffic didn't reach our alley set within a maze of alleys, all too narrow for cars. I could hear her words clearly, though she spoke very softly. She rarely made me feel as if she were preaching at me or trying to correct my ways.

I went to my room, trying to engage my mind with my own daily concerns—doing my school work well, wondering if I would spend a night with Batul at the end of the week. Through the open door to the courtyard I could hear the murmur of various sounds—the chirping of sparrows, the tumbling of fish in the pool (when it became cold, Maryam put them in a tank inside), the cooing of mourning doves Maryam kept in a cage, the rippling of water in the *joob* outside, from which water was channeled into cisterns inside houses. A motley, orange-and-yellow-haired, flat-faced alley cat wandered in from outside and mewed as he headed for the food in the saucer we had set down for him, then went to sit at the edge of the pool and stared longingly at the goldfish in the water. The parakeet in a large brass cage said, "*Salaam, halet chetoreh* (Hello, how are you)?"

Later in the day I joined Maryam and Hamideh and Ezat Sadaat for dinner in the courtyard. The three of them had prepared dinner together, as they often did. They were comfortable with one another, shared the kitchen, the courtyard with its rectangular pool. They used the pool's faucet for ablutions before their prayers.

We sat on a *sofreh* spread on the rug on the ground. It was a pleasant spring day. The air was filled with the fragrance of flowers, mingling with the scent of spices—saffron, turmeric—used in the food.

They bought the ingredients for the food mainly from vendors passing through the alley, carrying their merchandise on round wooden trays on their heads. They called to people, "Come and quench your thirst with the best ruby red pomegranate juice." "Come and taste the biggest and freshest figs with red flesh inside." "Come and see the freshest and tastiest herbs you can imagine."

They prepared everything from scratch. They stripped the wheat, then crushed the grains between the two round, heavy stones of a grinder. With the flour, they made pastries and cakes. They made their own pickles, a variety of them, and their own vinegar. They ordered specific cuts of meat for *khoresh*es and *kabab*s from the butcher on Khanat Abad, who was known for being meticulous in observing the halal rules on slaughtering animals. The women loved the cooperative creation of the food, which came out differently each time.

As we ate, the three of them focused on me; Hamideh's two daughters were married and on their own, and Ezat Sadaat, like Maryam, was unable to get pregnant. They said they hoped I would have many children when I grew up, as having children was a woman's best fortune.

I was happy in the company of my aunt and the other women. But as the day wore on and I could hear the hooting of an owl on the eaves, my heart beat with sadness, thinking of the shrouds they had been preparing earlier in the day.

Since there were no phone lines in Maryam's neighborhood, people just dropped in. A rap on the door with the bronze lion-head knocker meant visitors, including my other aunts and their children, who stayed for lunch or for tea and pastries. The house became vibrant with the women's conversation, stories exchanged, while we children ran around the courtyard, chased the butterflies, or played hide-and-seek. My cousins often stayed the night, as I sometimes stayed in their homes. We went to the roof and our male cousins helped us fly kites. In the evenings the sky was filled with kites of various shapes that neighborhood children flew, some tangling with one another.

Monthly, my aunts and neighborhood women came in to hear the *aghounds* whom Maryam invited to her house to give sermons. For the occasion she covered the walls of the living room with black cloth and set out an armchair for the *aghounds* to sit on. The *aghounds* came one after another and their sermons mainly revolved around various events related to the Imams' martyrdom. The women sat on the rug, leaning against cushions. They cried at the suffering of the Imams, which the *aghounds* recounted in great detail and in dramatic tones. After Maryam paid the *aghounds* and they left, the women let their chadors slip down. Maryam served them tea from a large samovar, with a teapot on top of it, standing in the corner of the room, and as they drank they talked.

The women, like the *aghounds*, talked about the events that happened nearly fifteen hundred years ago as if they had just taken place. They spoke of Prophet Mohammad and Ali and Yazid, and Umar, their differences, degrees of justice and generosity. They referred to Ali, Mohammad's son-in-law, who they believed should have succeeded Mohammad (an issue that divided them from the Sunnis, who didn't). They condemned Umar, the caliph who succeeded Mohammad instead.

I didn't miss the presence of a father. Other girls rarely had real relationships with their fathers and almost never spoke about them. Fathers were distant figures in the lives of Iranian girls—except when it came to rules and punishment.

Tehran streets were filled with adventures and mysteries for my cousins and me; we ran through them, our shoes pounding against the cobblestones. Unaware of the limitations that choked the hopes and aspirations of the young women all around me, I felt a boundless sense of freedom. We sneaked into little neighborhood bazaars filled with the scents of fruit, herbs, and spices, and bought bags of roasted pumpkin and watermelon seeds. We watched the greengrocer weighing a batch of vegetables on a scale, a copper-shiner filing a copper pot, sparks jumping from his instrument into the air. On Khanat Abad Avenue we went to the stationery store that stocked stacks of colorful stickers, and we bought angel and flower stickers to take home. Back home, our aunts held and kissed us, gave us handmade toys—rag dolls, pinwheels, clay animals. We were unaware then of the asperity of their lives.

Only in the public baths did I come to understand the difficulties of being a woman. In the large steamy room, with red loincloths wrapped around their hips, the women spoke of the unfairness of the system that gave women so much less power than men. The Shah's claim of equality for women was nonsense, they said. Didn't sons inherit twice as much as daughters when their parents died? And weren't men allowed to marry more than one woman? Didn't fathers automatically get custody of the children in cases of divorce? Wasn't it the simplest thing for a man to divorce his wife, whereas if a woman wanted a divorce she had to give up everything—the right to money and her children? How sad it was that the Shah divorced his wife, Fowzieh, because she didn't give him a son. Now he was married again and no doubt Sorraya, his new wife, would suffer the same fate if she didn't produce a son. The Shah had changed nothing for women, other than making it optional for them to wear the chador—but what good did that freedom do when it was the husbands who dictated to them whether or not to wear the chador?

"The Shah could learn something from Prophet Mohammad, who believed in equality for women," Maryam said as she wiped soap from her forehead.

"Yes, the prophet married a woman fifteen years older than himself, was devoted to her, and didn't divorce her even though only a daughter, not a son, by her survived," another woman joined in.

"He never married another woman until Khadijeh died," Aunt Roghieh, Maryam's middle sister, said.

"He was so unassuming, and, unlike the Shah, lived sparsely. He gave away everything extra," Maryam agreed. "His house, with its mud walls, its roof thatched with date-palm leaves, often remained dark for want of oil for the lamp. He was compassionate. Remember what's said about him? That when he saw a poor blind woman stumbling in the street in Mecca he led her gently to her home and took meals to her daily thereafter."

"You know how Agha brought another wife on me?" Aunt Khadijeh, who was named after the prophet's wife, said in a near whisper. "I can't say I was really upset when his truck turned over and killed him. It was God's doing, to answer my prayers."

Aunt Khadijeh was a vivacious woman now but I had heard Maryam say to her tenants that Khadijeh had been depressed for years.

"Didn't I give him three sons? What else did he want from me?" Aunt Khadijeh added.

Aunt Roghieh shook her head from side to side. "Dear sister, what happens on this earth is insignificant." She was the oldest of the sisters and had a retiring manner.

"And you know how I waited on Fatollah, and all I got was criticism for not giving him a child," Maryam remarked. "I was sure he was going to take another wife, but then he died." She began to massage the back of Khadijeh, who looked stirred up and upset by the memory of the other wife her own husband had brought on her.

The sweet intimacy among the sisters and the support they gave to one another gradually relieved their pain, and finally they could relax, joke, laugh. Then more cheerful subjects were introduced.

"A nice man from a fine family has come for Narghes's hand," Aunt Roghieh said, speaking about her fourteen-year-old daughter. She had been worried that no one would marry Narghes because she had bald spots on her head.

"See, when all the doors are shut on you, God opens a window," Aunt Khadijeh said.

"We're a part of an intricate design by God that unfolds itself in ways that we don't always understand," Maryam remarked.

Three

During those years of my living with Maryam, my birth mother was just a shadow. I saw her only once a year when she came to Tehran to visit her relatives. She always stayed with Maryam but she paid no particular attention to me; there was no bond between us.

One year when I was about seven, Mohtaram brought along a vivacious, curly-haired child of about two who kept moving around in Mohtaram's arms, staring at everyone, smiling at them. It was Mina, my younger sister, whom I had never met.

They stayed with us for a week and my other two aunts and their children came over daily to visit. Mohtaram stood out among her sisters because she had become modern, wore makeup, didn't cover her hair in the presence of men, and didn't pray. But still her sisters doted on her. They excused her, blamed her modern ways on my father. Men had all the power and it was dangerous to go against their will, they said.

"You were such a lively, pretty little girl," Maryam said to Mohtaram.

"No wonder Manoochehr *khan* waited until you reached the right age to marry," Roghieh said.

"And God has blessed you with so many children," said Khadijeh, who herself had three sons.

23

Mohtaram paid particular attention to her favorite sister, Maryam. "You were the most beautiful of all of us," she said to her. "Remember Reza Shah sent a woman over, asking if you would become one of his wives."

Reza Shah, the father of Mohammad Reza Shah, had a small harem and told women in his circle to look in public baths or streets for the most beautiful women, whom he could bring to his harem.

"Our mother didn't want you to be in a harem," Mohtaram went on.

"None of us sisters wanted to marry anyone," Maryam said. "We were happy to just stay home and be with each other."

Hossein *khan,* my grandfather, was a wealthy tobacco merchant and provided well for his family. They lived in a large house in Khanat Abad, this very neighborhood, and also had a summer villa in a village in the Alborz Mountains. He had set traditional values for his family. He believed education was for boys and boys only. His sons had gone as far as finishing high school. He encouraged his daughters to marry as soon as suitable men came along.

Maryam had completed the sixth grade and had some grasp of reading and writing. Mohtaram, after she was married, had tutors—my father's idea. My other two aunts were completely illiterate. All the sisters were married by the age of sixteen, as were almost all the other girls in the neighborhood. Mohtaram married at nine, the legal age then for marrying. My father was the only one among the sisters' husbands with a higher education. Not only had he finished college, he had continued his schooling and become a lawyer. My aunts' husbands all owned shops: Maryam's owned bakeries; of the other two, one sold produce, the other carpets.

My father had traveled and been exposed to other ways of thinking, but still he adhered to the tradition of arranged marriage and wasn't troubled by the age discrepancy between him and his bride, or by the fact that his bride was a mere child. He was Mohtaram's second cousin; he had watched her grow and anticipated marrying her one day. When they married he was thirty-four. After the wedding he set up a separate room for his child bride until she was old enough to perform properly as a wife.

Once the girls were married, they immediately started having children. All the sisters, that is, except for Maryam.

At the end of her visit Mohtaram cried. She couldn't bear to part with her sisters, particularly Maryam. Maryam promised to visit Mohtaram in Ahvaz but she never did. Without speaking a word, my father made it impossible.

Mohtaram kissed my cousins and me good-bye, showing no more love or affection for me than for my cousins. She made no attempt to instill in me the fact that she was my real mother. And I felt nothing special for her.

"Which one do you like better?" I asked one of my cousins after Mohtaram had left and Maryam had disappeared into the courtyard. "Maryam or Mohtaram?" I was devastated when my cousin said she liked Mohtaram because she had many children.

Something about that visit upset me. That night in bed I lay awake for a long time. I wondered for the first time why she had given me up so easily. Why hadn't she given one of her other children to Maryam? Was there something wrong with me? Why had I been so quickly surrendered? She held Mina in her arms so lovingly.

I stopped every few days at the stationery store on Khanat Abad Avenue that carried the magazine *Gheseh* (*Story*). Each issue contained a few "true" stories and one piece of fiction, all written by unknown, sometimes anonymous writers. At home I read every piece. Perhaps those words, those stories, would provide me with answers.

Because of all the reading I did I came out first in the third grade at Tehrani School. At the end of a school day the principal gathered everyone in the courtyard and announced who had come first in their classes. Then one by one she put crowns, made with gold-and-blue paper, on our heads. I didn't want to remove the crown too quickly, so I went home by the quiet, empty, backstreet that led to our alley. At home I found Maryam in the courtyard, watering the rosebushes with a tin can. I stood in front of her. She turned to me and noticed the crown. "I came first in my class," I said.

She put the can down and embraced and kissed me. "You're a wonderful girl in every respect," she said.

Why did Mohtaram give me away, then? I asked myself, still searching for an explanation.

Maryam and Hamideh were talking in the courtyard while they chopped vegetables. On the porch, I strained to catch every word.

"You know, Banu *khanoon* put her one-year-old baby girl in the doorway of that house at the end of the alley and walked away. The poor child is blind," Hamideh said to Maryam.

"Oh no, why did she do that?" Maryam said. "What happened to the child?"

"Banu had a suitor, that butcher at Asghari shop. His mother told her that he wanted her to place her child with one of her relatives. Her son wouldn't want that blind child around. Banu couldn't find anyone to take the child. But Banu changed her mind—she ran back and picked up the child."

I was chilled by what they were saying.

A little later Hamideh went into her room and Maryam came up onto the porch and went into the living room. I followed her.

"Mother, is something wrong with me that Mohtaram gave me away?"

"You're a perfect creation of God, my dear girl. It was your destiny to be my child. As soon as a baby comes into the world an angel writes its destiny on the baby's forehead."

"I don't see any writing on my forehead," I said.

"It's written with a special invisible ink."

"Does what the angel writes stay there forever?"

"Sometimes if a person pleads with God, he might decide to tell the angel to change the writing. But no one is praying to change your destiny. I want you with me forever."

Four

S uddenly Ali, the servant, was knocking on the door and calling me to breakfast. I didn't answer, and he left only to return and call me again. I finally roused myself, went to the bathroom, and washed up. Reluctantly I headed to the dining room to have breakfast with my new family.

Though it was early morning the sunlight pouring into the dining room was already glaringly bright. My siblings were there, sitting at the long wooden table and talking among themselves. I had met them all once or twice during Mohtaram's visits to Maryam, so I wasn't introduced to them. I took the empty seat next to Father.

"Here is Nahid, back with us," he said.

Everyone turned to me but we were all speechless. My brothers were grown now, Cyrus, eighteen, two years older than Parviz and in the last year of high school. They were attractive boys and exuded self-confidence. Pari, thirteen, was three years younger than Parviz and had robust good looks. Manijeh, two years younger than Pari, was pretty but had a wan, remote air about her. They were all dressed in imported clothes, like the ones I saw in boutiques in north Tehran. Pari was in a blouse and a skirt with shoulder straps, Manijeh in a white print dress with ruffles at the sleeves, Mohtaram in a striped black-and-white dress. Father and my brothers were wearing suits and ties, very formal. Suddenly my dress, made by the seamstress, seemed crude. I felt that I did not belong with these people.

"Now all my children are here with us," Father said, trying to pull me in, his stern face brightening.

"But my dear Maryam," Mohtaram murmured, looking down.

"Don't mention that," Father said sharply.

Pari smiled at me as if trying to comfort me, the first acknowledgment from a sibling of my presence.

Ali came in and put a glass of tea before me.

"Eat something," Father said, addressing me.

I began to serve myself cheese, bread, jam, dates.

"Take some *khameh*, too," Pari said. "It's good." I reached for the thick, almost solid cream and put a spoonful on my plate.

The bread was thick and cold, the tea didn't have mint fragrance like the one Maryam served. As I played with my food, my brothers talked among themselves, and Mohtaram focused on Manijeh, asking her what she needed that day for school. Pari glanced at me and smiled again.

"There's so much to do today, shopping, cooking," Mohtaram suddenly began to complain to no one in particular. "We need to get a new oven, a new fan for the salon. And all the children want one thing or another," she said. "Nahid needs a uniform to wear to school," she added.

There was no warmth in her words. I felt it was only me she was complaining about, as if I had somehow tipped the scales and now she had far too many children to attend to. The others, after all, had always been there.

Father got up and pulled the shades over the windows to cut the merciless light. When he sat down again he looked very serious, as if about to give a lecture. A hush fell over the table. After a few moments of tense silence, he said, "I have to take Nahid to school her first day."

Everyone finished eating and left the dining room one by one. The early morning havoc followed—the children flitting around the large house, looking for something or other—a misplaced shoe, the collar of a school uniform. I went into my room and waited quietly.

Finally Mohtaram came in and handed me a gray uniform with a white collar.

"Here," she said. "Wear this until we get you your own. It's Manijeh's from last year."

"I don't want to wear it," I said, rebellion bubbling up inside me. We didn't wear uniforms in my school in Tehran. Mohtaram walked away without another word.

After a few moments, Father appeared in the doorway. "Hurry up and put on the uniform, we have to go," he said.

Reluctantly, I put it on. It was too big for me.

"We'll get you your own uniform soon," he said once we were outside. "You're nine years old now, a woman," he added as we began walking. "You need my supervision."

I said nothing, filled with anxiety and fear of his power over me.

"I want you to start calling your mother 'Mother,'" he said. "She is your real mother, she always has been."

"I don't want to stay here," I said.

"You must stop talking like that," he said firmly.

We turned from Pahlavi Avenue onto another, smaller street lined mainly with houses, most of them modern, not inside courtyards. Palm trees, some with dates clustered between their branches, stood everywhere. There were no *joob*s in sight. It was much warmer than yesterday in Tehran and I was hot from walking. I felt I had been plunged into a different, alien world.

The school, a modern building on a long street, finally came into view. "Your sisters went here, too," Father said. "It goes through the sixth grade."

Other girls in gray uniforms swarmed in the street, some walking, some dropped off by chauffeurs. They greeted one another and disappeared inside.

As we reached the entrance Father said, "I'm sure you'll like it. You're only a week late for classes here."

I stood by the door, not wanting to go in. He took my hand and led me inside into a large yard. The yard was open on the other side, except for a short fence. Palm trees stood in clumps in several spots. The classrooms and offices were inside a large grayish two-story modern structure. Father led me to the principal's office on the second floor.

A woman in a stiff navy blue suit opened the door. Her dark hair was pulled back tightly and she wore a touch of makeup on her face.

"Oh, Mr. Ghazi," she said, using the word for "judge." "I am so pleased you believe this school worthy of your daughter." She turned to me. "Welcome. You look healthy. It was good of your parents to send you to Tehran to recover."

I blushed. What was she talking about?

"We'll be off now. I wanted you to meet her," Father said to the woman.

"We'll take good care of her," she replied, smiling at me.

"Go and join the other girls," Father said to me as we walked back to the yard. "Find out where your classroom is." He walked away, leaving me alone in the courtyard.

Girls in uniforms stood in groups in patches of shade or under canopies. I felt self-conscious in the too-big uniform. All the girls seemed to know one another well and I felt too upset and shy to even try to strike up a conversation with any of them.

Back in Tehrani School my friends now were talking to one another, comparing notes about other girls they liked or didn't like, teachers who were nice or not nice. Maybe they were worried about me, wondering what had happened to me, or why I was abducted by that man. Or maybe by now they knew what happened. Father had spoken to the principal there and she might have announced it to the students.

Most likely Batul must have gone to our house and found out from Maryam what happened. I missed my friends and Maryam. Was Maryam on the way to get me? Would she be waiting for me when I returned to the house? It was hard to believe that just twenty-four hours earlier I had been in Tehran with them.

A man walked over to the large bell hanging from the ceiling of the school porch and banged it with a brass pole. The girls began to line up for classes. I asked a girl where the fourth grade was. She scrutinized me and then pointed to a line. I went and stood at the end of it.

The bell rang again and everyone began to sing the national anthem, routine at all schools, but I joined in with difficulty in this new place.

Our Shah-anShah, may you live long
Iran, oh, land full of jewels
Oh, your soil is the source of art and virtue
May my life be sacrificed for my Motherland
Love for you has become my occupation
May my thoughts not be far from you
The rock of your mountains is pearl and jewel
The soil of your plain is better than gold . . .

After we finished singing we went into our classrooms and I sat close to a window, so I could look outside.

The teacher, a middle-aged man, walked in. He began to write words on the blackboard and asked us for the meaning of each one. He didn't seem to notice me, didn't ask my name or why I was there. He just droned on about all the conquests the Iranians had made of other countries. He frequently glanced at the large photograph of the Shah displayed prominently on the wall, as if he were afraid that the Shah was listening.

I took a notebook from my bag and scribbled in it. I shifted in my seat and glanced out the window. A blackbird jumped from branch to branch in a palm tree, pausing for a moment and then starting up again. A lizard sped around and around the trunk of another palm tree. I heard the hooting of a train and fell into a fantasy that I was on it, going back to Tehran.

After school I walked to the house, on the quiet backstreets to avoid the students who walked together on Pahlavi Avenue.

When I approached the house, I found the twin wooden doors both open. I went in through the door that led to the courtyard, hoping Maryam would be there, sitting with Mohtaram, talking to her about taking me back. But there was no one there.

I climbed the steps to the second floor, looked around, and saw no one there, either. I went into my room and sat on the bed in a state of uncertainty. What was going to happen next?

In a few moments Father came in. "We're going to take photographs of all of us. We can send one to your aunt."

Mohtaram joined us. She put some clothes on the bed. "You look sweaty," she said. "Go take a shower first and then change into these."

I took the clothes and went downstairs to the bathroom. Its floor was covered by plain white tiles, as was the shower area. Between our trips to the public baths Maryam would bathe me in a basin on the kitchen floor covered with green tiles. She used a cloth made of woven straw and dipped it in soap, to wash my skin. She washed my hair with another soap. Then she rinsed me with warm water she poured from a pitcher and wrapped me in a large, soft towel and kept me warm. But in this new household everything seemed cold. I stepped out of the shower and dried myself with a towel, then put on the clothes Mohtaram had given to me. They fit well enough but they weren't my own clothes.

Out on the terrace, my siblings and Mohtaram and Father were standing around, already dressed for the photo. A young man stood behind a camera on a tripod, fiddling with the film. Pari took my hand and asked me to stand next to her. At the photographer's suggestion we all changed position a few times. I struggled to smile but couldn't. After finishing with his task, the photographer and Father exchanged some words; then he picked up his tripod and left. The children all scattered to their rooms.

Later that evening, Father called me into the dining room for dinner. There were guests, friends of my parents. I sat with them at the table while Ali and Mohtaram brought in the food—whitefish, lamb *khoresh,* and saffron rice. The guests were two couples and their children; one had two girls and the other, one.

Father and the men talked about how Ahvaz was expanding, how the oil business, central to the city's economy, was thriving. Ahvaz, with its large oil fields and pipelines, was a major supply and distribution center, they said.

"But most of the money goes into the pockets of American and English technicians," one of the men said, shaking his head.

"Yes, they come here for all the work generated from the oil fields," the other man said expansively, waving his hands in the air. "Factories, foundries, distribution of oil to cargo ships sent to Khoramshahr and the oil refinery in Abadan. Why can't our own men do the work?"

"You know, dear *agha,* that we don't have enough qualified technicians of our own," Father said.

"All that money from the oil could be spent on useful things like medical care," the first man remarked.

Mohtaram talked to the other women about all the heat and dust, the flies, the rising prices of everything, how she missed being near her family in Tehran. Like Mohtaram, the two women had makeup on, their hair was set in permanents, and they wore imported clothes. The women didn't focus on religion, as Maryam and other women in her neighborhood did, but they didn't talk about the issues Father and the men were expressing opinions about. True, they weren't covering up in front of the men, but they weren't really mingling with them in conversation, as if they were in different worlds. The three girls, two a little older and one a little younger than me, were wearing dresses with pleated skirts and shiny patent leather shoes and white socks. My parents, sisters, and I were still wearing the clothes we had been photographed in earlier. Father and the two other men were wearing suits and ties, even though it was hot. The ceiling fan, turned on high, wasn't helping.

The three girls and their mothers kept staring at me, maybe trying to figure out why I hadn't been a part of the family until now. Mohtaram noticed their staring. "Nahid was a sickly, thin baby and we thought she'd do better in Tehran's more temperate climate."

This was similar to the explanation Father had given to the principal. I felt shame that Father and Mohtaram had to find some explanation to give to everyone for my having been away all those years.

"And my sister was desperate for a child," Mohtaram said finally.

"You must be so happy to have your child back again," one of the women said.

"Yes, I missed her so much," Mohtaram said flatly.

I knew she was lying.

After the guests left, my parents went to the porch to talk. As I got ready for bed, I heard Mohtaram say, "She's my sister's child. It's cruel to take her away from her."

"You gave her to your sister for a little while, that's all. It's for Nahid's own good. Your sister should understand that."

After that there was silence and then the sound of footsteps receding in different directions.

Five

N ahid *joon,* Nahid *joon.*" Maryam was sitting in one of the wicker chairs on Mohtaram's porch. Only two days had passed since I had been taken from school but it felt like an eternity. She was wearing one of her special dresses, navy silk with light blue flowers on it. She had taken off her chador because no men were around, and her hair flowed over her shoulders.

"Nahid *joon,* Nahid *joon,* he came and took you away," she said in a choked voice. She got up and held me to herself. As we embraced I could smell the familiar rose water on her skin, feel the incandescence of her love.

Mohtaram came out of the kitchen and sat with us. She was tense and jittery.

"You must talk to Manoochehr *khan,* make him understand. It isn't right to take her away from me," Maryam pleaded with her sister, tears collecting in her eyes.

"If Manoochehr would ever listen to me," Mohtaram said, trailing off. "Don't worry, she's still your child, I won't steal her heart from you."

Mohtaram's words hurt me, and also relieved me; Mohtaram didn't value me but also wanted Maryam to have me back.

"My dear, don't ever think that I'm not grateful to you for having been such a good sister to me all my life," Mohtaram said.

"You have everything—a husband who provides well for you, you're blessed with so many children. What do I have? No husband, no ability to have children. My womb has been cursed." Maryam started to weep.

I leaned against her and put my arm around her and tried to fight tears.

"Oh, my poor sister. But one of Manoochehr's clients is looking for a wife," Mohtaram said. "He isn't young but he's nice and very rich. He lives in Khoramshahr. Manoochehr asked me to talk to you about him."

"I already buried an old man," Maryam said. "I don't want more headaches."

"He may give you children of your own."

"One husband didn't give me any children. How can another?"

"You'll have someone to take care of you."

Maryam shook her head and pulled me closer.

I wished Mohtaram would leave me alone with Maryam. It was difficult for me to reconcile my love for Maryam and the resentment I felt toward Mohtaram.

Maryam looked startled and suddenly collected her chador and put it on. Father was walking over to us. At his approach I could see Maryam's face darken.

"Welcome," he said to Maryam. "This is your home."

Maryam kept her eyes down and said nothing and he walked away without any conversation exchanged between them.

Ali called Mohtaram into the kitchen. As soon as she left, I looked at Maryam and said, "Take me back with you."

"That's why I'm here, I want to take you back," she said. "My house is empty without you."

Maryam stayed for three more days. Every time I came home from school the first thing I asked her was if I was going back with her. On her last day she said, "Mohtaram asked your father, and I begged him myself, but he said no. Pack everything, let's leave while no one is home."

I put a few of my belongings in my schoolbag and we headed outside. As soon as we entered the courtyard, the outside door opened and Father came in from the street. He greeted Maryam and, seeing the small suitcase in her hand, said, "I'll take you to the station."

Maryam froze and didn't say a word. I was silent, too. I could feel a dark current locking me to her, as if we were caught in the same nightmare.

"You aren't taking her back with you," Father said firmly.

"She's my child, how can you take her from me?" Maryam finally said in her shy, diffident voice.

"If you love her you should know it's better for her here. She needs a father to look after her."

Mohtaram walked into the courtyard. Maryam again begged her sister to let me go back. But this time Mohtaram said nothing.

"Stay here with me," I said to Maryam.

Maryam looked at her sister. Mohtaram offered no encouragement, perhaps afraid of other scenes between Maryam and Father. She looked shaky and upset.

"Come with me," Father said to Maryam. "The car is outside, the chauffeur will drive us to the station."

"I'll go to see you off," I said to Maryam, still hoping that at the last minute Father would change his mind and let me go with her.

"You stay right here," he said to me and turned to Maryam. "Let's go, Maryam *khanoon*."

She kissed me. Her face was wet with tears. I began to cry, too. Father was unmoved.

As soon as they left I ran upstairs to the balcony that wrapped around the second floor, and watched the steel blue limousine zigzag through the traffic and disappear.

Later that afternoon Father came to my room and, taking my hand, brought me to Mohtaram. She and Ali were on the porch, crushing a block of ice to supplement what the refrigerator made.

"Say 'I love you, Mother,'" Father said.

I said nothing.

"Go ahead," Father said, the muscles of his face tightening and his voice rising above the sound of the ice chips being put into a pail by Ali, while Mohtaram stood and stared into space.

"I want to go back to my own mother," I said.

"This is your home," he said. "Say 'I love you' to your mother and everything will be fine." He grabbed my arm. "Go on, say it."

I pulled away and ran to my room.

"She's here to stay," I heard Father say to Mohtaram.

"We can't let Maryam suffer like that."

"You can ask her to come and stay with us for a while."

"She won't feel comfortable here."

Several months later Maryam visited again, this time with my grandmother. Aziz was sitting alone on the porch and running between her fingers her rosary with its ninety-nine amber beads and yellow tassel, and repeating, "Allah, Allah." She looked so different from the year before, when she had visited Maryam and me in Tehran. It was as if she had suddenly aged—her hair was almost totally gray and there were deep wrinkles on her face. She got up and we embraced tightly.

"Maryam is in your room, go see her," she said as we pulled apart.

I found Maryam sitting on a mattress in the corner of my room, staring into space. Her hair was uncombed and disheveled. She got up and grasped me in her arms, holding me very tight. As I sat with her I could feel that dark current again.

"Can you take me to the river and drown me?"

I was overwhelmed by sadness and a sense of helplessness. "Please don't talk like that, please, please," I begged, holding her hand in mine.

"I caught Maryam sitting at the edge of the cistern," Aziz told me later. "She was staring into it. I had to remind her that it's a sin to kill yourself. I wanted to take her to the hospital but she begged me not to. A doctor came and gave her injections and she felt a little better but then she got worse. The doctor gave her pills, too, but she won't take them." Aziz said she put ground herbs in Maryam's food, pinned turquoise clay beads to her dress, and burnt *esphand* in the room, but nothing was working.

This time it was Aziz who pleaded with Father to let me go back with them and live with Maryam again, be her child, but Father adamantly refused.

"You're like my own mother," he told Aziz. "You bring light to our household. You and your dear daughter Maryam should consider this your home and stay as long as you like. But you can't take my daughter far away again."

It was clear that I was there to stay. And hope slowly drained away.

❋

Every time I thought of the home I had lost, my chest filled with a heaviness, a pressure. I would cough until I turned red and tears pooled in my eyes. It happened at all times of the day and night.

Finally Father took me to a doctor, a taciturn middle-aged man with an authoritative voice. The doctor asked me a few questions and examined my ears and throat.

"Nothing is wrong with her," he told my father after the exam. "It's all nerves."

"You heard the doctor," Father said when we were outside. "Your cough doesn't have a real basis. If you try to relax and view your mother as a mother you'll be fine." He took me to a café close to the doctor's office and ordered *falute,* ice cream mixed with strips of fruit, for both of us. "You could fill the hole Mina has left in your mother's and my heart, if you only try," he said.

I recalled Maryam and her sisters talking in sorrowful tones about the lovely, curly-haired baby Mohtaram had brought with her on one visit. Mina had contracted malaria, become feverish, her skin had turned yellow, and then she died. I felt a renewed sadness at the thought of her death. But I soon became aware of a weight on my heart—Father was giving me what seemed to be the impossible responsibility of filling the hole Mina had left in their lives, especially in Mohtaram's life. Mohtaram had lost a daughter and perhaps because of that Maryam lost a daughter. It was almost worse than if I had died. Maryam and I were so close but now I would grow up here in Ahvaz in my parents' house, far from her. Would we forget each other? Father had also said to me on that first day when he walked me to school that I was nine years old and needed supervision. Perhaps I hadn't been told the whole truth. There were things no one was telling me.

"The doctor said it's all nerves," Father explained to Mohtaram at home.

"I thought so," Mohtaram said distractedly.

In the coming months I was in and out of the doctor's office. There were germs in Ahvaz I wasn't immune to. An eye infection caused swelling in my lids; I had an ear infection and I couldn't hear well for a while; a large boil appeared on my back and a fever accompanied it. Mohtaram always asked Father to take me to these appointments.

Father also tried to get me to eat more. "You're starving yourself," he said, as he kept adding food to my plate. I had lost weight rapidly since coming to Ahvaz, too sad and anxious to have much of an appetite and, anyway, missing Maryam's cooking. Mohtaram supervised Ali making the meals—usually whitefish, smoked or fresh, *khoresh* served with dill and lima beans, rice, some of the same dishes Maryam made. But they didn't taste as good to me. What Maryam and Hamideh and Ezat Sadaat prepared was much more flavorful because they knew how to use just the right mixture of spices.

My father was attentive, but I couldn't warm up to him. He had too much power over me. He had single-handedly changed the course of my life. He was stern, and along with his attention to me came bursts of anger and criticism that I didn't do anything right.

One day I was sitting in my room when Father came in unexpectedly. He took my hand, brought me over to Mohtaram, who was on the porch, alone, reading a fashion magazine. Although it was in Farsi, it contained the latest fashions in Europe and America.

"Tell her, 'I love you, Mother,'" Father said, trying again.

I distracted myself with the sounds coming from outside—traffic going by, mixed with voices of vendors hawking their merchandise in the square.

Mohtaram looked up from the magazine and stared at me.

I pulled my hand out of Father's. As I turned to leave he slapped me across the face. "Stubborn child," he said.

I ran back to my room and shut the door. I wanted to shout, "I hate you," but my throat was clogged. Later I looked at myself in the small, rectangular mirror on the wall. His handprint was still on my face.

My new home was chaotic, filled with a clashing and confusing mixture of traditional Iranian/Muslim customs and values, and Western ones. None of us prayed, followed the *hejab,* or fasted. But my parents believed boys and girls shouldn't mingle with the opposite sex until they were married by the religious law, that marriages should be arranged by parents, that unmarried girls shouldn't draw boys' attention to themselves by wearing makeup or suggestive bright-colored clothes, that education was for sons. Daughters should marry as soon as a suitable man came along. Tension from unexpressed desire permeated the house—desire of any kind—for more clothes, a different type of clothing, to say certain things, to be with a particular person.

The mixture of values at home mirrored the ones among the people of Ahvaz. Ahvaz's population, consisting of a few thousand Americans and English, about seventy thousand Iranians, and a few hundred Arabs, mainly immigrants from Iraq, was an amalgam of the modern and the old-fashioned. There was a great deal of antagonism in the city among people with opposing views. There were the conservative Iranians and the half-Westernized ones, like my parents. Then there were the Americans and English employed by the oil companies, not to mention the Arab immigrants who were Sunnis (in the midst of Shiite Iranians). They mingled uncomfortably. As people lined up in front of the cinema that showed American movies,

Mother and Father

a mosque across the street broadcast a sermon warning people against worldly pleasures such as seeing movies. Romance was forbidden and yet romantic songs were always blaring out of radios.

The Shah himself, caught between America's pressure and the mullahs opposed to his Westernization, allowed certain things but not others. His alliance with the United States was rooted in what happened in 1953. At that time Prime Minister Mossadegh was distressed over how much profit the British, who controlled Iran's oil industry, were making. He tried to initiate certain reforms. The British resisted. Unable to resolve the issue single-handedly, Britain turned to the United States to settle it. It seemed to the CIA that Mossadegh was a Communist and would move Iran into the Soviet sphere at a time of high Cold War fears. An internal struggle between the Shah and the prime minister followed, culminating in the Shah fleeing Iran. With the help of the CIA, the Shah was restored to his throne and the prime minister was arrested (Operation Ajax). The Shah then reached an agreement with foreign oil companies to "restore the flow of Iranian oil to world markets in substantial quantities." But now instead of the British it was the United States who had most of the control over the oil industry, because of the bigger part it had played in helping the Shah back to his throne. America even helped form SAVAK, the Shah's powerful secret police.

To remind people of the Shah's power, his portraits and statues were ever-present in all public areas, schools, parks, squares, and offices. Artisans were encouraged to weave his portrait into small rugs and tapestries; his face was of course on coins and *tooman* bills.

Tehran had a similar mixture of people and values, but it was a much larger city and the tension hadn't been as apparent to me.

Six

Weeks went by and I didn't get any letters from Maryam, even though I wrote to her weekly, sometimes daily. The only news I had about her was through bits and pieces I heard exchanged between Mohtaram and Father. Maryam's depression wove like a dark thread through their conversation.

I was lying on my bed crying when Pari knocked on the door and came in.

"Come with me, I want to show you my room," she said, putting her arm around me. I dried my eyes and followed her. Her room was between mine and Manijeh's, along a row that included our brothers' and parents' bedrooms.

"I still remember when Aziz took you away," she said. "I was almost five then but the memory stayed with me because I missed you. Poor Aunt Maryam to have lost you, but I'm happy to have gained you back."

Pari opened an album with a red leather cover. "American movie stars," she said. She pointed to each photograph and identified the star. "Elizabeth Taylor, Paul Newman, Marilyn Monroe, Kim Novak, Ava Gardner, Montgomery Clift." Then she pointed to a poster on the wall and said, "That's Judy Garland, she's my favorite."

Pari was wearing a white dress with yellow and red flowers on it, and a white ribbon held her hair back. It struck me that she looked like a younger version of the actress in the poster, with the same lively and expressive face.

"I want to be an actress, if they let me," she said with excitement.

She began to tell me about some of the American movies she had seen. One was called *A Place in the Sun*; the photographs of Elizabeth Taylor and Montgomery Clift in her album were from that movie. "It's mainly a doomed love triangle," she said. "A man and woman from different classes fall in love. A simple, plain woman in love with him pays the price."

I had never gone to a movie. The stories Pari was telling me were so en-

Pari

tirely different from the passion plays Maryam took me to—dramatic reen-
actments of the battle that led to the murder of Prophet Mohammad's
grandson, Hussein. The last one I saw was in the yard of a boys' school, not
far from where we lived. For the occasion I had to wear the chador, otherwise I wouldn't be allowed to go in. The same rule applied to mosques, even
for girls as young as eight years old, as I was then. The production was elaborate, with live camels and a good imitation of a battlefield scene. They set
fire to an effigy of Umar, made of tissue paper. They condemned Yazid, who
had ordered the assassination of Hussein, as a drunkard who disobeyed the
rules of Islam.

Through dialogue the actors told the story of how Mohammad became
a prophet. Mohammad was born around 570 AD (no one knew the exact
date). He was raised by his grandfather and uncle, as he had lost his parents
at a young age. He frequently went to a cave in the desert, three miles from
Mecca, and meditated. He was sleeping on Mount Hira when the angel
Gabriel descended from heaven to give him a message. It contained only
one word, "Recite." Mohammad asked, "What shall I recite?" Gabriel said,
"Recite in the name of the Lord who created all things, who created man
from clots of blood." Mohammad was thus filled with divine majesty. What
was revealed to him was recorded and became the text of the holy Koran.
The Koran was a direct revelation of God. When Mohammad informed his
wife, Khadijeh, of his vision, she said, "You never utter a word that
isn't true." Khadijeh was his first disciple and the first follower of Islam.
Mohammad delivered public sermons on his faith. He converted people
through his compassionate personality, charming demeanor, and force of
divine virtue.

I was brought back to the present by Pari's voice. "I will have to ask Mohtaram to take us to an American movie. Father wouldn't want us to go
alone."

One afternoon Pari picked me up from school and took me to the Karoon River, which ran through the center of Ahvaz. We took our shoes off and walked barefoot on the moist sand. As we walked we could hear the singing of the Arab boys who owned and rented out rowboats. Their voices mingled with the *flap flop* sound of the waves. We passed mud and straw houses, where mostly poor fishermen lived, rows of palm trees so tall that they seemed to be touching the sky. The water was streaked with black from petroleum deposits, but the sky above was a cloudless deep blue. Shells were strewn on the sand. We picked up a few bright orange and pink ones, washed them, and waited for them to dry before putting them in our schoolbags.

After leaving the riverbank we went to the shop on Pahlavi Avenue that carried actors' and actresses' photographs, for Pari to buy more to add to her album.

"There isn't really much in this town, just the river, the park, Pahlavi Avenue with its few shops and restaurants. There's the nightclub, too, but that's for men. They drink and watch belly dancers. Father goes and sometimes Cyrus and Parviz, too. Our brothers can stay out late, do what they want."

"They're never home."

"I'm grateful to have one cinema that shows American movies with subtitles. The other one shows only Iranian action movies, poor imitations of American ones. I wish we didn't always have to go to the movies with Mother."

"In Tehran there are so many things to do. But truthfully I rarely left our neighborhood. Pari, I'm miserable. I miss Maryam terribly."

She put her arm around my waist. "You can rely on me anytime. I know how sad it is for you and Maryam to be pulled apart like that." She came to a stop by a shop. "Let me buy you something. I want to." We went inside. The shop had a variety of accessories. She asked me what I wanted. I pointed to a tortoiseshell comb and she bought it for me.

Then she took me to Café du Park inside the Melli Park. We sat at a table in the shade of a tree and she treated me to lemonade and pastry.

We walked back through the cooler backstreets lined with brick houses and palm-filled gardens. It was dark by the time we got home.

"Pari, Nahid, don't you know you should be home before dark?" Father said when we walked in. "This is the last time I want to see you returning home late."

❋

Father had recently resigned from his judgeship and was now in private practice as a lawyer. He did some of his work at home now, in his office, one of two salons in the house, both near the bedrooms. He emerged from his office periodically to supervise, to ask Mohtaram about domestic affairs, and to discipline us. He commanded and criticized.

"Mohtaram *joon*, when are you going to learn to run the household well?" he'd say. "Look at the way you shop. We either don't have enough fruit or we have too much of it; the porch is full of pigeon droppings, and can't you at least tell Ali to clean it? Or get Fatemeh to come and help out? You're a grown woman now, not that little girl I married." Then his tone would soften and he'd add, "Remember, on our wedding night I had to pick you off the ground and put you into the carriage transporting us to our hotel?"

"Ali, Ali, stop staring at pigeons and do your work." Ali often sat in front of his room on the first floor and threw seeds on the ground for the pigeons.

"Nahid, it's time for you to gain some weight."

"Manijeh, don't cling to your mother all the time."

"Pari, how many times do I have to tell you not to wear that red dress? Go take it off right now."

He didn't criticize our brothers, at least not in front of us women.

In the evening Father was rarely home and that was a relief, except per-haps for Mohtaram, who complained, "He goes out to the nightclub with his friends and they drink *arak* and watch belly dancers and I have to stay behind."

As Pari and I spent more time together, Manijeh, who had been cold to me since I arrived, became outright antagonistic. She was the only sibling who addressed Mohtaram as Maman; the others called her Mother, and I noth-ing. If I absolutely had to talk to her I went and stood in front of her un-til she looked at me and then I made my request. I never addressed her directly.

"Maman bought this for me," Manijeh said, showing off her new dress as I passed her on the porch one afternoon. The dress was white linen with a pattern of pink and yellow cherries. She suddenly pulled my hair so hard that tears came to my eyes. "You aren't really hurt," she said. "I just touched your hair. And don't go and complain to Maman; she won't listen to you. No one wanted you, that's why they gave you away." She spoke in a slow, slurred way, her eyes narrowing in hatred.

"Spoiled brat!" I said. "I hate you."

"I hate you, too," she said and then called, "Maman, Maman, did you hear what she said?"

Mohtaram rushed to the terrace. "Apologize to your sister," she said im-mediately.

"She started the fight," I said.

"Liar," Manijeh said.

"You're the liar," Pari said to her, joining us from her room.

"Pari, stop that," Mohtaram said. "Ever since Nahid came here you've be-come nasty to Manijeh."

"Nahid has nothing to do with it."

"All of you be quiet," Father called from his office.

Mohtaram went into her room and the rest of us dispersed to ours, our sanctuaries from always colliding on the porch. I often wondered what Father and Mohtaram talked about in the privacy of their bedroom. Did they have the same kind of conversations as they had in the open or did they say certain things to each other that they didn't tell us? They appeared like a fortress to me because Mohtaram almost always took Father's side, but what about when they were alone together? Mohtaram certainly was mysterious. For instance the way she went to Manijeh's aid as soon as she asked for something. Pari had to keep repeating her requests before Mohtaram would pay any attention; and she ignored me.

"She looks like an angel," Mohtaram praised Manijeh to whoever was nearby and, "Isn't she becoming more and more beautiful?"

Of Pari she said, "She's healthy-looking."

But to me Pari was more beautiful than Manijeh. True, Manijeh, with her mass of wavy brown hair, light hazel eyes, and well-proportioned features, was pretty, but Pari's face projected a vibrancy that Manijeh's lacked. What did Mohtaram think of my appearance? I had no idea. She never said what she thought. I knew what Father thought: "If only she weren't so thin."

Father didn't treat us sisters with particular favoritism.

Both Father and Mohtaram had respect for and encouraged their sons in whatever interests they had. Cyrus wanted to become an engineer and Parviz a doctor. Father and Mohtaram encouraged their desire to go to America to pursue their education.

Father believed his sons would go even further than he himself had— they had inherited his intellect and determination and had the additional advantage of his financial support. Father had put himself through school. He lost his father at an early age. His father had been mayor of a small town, and his mother mismanaged the money they inherited. Father worked to help support the family and went to school at the same time.

In spite of the fact that our brothers were so high up in the household hierarchy and had much more freedom than us sisters, Pari and I didn't re-sent them. There was no competition between us and them as there was between us sisters. In fact we felt they added something to our lives by introducing us to certain things.

Sometimes Parviz put on records and, holding us sisters one at a time, led us through the tango, fox-trot, and a slower dance he said was popular in America. He played Ping-Pong with us at a table that Father had set up on the terrace mainly for him and Cyrus. He joked with me that he and Cyrus had found me inside a large watermelon on the Karoon River's bank and brought me home to our parents. He praised me for reading a lot.

Cyrus was more reserved than Parviz but still he bought American items for us from a store near the oil drilling company, where he worked a few hours a week to learn certain skills in preparation for engineering school. They were ordinary household products such as Jell-O or Nescafé but Pari and I felt we were getting a piece of America, as we did from American movies.

Seven

"Maryam is much better." I'm not sure how much time had passed before Mohtaram was saying that to Father.

I saw Maryam once or twice a year, when she came for short visits. I still considered her my mother, but now she had no say in the course of my life. Everything was up to Father. Parting after each of her visits was unbearable for both of us. We considered my sudden departure a kidnapping.

Pari became my only consolation. She was happy to have me, the little sister she had once lost, back with her. She told me how nice it was for her to be able to share things with me and have a friend in the household, ignored as she felt by Mohtaram and angry at her favoritism of Manijeh.

Indeed Mohtaram's extreme attention to Manijeh at Pari's and my expense was strange and continuous. One evening, at Pari's suggestion, Mohtaram agreed to take us three sisters to see *Giant* at Javani Cinema. Sahara Cinema was on Pahlavi Avenue, within a block of our house, but Javani was farther away. Pari and I were excited about the movie and had been talking about it all day.

"Maman, I'm not feeling good," Manijeh said, as we were getting ready to leave.

"What's the matter, my dear?" Mohtaram asked.

"I have a headache."

Mohtaram felt Manijeh's forehead with the palm of her hand. "You don't have a fever but you should rest. The movie can wait for another night."

"Nahid and I will go by ourselves," Pari said.

"You know your father doesn't allow that. I have to take you."

"Manijeh becomes sick whenever she wants to get her way," Pari said.

Manijeh's face became red and she put her tongue between her teeth and pressed on it.

"Don't you talk like that to your sister," Mohtaram admonished Pari.

We had to skip the movie that evening.

Pari and I started to cut classes in the afternoons and secretly went to Javani Cinema. Father gave us allowances, graded according to our ages and gender, with a big jump from Pari to Parviz. We sisters got enough *toomans* to be able to go to the movies, or to a café occasionally, or buy a few desired items. If I ran out of money Pari paid for me.

Usually very few people were in the cinema in the afternoons and we felt safe that no one we knew would see us and report to our parents. Watching the American characters on the screen was magical for both of us, transporting us to another way of life. Once Pari took me to see *A Star Is Born*. Judy Garland portrayed an actress whose career blossoms as her husband's declines. Pari was particularly excited by the story.

"Those women can choose a career, marry the person they love," she said as we walked home. "We aren't given any options. Freedom is just a trophy the Shah dangles before us." Pari was wearing the bright red dress that Father had told her not to wear. I interlocked my arm with hers, wanting to protect her, as well as be protected by her.

When we got home, Mohtaram and Father and Manijeh were sitting on the terrace having tea and pastries. "I want to become an actress," Pari announced.

"Stop that nonsense," Father said sharply. "Didn't I tell you an actress is no more than a whore?"

✶

It soon became clear that Pari and I were in our own world within the household. Like her, I resisted the roles prescribed for us by our parents, our school, and the wider society. Manijeh's dream was closer to what was expected of her. My brothers wanted to go to America to study and planned to return and put their education to use in their own country.

My former life with Maryam—once my obsession—became more and more remote as I grew closer to Pari and adopted her views and interests. Of Maryam's religious devotion, Pari said, "It's a way of coping with all that's lacking in this life."

It was true that it was almost a refrain with Maryam and others around her to say, "It's the life beyond that matters." How could they believe in God when he was so unjust? How could they trust that he would lead them to a better life beyond? Those thoughts that had come to me vaguely in the past were now suddenly solidified.

✶

My brothers were leaving for universities in America in the summer of 1958, when I was twelve and Pari was sixteen. Cyrus had waited for Parviz to graduate so they could go together. They seemed to be on top of the world, with an air of determination and superiority. They spoke in confidential tones between themselves and had "conferences" in Father's office. Sometimes they sat together and smoked Winston cigarettes, holding them with poised hands, puffing exaggeratedly.

"I had to pay for every bit of my education, working long hours and studying," Father told my brothers at breakfast one morning. "You're lucky to have a father who can support you."

"We really appreciate all you have done for us, Father," Parviz said.

"You've given us so much," Cyrus said.

"We'll return and put our education to use," Parviz said.

Cyrus nodded in agreement.

"Of course that's what I hope for you to do," Father said. "Then you'll marry nice Iranian girls your mother and I will find for you and you'll give us wonderful grandchildren."

"We hope so," Parviz said.

They drifted to other subjects, mainly politics. Father's voice grew fraught with tension. In the privacy of our home he criticized the Shah for giving SAVAK so much power. They could, at any time, declare someone guilty, arrest them, and even execute them for speaking against the Shah.

My brothers agreed that it was ridiculous that different parties and affiliations—leftist Tudeh, Constitutionalist, Regionalist, Nationalist—and many others were declared illegal at different times.

Father had resigned from his judgeship because it had become too risky, he said. SAVAK members tried to dictate decisions to him. He had also resigned from the textile company where he had been president for a while, because he didn't like the working conditions, the poor health benefits, and the low salaries, and because he was unable to get enough support to improve the workers' lot. As president, he complained, he was a figurehead. The boss, the person in charge of finances, was affiliated with the government and Father had to take orders from him.

It surprised me that Father was so compassionate in his public life, considering his sternness with us girls and with Mohtaram.

"The wheels of this country are turned by the Shah and his circle," Parviz said. "Or Shah and America."

"Parviz, are you careful when you give talks?" Father asked. Parviz often gave talks at his high school's adult education program about public concerns like sanitation and disease control.

"Don't worry, Father, I stay on safe ground."

Father got up to leave; so did Cyrus. Parviz and I lingered.

"I wish I could go to America, too, one day," I said.

"Nahid *joon,* I hope you will. You're my studious sister."

Then he got up to leave as Father called him.

It was even hotter than most summers that year, with temperatures reaching 110 degrees. Damp winds blew in from Shatt-Al-Arab, the river at the Iraqi border, a marshy channel contaminated with oil. Homeless beggars died on the street from heatstroke. The asphalt melted and stuck to our shoes. The dank air brought many mosquitoes, and Ali constantly pumped mosquito repellent into every room.

On the long, hot summer days when every moment was like an eternity I had only Pari to make the time move. Pari and I dipped our feet into the pool in the courtyard to cool off. The pool was shallow and full of frogs. Lizards emerged from behind palm trees, looked around, and went back to their shady spot. We dampened our clothes and sat under the fan turned on high in Pari's room. Sometimes we climbed the stairs to the roof and watched the scenes on the outdoor screen of Sahara Cinema across the street. Though they showed mediocre movies, we still liked watching the images on the screen and catching some of the dialogue. We drank glass after glass of *doogh* to quench our ever-present thirst, and indulged in flights of fantasy about what we could do with our lives, and were full of hope that we could resist our parents' pressures.

One evening, in the middle of August, Father took the family to Akbari *chelo kababi* restaurant on Pahlavi Avenue, as a farewell dinner for our brothers. Father chose that old, traditional restaurant because my brothers most likely wouldn't have that kind of food for a long time. Parviz was going to a university in St. Louis, and Cyrus to an engineering school in Indiana. My brothers said again how they intended to return home after completing their education. They agreed with father that it was a pity we didn't have enough Iranian experts and that foreigners had to do those jobs. The unfavorable exchange rate from *tooman*s to dollars made my brothers' education in America very expensive, but Father was willing to make the sacrifice for the good it would do. American universities were considered to be far superior to Iranian ones.

The next day after breakfast our brothers kissed us good-bye and left, with Father accompanying them to the airport. The moment they were out of the house, the rest of us fell into silence. It was as if a limb had been cut off and we were watching it bleed, not knowing what to do about it.

I found a package on my bed, put there by Ali—as he did with my mail. It was the tapestry depicting paradise, which had been in my old room. With Ali's help I hung it on the wall of my new room. Maryam had embroidered the tapestry for her own dowry. In the middle of the lush green square cloth a stream meandered; trees full of exotic flowers stood on the four sides; birds flew out of the center to the edges; *huris* carried platters of fruit to men and women who reclined against cushions set under the trees; angels clustered in the air, ready to be of service. I found something new in it almost every time I looked—a rabbit peeking out of a bush, a gazelle half hidden behind a rock. But what I liked most about it now was that in the sky the birds were in flight.

Eight

In the fall I entered the seventh grade and joined Pari and Manijeh in the same school. Pari and I walked back and forth together; Manijeh chose to be driven by the chauffeur in the family limousine. Students in Nezam Vafa High School came from the same family background as our parents, middle to upper-middle class, as had been the case in the elementary school. Having a high income, as we did, didn't make a family more or less western. The same conflicting attitudes and values dominated most families, rich or poor.

Pari and I were keenly aware of how different we were, not just from Manijeh but also from most of the girls in the school, who accepted their prescribed roles. Many of the girls were already engaged to be married as soon as they reached legal age, which had been raised to sixteen.

The engaged girls formed a clique of their own. All their fiancés were much older. This was due partly to the fact that ideally husbands had to be "established" to be able to support a family. If you married someone who was not established you would be forced to live at the groom's parents' or siblings' homes until they saved enough money to have their own places.

Jaleh Yazdan, with her olive skin and curly dark brown hair, was engaged to a colonel twice her age. Minou Tajar and Shahla Sadeghpour, cousins, were engaged to brothers, both doctors, both twice as old as their brides. Girls referred to their fiancés by their titles, colonel, doctor, engineer. They whispered to each other as they stood under trees or in other shady spots. In public they were polite, proper. They addressed people with *taarof*, self-deprecating remarks combined with flattery. "I'm not worth your trouble." "It's the beauty of your eyes that cast the glow." "Please forgive me, I'm less than a particle of dust." *Taarof*, which Pari and I criticized between ourselves, was a traditional code of behavior that played a double function. It showed good manners and politeness and at the same time put you at a distance, so that you could guard your privacy in a culture full of taboos.

Girls didn't ever run, laugh out loud, or look at boys standing in doorways or against walls. Boys were waiting for them to pass by, to put letters in their hands inviting them to secret meetings. The engaged girls moved in a slow way, spoke softly; any raised voice, any swift or jerky movement was considered unfeminine and not in good taste. They had to be careful not to do anything inappropriate for fear that they would drive the men away. Those who didn't have anyone yet had to do their best to attract suitable men. To that end the wealthier girls underwent plastic surgery to make their noses smaller or to take the hook out of them. Some even had their breasts enlarged.

Rumor had it that if anyone "slipped" and lost her virginity, she would have her hymen sewed up by a special surgeon so she wouldn't be discovered on the wedding night.

"Modern" girls, too, were afraid of the power men had, no less so than Maryam and other women in her ancient neighborhood. "Men are murky, inscrutable," one girl said. "You never know what they may do to you. For one thing, they flatter you and then once they get their way they abandon you."

I was now at an age when my breasts were budding and I had an awareness of men.

"When you have your periods, can you become pregnant if you let a man . . . ?" I started to ask Pari once, as we walked back from school.

"Go all the way," Pari said. "Yes, you can get pregnant."

Two boys began to follow us, coming close and brushing against our arms, whispering endearing words. They were only two among many *lati*s, lechers, who followed girls on the streets. When we entered crowded Pahlavi Avenue the boys melted away and disappeared among the people on the street.

"There's only one man I like," Pari whispered.

"Who?"

"Majid. He's nice, not one of the *lati*s. And he's different from most men, not tyrannical. I met him when I auditioned for a play they're putting on at school. He came a few times to discuss the play with Miss Partovi. I'm filled with desire at his mere sight. It's like being inflamed."

I thought of Maryam talking with other women about sex as something a woman performed only for the sake of her husband. It was a sin for a woman to enjoy sex or to feel desire. The model for a woman in Maryam's neighborhood was Fatemeh, Prophet Mohammad's daughter. They believed she was a virgin when she gave birth to a son. She had gone bathing and emerged from the water pregnant. The pregnancy lasted for six months; during those months her womb glowed with incandescent light. Angels came to her and helped her give birth.

"Aren't you afraid to feel that way?" I asked Pari.

"Don't you see how men and women desire each other in American movies?"

"Yes . . ."

"Nahid, they gave me the part I really wanted, of the girl Laura."

"Oh, Pari, I'm so happy for you."

"*The Glass Menagerie* is a serious play by an American. Miss Jahanbani, you know, the principal, said there's no point having a play at school. But Majid and Miss Partovi talked her into it."

"How exciting," I said.

"The play has been changed a lot from the original. Miss Jahanbani insisted on certain changes. But the grain of it is still there." Pari turned to look at me. "Don't tell Father I'll be in it."

"Isn't he going to find out? Manijeh will tell him. Maybe it will be in the newspaper."

"Manijeh doesn't pay attention to such things at school. She may not even know about the play. And I doubt it will be in the newspaper."

That evening we went to the balcony and looked out on the street. Groups of boys stood talking under streetlamps or trees. Some had lined up in front of Sahara Cinema. We had seen them around the town. They tried to amplify their individuality by their clothes. One always wore a black shirt to show his affiliation with the conservative Nationalist Party, one wore a red kerchief in his jacket pocket to indicate he supported the Tudeh Party, or Communism, which was outlawed; its members were arrested if they were caught. He was taking a big chance by wearing the kerchief.

"The handsome but conceited one," Pari referred to the boys. "The one trying to imitate Marlon Brando." "The one with the tiny eyes and funny-looking head."

She sank into a somber mood. "I know Father and Mother are going to try to force me into marrying some old man," she said. "I won't give in."

Later that night, Pari practiced her part for me, playing Laura. She contemplated how to move or hold her hand, how simple or complex her facial expressions should be at any moment. The story of a girl whose mother's hope for her and the family was to find her a suitable husband was not unfamiliar to us. It was the sole wish of almost all parents to match up their daughters with the right man as soon as possible, to avoid the danger of their becoming "old maids," and "sour," like some of the teachers and nurses. Higher education was for girls who couldn't find husbands. Girls without husbands would be pitied or shunned. After their parents died, they would have to live with family members willing to take them in.

Pari's ability to put herself in the head of the shy American girl filled me with awe and admiration.

When Pari stayed at school to rehearse I eagerly awaited her return as the household went through its slow, anxious routine. I was worried that Father might notice Pari's delay in coming home as he came out of his office periodically to check up on what everyone was doing. Mohtaram fretted over her domestic tasks, Manijeh hovering around her, Ali watching or feeding the pigeons between his chores.

After I did my homework I read or wrote. I wrote little sketches and stories, aside from my assignments for composition class. I fantasized that one day I would write a play and Pari would act in it. As soon as Pari came back, the pulse of the household returned.

❁

On the day of *The Glass Menagerie* opening Pari was ecstatic.

"What's the most exciting thing for you about acting?" I asked.

"To get to a point where I feel I'm the character."

"I like to write fiction so that I can shape a character's life, make sense of it."

She had managed to keep her part in the play a secret from Father. But then Father came into her room, where I was sitting with her, and said, "I don't approve of your involvement with that school play. We can get into trouble." He threw a cutting from *Etalaat*, the daily newspaper he subscribed to, on the floor and left.

Pari picked it up and we both read it.

Iraj Moghadessi, the producer, Parviz Ahmadi, the director, and all the actresses, among them Simin Baghouli, were arrested for participating in Ibsen's play *Public Enemy* at DadeBad Playhouse in Abadan. . . .

"I wonder how Father found out about your being in the school play," I said.

"Miss Jahanbani must have told him. You know Father talks about us with her all the time. But *The Glass Menagerie* doesn't have anything anyone could possibly misconstrue as anti-government."

Pari went to Father, cried and begged, and he finally told her she could go ahead this one time. But he didn't come to see the play. Neither did Mohtaram, going along with Father's wish. Manijeh wasn't interested. I was the only one in our family who went to see it.

The stage was designed to look like a shabby St. Louis tenement apartment: two soft armchairs, with exposed stuffing and faded floral upholstery, a worn rug on the floor, a table covered with a checkered plastic tablecloth, and four chairs. The audience, not a large one, consisted of teachers, some from other schools, a few parents and students. I sat in the first row. The stage was dimly lit but a spotlight focused on Pari's face. I couldn't take my eyes off her. She had become Laura. Wearing a full-skirted dress falling below her knees, with puffy sleeves and frills at the neckline, she sat at the table and played with small glass animals. The mother, Amanda, wore a long silk dress and pumps. She pressed her son to find a "gentleman caller" for his sister while Laura avoided them by engaging herself with the animals.

Two of Pari's friends, Ziba and Fereshteh, played the male parts—Tom, the restless, poetic brother, and Jim, the gentleman caller. Tom wore a suit and tie, and Jim a suit and bow tie.

When the play ended, there was long, loud applause. People were saying how good Pari was. I beamed with pride. As Pari had explained to me, they had left out or changed from the original what would look immoral to an Iranian audience. They didn't show that Laura once had a crush on Jim, that he used to call her "blue roses." They didn't show them alone together onstage at any point. They had changed the fact that Jim told Laura directly that he was engaged. Instead the mother drew it out of him.

I headed backstage immediately after the applause stopped. "Pari, you were so good," I said, as she changed into her clothes.

A girl who had worked as an usher came in with a bouquet of flowers and gave it to Pari. "For you," she said and walked away.

Pari looked for a card but there wasn't one.

As we walked home with Pari holding the bouquet, she said, "It has to be from Majid. Did you notice the man sitting on the side in a plaid maroon and blue shirt?"

"Yes, he looked very excited watching."

"That was Majid. A few days ago, after a rehearsal, he was waiting for me outside, just standing next to his cherry-colored Buick, his arms folded. It was like we had an appointment. The street was empty then and I dared to get into his car. He drove through backstreets and we talked like two people who know each other well. He teaches in a boys' high school but he's interested in all sorts of things. He loves movies and plays. He believes women should have equal rights." Pari paused, then said, "I let him kiss me."

My heart was pounding loudly in my chest. Pari had entered a forbidden realm, condemned not just by people in Maryam's milieu but even by the more modern Iranian society.

"He's going to send his mother over to ask for marriage."

"But, Pari, do you want to get married?"

"I know I will have to. It may as well be Majid. Just a few days ago Father said to me I should be seriously thinking of marriage. He said someone appropriate has asked for me, but didn't say who."

The blind flute player who usually sat on the Karoon Bridge was sitting against a wall on the path, singing and playing his flute.

On that moonlit night in the alley,
You stole my heart.
Spring came to town with you holding a bunch of wild violets;
And when you went back through the
Doorway there was a smile,
Alive, on your lips
And your eyes spoke memories of our love.

"Why do we have to be content to exchange notes and look at each other from afar?" Pari said, half to me and half to herself.

At home we used the door that led directly to the second floor and to her room so we wouldn't have to go through the courtyard or the porch in front of our parents' bedroom. Pari put the flowers in a vase and the room filled with their scent.

Nine

"hat would look really good on you," Pari said as we walked on Pahlavi Avenue. She was pointing to a dress in a shop window.

"I'll try it on," I said.

The dress wasn't my size and they didn't have it in other sizes, so we bought another dress, dark pink with white circles on it, and headed home on a quiet path that ran parallel to Pahlavi Avenue.

As we were passing a field filled with wild sumac and jasmine bushes, a little boy rushed over to us and handed Pari a rose. A small envelope was tied to the stem with a ribbon. The boy walked away quickly and disappeared into another street. The path was empty and quiet and Pari opened the envelope. I watched her read the note. She was so absorbed in it that I lost her for an instant. Then she came back to me, her face radiant. "Here, I'll let you read it," she said.

My dear Pari, I can't get you out of my thoughts and heart. I know we're for each other. Your parents have sent my mother back with no promises of any kind. Are you aware of that?

"Were you?" I asked Pari.

"No, they never told me about his mother coming over. I was despairing thinking he had changed his mind," Pari said, suddenly looking perturbed. "I'll have to talk to them."

At home, Pari put the rose in a patch of sunlight on the terrace to dry, so that later she could put it in her bureau among her clothes, as she had done with the flowers in the bouquet.

"Wear your dress, I want to see it on you again," she said when we were in her room. "You look grown up. Soon many boys will go after you and you'll fall in love, too, if you let yourself."

We promised each other that we would marry only for love. Arranged marriage was a disaster, we decided. Look at Mohtaram and Father; they were more like father and daughter than husband and wife. Look at all the girls at school, engaged to men they hardly knew and had to share a life with. We didn't want to be links in that long chain of tradition that went back to our ancestors. Pari and I had to break the pattern.

"Where did you get those foolish ideas, love, love? American movies!" Father shouted at Pari on the porch.

"Many families in northern Tehran approve of their daughters going on dates and getting to know a man before marrying him," Pari retorted.

"Ahvaz isn't north Tehran. And nobody in Tehran is so foolish as to leave such decisions to a girl," Father said.

"Romance doesn't fill empty stomachs," Mohtaram offered. "Why would you marry a teacher who won't be able to provide well for you and your children?"

"I want to marry for love," Pari insisted.

"Your head is in the clouds! You don't know what's good for you," Father shouted. In a burst of rage he took hold of Pari's arm and dragged her across the porch, then threw her into her room and slammed the door. He walked away briskly to his office.

I ran to Pari.

"I feel this ache in my heart from the way they talk. It hurts when I breathe," Pari said, her voice shaky. "Mother should be on my side. She should understand her daughters. Instead she always takes Father's side."

"Father knows so much about world history and politics. He speaks French. His office is filled with all those leather-bound books, and those dictionaries. But when it comes to Mother and us, he's a dictator," I said.

I thought of the two framed tapestries that Mohtaram had made and a few days ago hung in the salon, where they entertained guests. They both depicted ponds with ducks floating on them. In the upper right-hand corners were suns. The ponds shimmered in spangled sunlight.

"Did you see those tapestries Mohtaram made?"

"That's where she's allowed to express herself," Pari replied.

"Do you think she ever felt for Father the way you feel about Majid?"

"How could she? She was just a child when she was forced to marry." Pari was lost in thought. "But she may have felt that way about another man," she said after a pause.

"What?" I gasped. "Who?"

"I still remember years ago, when Father traveled a lot, there was a handsome man, the owner of a jewelry store on Pahlavi Avenue. Mother kept going to the store all the time. I saw her once when she came out; her face was glowing as if inflamed, the way I feel when I see Majid."

After I left Pari's room, I came across Mohtaram standing in front of the tall mirror next to the gauzy white curtains in her bedroom, studying her appearance. She had her hair in a flattering permanent wave, had red lipstick on. With the wistful, soft expression on her face, she was so different from the woman who was trying to put practical sense into Pari's head.

What Pari and I had talked about tantalized me. Unable to sleep that night, I sat in bed and constructed how an affair could have happened between Mohtaram and the jeweler.

At first, when they passed each other on the streets, she and the man exchanged glances. Then she began to visit his jewelry store on one pretext or another. Finally, he begged her to meet him somewhere. At first she resisted the idea. One day, she went to the balcony and saw him standing in the square, looking up as if hoping she would come out. Mohtaram remained on the balcony, her eyes locked with the man's, until one of her children started crying and calling her from inside the house.

Finally, when Father was away on a business trip, she succumbed to temptation and met the man, maybe in a quiet corner of a park. She felt faint with desire just being near him. Maybe she had a moment of panic and began to walk away from him. But he went after her and said, "How can you walk away from me? Don't you see how I follow you everywhere just to get a glimpse of you, hear your voice?"

He pointed to a blue wooden chalet. "Will you come there with me? I know the park guard. We can stay there without being interrupted." The chalet stood in a date palm garden, set off from the rest of the park. Its door was open and they walked in. A rug covered the floor and an earthen jar stood on the mantel, but otherwise it was bare. He latched the door from the inside and took her in his arms. "Don't worry," he said. "There is no one around." Did he make a practice of bringing women there? The question passed through her mind but she was too far gone in her desire to resist him. The palm fronds were whispering in the breeze outside. A patch of sunlight skipped in through the dormer window and danced on the wall before them. She was wearing a blue skirt and sandals and a white blouse with a row of red, yellow, and blue flowers, embroidered by her mother, at the neckline.

Then he was undressing her and himself. She went along with it, mesmerized. She was shivering—it was exhilarating to be with someone close to her own age. She sensed her own attractiveness as she felt the young man's touch and heard him whisper, "You're beautiful."

After that, as if pulled by a magnet, she met him again and again, whenever Father was away on business.

One day she went to the chalet and the man wasn't there. Later she found him in the store but he avoided looking at her. He no longer stood in the square, staring up at the balcony to get a glimpse of her.

I wrote it all down and hid the notebook under my mattress so that Father wouldn't see it, as he frequently dropped into my room to check to see what I was reading and writing.

The next day I read it to Pari. We almost convinced ourselves that it was true, that it had to be.

Arguments between Pari and our parents about Majid, who sent his mother over several more times, continued for months.

"I won't marry anyone else except him," Pari said, but Father always said no.

Pari locked herself in her room for a week. Her skin became sallow and she had nosebleeds. Ali or I brought food to her. I ate my meals with her and tried to comfort her, telling her that maybe it was just as well if she didn't marry now, but she was disconsolate. She reminded me that our parents were going to force her to marry someone else. At times she was uncommunicative, wanted to sleep or just be alone with her thoughts.

"What are you doing, what's this silly strike?" Father would say as he pounded on her door. And Mohtaram told her she was torturing herself for no reason. "There are much better suitors for you."

I wondered if Father and Mohtaram were evil. But my grandmother, whom I loved so much, had done the same to her daughters, had forced them to marry men she and my grandfather chose. They themselves were victims of the oppressive system that dictated to people how they should feel and live their lives. This was the time Pari should resist marrying anyone but Majid, break the chain, as we had promised each other.

Miss Partovi sent a message through me to Pari, telling her she should audition for a part in *My Fair Lady,* an American musical. Pari's spirits lifted at once. She took the chance that Father wouldn't stop her if he found out about her participation in the play, that he'd hope her involvement in something she liked would heal her wound.

But Father said no. "Father has forbidden me to participate in the play, now that I actually got a part," Pari cried to me. "He told me he doesn't want me to stand onstage and represent a woman as an object of a man's lust."

"Pari, that isn't all there is to *My Fair Lady.*"

"I told him the same thing but it fell on deaf ears. He told Miss Jahanbani that he doesn't want me to be in any more plays and that's the end of it."

To help Pari calm down, we went to see a movie that was showing in the auditorium of the American high school on the other side of the river, in a neighborhood where many Americans lived. Though there were many Americans in Ahvaz, we didn't have a single American friend. I understood why; all the differences in values kept them apart from Iranians. Most Iranians, even many of the Westernized ones, were still bound, at least partly, to their cultural-religious values and traditions, as the Americans were to their own. Iranians referred to them as "the Americans," and I assumed the Americans referred to us as "the Iranians." We were categories to each other.

The movie, *Separate Tables,* was in English with Farsi subtitles. On the way out we saw a notice on a bulletin board in the hallway that a studio was looking for people to dub movies from other languages into Farsi. Pari wrote down the information. She said, "I'm going to try for that, hope that Father won't find out."

Pari was accepted by the studio to dub *Bitter Rice,* an Italian movie, into Farsi. She cut classes several afternoons and went to the studio. For a while, she managed to keep her part-time job a secret.

"Father isn't the only one who thinks of actresses as whores," Pari told me one day. "The people in the studio seem to be of the same opinion. One of them asked me to take my clothes off. I just ran out of there."

Ten

One afternoon, as I was taking a different route home, I noticed a bookstore on a narrow street off Pahlavi Avenue. The street was lined with a few run-down and some closed-down houses and was very quiet. I walked in and looked for books. A few boys were there, but no girls. Among the boys was the one I had seen with the red kerchief. That day he wasn't wearing it.

The store wasn't large but it was brimming with books. On a table I found books by revered Iranian poets, Saadi, Hafiz, and Omar Khayyam. These ancient poets spoke to all strata of the population in Iran; each interpreted the poems in his own way. Hafiz's poetry was often used to tell fortunes. The person would open the book randomly to a page and whatever was written there was interpreted to mean something about the person's future.

On the same table were several books translated into Farsi, among them *Pride and Prejudice, The Sun Also Rises, Crime and Punishment.* They must have passed censorship, I thought. Operating under the Ministry of Information, the censorship authority controlled the publication of all manuscripts, original or translated. Books that either contained a political message or could be interpreted that way were banned. Sometimes a book passed censorship but, after some new meaning was found in it, was taken off the market and all copies destroyed. SAVAK was always on the lookout for any-thing even remotely threatening to the regime. Restlessness aroused in peo-ple by reading certain books could eventually lead to an uprising, they believed.

I picked out *The Sun Also Rises*. When I went to pay, the owner looked at me quizzically, as if wondering what a young girl was doing buying a book by a foreign writer. He was a thin, tall, sensitive-looking young man with grave dark eyes. As I was leaving the store he said, "Come back. I get new books all the time."

At home I devoured the book. I began visiting the Tabatabai Bookstore weekly to buy more. The owner, Jalal, told me a little about the translated books he had in stock, which he ordered as soon as they were available. I liked reading those books; they gave me glimpses into other worlds, other lives, as American movies did.

Once when I came home, I found the door to my room wide open. Fa-ther was rummaging through my books. I stood at the door fearfully. Was he going to object to the books I was reading? What if he looked under the mattress and found the story I wrote about Mohtaram and the jeweler? I entered the room and just stood there silently.

"Nahid," he said in a tense, agitated tone. "Be careful about the books you buy; some of them can get us into trouble. You never know who might be a SAVAK agent. It could be someone disguised as a handyman or an electrician."

Then he zoomed out. I breathed with relief. He hadn't mentioned my story. I shut the door and, just to make sure, looked under the mattress. The notebook was there as I had left it. I picked it up, pulled out the pages con-taining the story, and tore them into pieces. I put them at the bottom of my schoolbag to discard in the large garbage pail just outside of school.

One day when I was browsing at Tabatabai Bookstore, Jalal said, "I just got a new book I can show you." It was as if we had an unspoken connection, trusted each other. There was no one else in the store at the time but he was whispering. His face, his voice were even more grave than usual. He reminded me of characters in *Brothers Karamazov*.

"What is it?" I asked, dropping my voice.

"*Les Misérables*. It was taken off the market. I managed to get a few copies before they shredded them. I tell you because I know you love books as much as I do and you hate many things about our society as I do."

"What's it about?"

"A man who, out of starvation, steals a loaf of bread and is hounded by the police for the rest of his life. SAVAK thinks the book might mirror some things in our society."

"I'd like to read it."

Jalal pushed aside a thick curtain in the back of the store, revealing a stairway. He climbed down and returned within minutes holding a book. He handed it to me. It had a plain white jacket on it, revealing no title or name.

After I bought it he wrapped the book in gift paper and gave it to me. "Be very careful," he said.

I put it in my schoolbag and headed home. His remark, "Be very careful," rang in my ears, and I was tempted to turn around and say the same thing to him. Terrifying images of Jalal getting arrested, his shop being shut down, his being thrown in jail for years or even executed came before my eyes. According to rumors people were punished that way for just that "crime" he was committing. How strange that in our culture books were considered dangerous, that the written word was given so much power, that a person was thought of as a criminal for owning or reading certain books. I had actually taken a few steps back to the store, I realized. I stopped myself. He was older than me, had owned the store for three years, he once told me. He was cautious enough to have gotten away with selling such books. He knew instinctively whom to trust.

I stayed in my room with the door shut and immediately started reading the book like a child starved for food.

I wrote a story based on the plight of the woman who had been tempted to abandon her blind child, the story Maryam and Hamideh had spoken of that day in Tehran.

When Shamsi and her two small children moved into some rooms in our house, they looked very poor and pathetic. My mother took pity on them and reduced the rent. Wherever Shamsi went her children followed. One of her daughters, Monir, the smaller of the two, was blind in one eye and the other eye could see only vague shadows of things. No one knew how Shamsi suddenly began to acquire new possessions. She got new clothes for herself and the children. She bought copper pots and pans, which she shined every day. And a faint smile lingered on her face. Then Monir disappeared. No one saw her in the mornings or at any other time and the smile on Shamsi's face also disappeared. One day she confessed everything. There was a man who was interested in marrying her but he would not put up with a blind child. So she had taken Monir to the desert at the edge of Tehran and left her there. Then Shamsi had run away and gotten into a jeep full of soldiers. The soldiers had teased and flirted with her but she covered her face under her chador, unable to cry or smile. I picture Monir standing in the vast desert, listening to the vanishing echoes of her mother's footsteps. Then waiting desperately for her to appear again until other frightening images and echoes swept over her consciousness. . . .

I showed the story to Pari, as I did all the stories I wrote. As important as it was for me to write, it was equally important to hear her reassuring, encouraging voice. After Pari told me she liked the story, I handed it in as my composition assignment at school.

"What do you think?" Mrs. Soleimani asked the class after I'd read it aloud.

"It's too sad," one of the girls said.

"It doesn't sound real," another girl said.

"But it *is* realistic; it captures the desperation of women all around us," Mrs. Soleimani said. She was married with a son, thus having fulfilled conventional expectations, and in addition she had managed to have a career. She encouraged us to strive for more than just marriage and children.

At her comment the class fell into silence.

"If you had a choice, would you have been born a man or a woman?" Mrs. Soleimani asked.

I raised my hand.

"Yes, Nahid?"

"I would still want to have been born a girl, but I want to go to America and live there." The idea of going to America had been in my fantasies ever since my brothers left.

A few others in the class of twenty raised their hands. One said she would want to be born a girl because she could become pregnant, something a man couldn't do. Another said she didn't understand boys, so she wanted to be a girl. Yet another said she thought life was harder for men because they had to be the breadwinners and be strong. Only one said she would want to be a boy so she could become a good soccer player like her brother and do other things her brother was allowed to do, like stay out late at night and take trips with his friends without parental supervision.

"Most of you are fourteen years old," Mrs. Soleimani said. "Some of you have been promised to men who are much older and know a lot more about life than you do and will no doubt be able to dominate you. You must fight being in that situation."

Some of the girls looked at her with awe for saying such things. Others seemed vaguely disapproving, as if she were attacking them rather than giving them guidance. But of course she was absolutely right, I thought. It was the way Pari and I felt, too, that we had to fight against that situation.

After class Mrs. Soleimani stopped me and said, "You look sad. Are there problems at home?"

I nodded.

"Come, let's talk in my office."

"I'm so unhappy," I said once we were in her office. I told her how abruptly I had been torn away from Maryam and now my mother was totally cold to me. How my father would force my sisters and me to marry whomever he chose for us, how he controlled every aspect of our lives.

"I'm certain if you were a boy your mother wouldn't have given you away, even as a kindness to her sister," Mrs. Soleimani said. "When something goes wrong with my car, male drivers honk and yell at me because I'm a woman. All the men in this school, and everywhere else, get paid much more than women. They're breadwinners and we women are bread eaters, they say. I had a very authoritative father, too, Nahid, but I fought him and pulled myself out of his grip and managed to go my own way." She pondered that for a moment, then added, "Within the limits."

The bell rang for the next class and we parted, but Mrs. Soleimani's words had moved me deeply. Back home, I told Pari what Mrs. Soleimani had said about fighting her authoritative father.

"Father's will is impossible to bend," Pari said, despair coming into her face.

"Why don't you ask him to send you to America to study? I want to do the same thing. Maybe he'll agree if you insist that you won't marry anyone."

"He isn't going to go along with such an idea. He said so many times that education is a waste on a girl."

"If you had a choice, would you have been born a man or a woman?" I asked Pari.

"I don't want to be a man, dictatorial," Pari said. She thought about that. "There are exceptions. Some, like Majid, are different."

"Parviz and Cyrus are different, too," I said.

Pari nodded. "The world would be a better place if there were more men like them."

Eleven

On a Friday, the Sabbath in Iran, I found Pari in her room getting dressed, putting on a blue dress and gold jewelry.

"A suitor is here, with his sister," she said. "Mother and Father made me dress up. They're going to call me in to meet them. I saw him going into the salon. He looks really tense. You want to see what he looks like?"

We crept slowly to the salon and took turns peeking through the large keyhole. Our parents were sitting on the maroon velvet sofa. The suitor and his sister occupied the two matching dark blue armchairs.

"Look how his ears stick out," Pari whispered.

Everything he did, all his gestures, seemed comical as I saw him through Pari's eyes. We crept back to Pari's room as we couldn't hold back laughter.

Moments later Father came to her door. "Come with me," he said. Pari followed him.

The air in Pari's room still had a faint scent of the flowers she had received from Majid. And here she was, pressured into being viewed by a suitor, perhaps soon pressured into considering him. Someone she had absolutely no interest in. How ridiculous and unfair it all was.

After the visitors left, I heard angry voices on the porch.

"I don't want to marry him," Pari said.

"Come to your senses," Father boomed. "Taheri is one of the richest men in Ahvaz. He has a share in the Dorang Petrochemical Company. He makes one million *tooman*s a year from his carpet shops in Ahvaz and Tehran. And he'll inherit a fortune from his elderly father, who has a thriving business in Tehran. And he's educated, a graduate of the Finance Academy in Tehran."

"He values you so much he's offering a large sum for your *mehrieh*," Mohtaram said. "You can't throw that away."

"You're trying to sell me."

"Pari, don't be so foolish," Father said.

"Let him marry Manijeh instead," Pari said defiantly.

"You know very well that as the oldest you have to marry first," Father said.

"You aren't thinking of me at all!" Seconds later Pari was in her room.

"What happened?" I asked her.

"I'm not going to give in to them," she said.

But Taheri was persistent. Since his parents lived in Tehran, his oldest sister, Behjat, was the one who mainly dealt with our parents. She was a widow and lived with her brother. He planned to sell the shop in Ahvaz and live in Tehran to be near their elderly parents.

Behjat was a little more old-fashioned than our parents, from what we could see. She didn't wear a chador, but she wore a head scarf and conservative clothes and no makeup. One afternoon when she was sitting with Mohtaram in the salon, Pari and I went to the big keyhole again, looking in and listening.

"My brother is an open-minded man," she was telling Mohtaram. "He doesn't want a chadori wife. He doesn't even like me to wear this head scarf. I'm an old woman now, I didn't wear it when I was young. He wants a wife who can dress well, like your daughter. When he first saw your daughter on the way to school, he knew immediately she is the one for him."

Mohtaram came to Pari after Behjat left and they had the same argument as before, with Pari refusing to give in to the marriage proposal.

"They keep at me," she said. "But I can't imagine sharing a life with that man."

Behjat visited a few days later and Pari and I again took our spot by the keyhole. This time Father was there with Behjat and Mohtaram.

"My brother is threatening suicide," Behjat said urgently. "He said if your daughter doesn't consent, he'd rather be dead. Taheri has a romantic soul."

"I admit my daughter is headstrong," Father said. "Bear with her, she'll come to her senses."

Later that day Mohtaram came to Pari's room and gave her a letter, which she had already opened. She left and Pari and I turned to the letter immediately.

With all respect, Pari khanoon, *the daughter of a distinguished father and respected mother, I can't imagine a life without you as my wife. I'd rather die than see you marry someone else. I have a plan to kill myself. . . .*

Pari grimaced. "This is just blackmail. He doesn't know me even slightly. We haven't spoken to each other once."

I felt anxiety in the bottom of my stomach from all the tension building up around Pari.

"I confess to you, I saw Majid," Pari said, holding the letter in her lap. "We went to his apartment near the river this time. We kissed. He stopped before going further. He isn't a selfish man. In fact, he told me we should stop seeing each other unless we can get married. He had actually heard about Taheri's interest; he said he hoped nothing would come of it. Majid is going to wait until Taheri finally gives up and then send his mother over again."

We sank into a contemplative silence.

"Pari," Father called from behind the door.

After Pari left, I wondered what was going to happen. Was Pari going to keep arguing until Father and Mohtaram gave up? Then would she and

Majid get married? What would be the consequences of that? Pari would have no support from our parents; in the future, if she needed help, they wouldn't be there for her. Then I grew apprehensive about Majid's character. Was he really any different from other Iranian men who expected their wives to be "pure"? Pari had broken a deep taboo by going to his apartment and letting him kiss her. Would he begin to disapprove of her for doing so?

"Father keeps telling me Taheri is such a good catch," Pari said, coming into the room. "Why won't he listen to me? My emotions are all tangled up with Majid. You know what Miss Partovi says, that a good actress should be able to present characters so that all different aspects of them come together in a coherent way? I want that for myself but I feel so fragmented under all the pressure."

What Pari said only added to my trepidation. It was as if she had turned into a delicate vase that might suddenly break into pieces.

On a hot April afternoon Pari and I were sitting at the edge of the pool, dangling our feet in the water. It hadn't rained for a long time and the date palm trees standing in a row on one side of the courtyard were shriveled and dusty, their fruit all dried up in clusters. Dragonflies darted around the dusty air.

"Nahid, I'm going to marry Taheri," Pari said suddenly.

"Pari, why? How did this happen?"

"Majid sent his mother here again, and Father and Mohtaram refused to accept the proposal. Even though we weren't going to see each other again, I did see him. But this really was the last time. It was too painful. Do you know what he said? That we should elope. But of course it's not possible. No one would marry us without Father's consent. Majid knows that; it was only a wild fantasy."

"You could wait awhile," I mumbled. "Maybe someone other than Taheri—"

"I have something to gain by marrying Taheri," Pari interrupted. "He'll take me to Tehran. I'll pursue acting there. People must be more open-minded there about actresses." Her face looked blurry in the dusty light and I couldn't assess her feelings clearly.

"I'm going to be lonely without you," I said after a moment.

Ali came out of his room and started throwing seeds on the ground to attract pigeons. Sounds from the streets were beginning to become muffled as dusk was approaching. Pari and I got up and started walking up the steep stairway that took us to our rooms on the second floor.

After Pari told our parents she would marry Taheri they praised her, telling her she was now finally acting her age of almost eighteen, a mature woman.

Our parents informed Behjat that Pari was willing to marry her brother.

"He will be so happy," she said. "You saved him from terrible things he was threatening to do to himself."

They proceeded with serious negotiations about the *mehrieh* and *jahaz*. *Mehrieh* was financial collateral or material backing given by the groom, in case of marital discord. If the husband decided to divorce his wife he would have to pay her the agreed-upon sum. He offered property but our parents decided they preferred a sum of money, which was large, half a million dollars in Iranian currency. For *jahaz*, or dowry, our parents agreed to send along with Pari old gold coins, silverware, dishes, and other household items. Pari hadn't participated in the negotiations, as that wasn't the custom. It was an agreement between our parents and Taheri's sister.

Twelve

In spite of all the pressure on Pari, I kept thinking if she were stronger maybe she could have gotten her way. I could see that at times her rebellion was mixed with a desire for our parents' approval. Occasionally she went to Mohtaram and Father and was full of smiles and friendliness to compensate for her defiance.

I still hoped she would try to get out of marrying this man. But close to the end of that year, when Pari was about to graduate from high school, she got engaged. They put off the wedding date until September, when the house Taheri was setting up for them in Tehran would be ready. The house was in a modern, bustling section of central Tehran, he said.

The engagement party was a small affair, with only the immediate family present. The big celebration was saved for the wedding itself.

After Taheri and Behjat arrived in the afternoon, we all sat on the porch at small tables set out by Ali. We were dressed up for the occasion. Pari wore a blue dress with designs of shiny, darker blue flowers in a thicker fabric. Her shoes were white and she was wearing white gold flower-shaped earrings studded with diamonds. Everything she was wearing, including the expensive earrings, were presents from Taheri. He was dressed in a wine-colored jacket, light gray pants, and a pink-and-gray-striped shirt. He could have been good-looking, had it not been for the extreme intensity about him that practically contorted his face. In the large space, Mohtaram, Manijeh, Behjat, Father, and I receded as Taheri focused almost entirely on Pari.

He was ten years older than Pari, not as significant an age gap as between many couples, but he spoke to her the way an experienced man would speak to a child.

"Pari, you aren't old enough to know what I have learned in life, such as the value of stability, a husband who provides well for you," I was startled to hear him say.

"I'm not a child," Pari said, as directly.

"I'll teach you many things when we get to our home in Tehran." Taheri took from his jacket pocket a box containing a diamond ring. He put the ring on Pari's finger.

"I wish you a long and happy future together," Behjat said.

"May your union be blessed," Mohtaram said.

We all began to clap. Pari was blushing, and I sensed she was uncomfortable with the formality of the remarks.

Ali brought over a tray of tea and passed it around. From a table set in the corner, Mohtaram picked up a large platter containing sweets, *bamieh*, *zulbia*, and other pastries and served them.

"Would you like some *arak*?" Father asked only Taheri, as alcoholic drinks were proper only for men, even among the modernized Iranians. Father drank *arak* (vodka) only with his male friends.

"I don't drink, I'm a good Muslim," Taheri said. "But don't get me wrong, I like many aspects of Western culture. I like my wife to look modern and speak well." He turned to Pari and stared at her face, as if he couldn't have enough of her.

Pari was *namzad*, an engaged girl. Father told her and Taheri they could be alone for a while in the salon.

In a few moments I went to the keyhole. The expression on Pari's face was conflicted. Taheri's was possessive, almost tortured. He made me uneasy. I watched as he tried to kiss Pari and she gently pushed him away. This was the accepted way for a girl to behave, to save herself until the wedding night. But I knew, of course, that Pari wasn't just playing a role.

Now Taheri was allowed to come and see Pari once a week and be alone with her for a short time in the salon during each visit. Whenever I could get away with it I spied on them. Every time Taheri tried to kiss Pari, she said, "Not until we're married."

"He keeps saying how I'm the only person he has ever wanted to marry," Pari told me. "That no one has ever stirred him to exaltation the way I do. He has promised to let me pursue acting. He said he wants me to be free and do what matters to me."

"Pari, is it wonderful to be so adored?"

"You know, Nahid, sometimes he frightens me, he's so intense."

I couldn't understand how Pari was going to tolerate Taheri day after day, live with him, share his bed. Neither could I see myself in the same situation, marrying someone I hardly knew or even liked. Resistance was only hardening in me.

Pari now had a high status at school because she was one of the engaged girls. And Mohtaram paid more attention to her, taking her shopping, adding various items to her *jahaz*, which she had started preparing for her daughter as soon as she agreed to the marriage.

They came back with packages of high-quality bedspreads, pillowcases, towels, china, and silverware, some imported, some made in Iran. Mohtaram had said to Pari, "Taheri loves you so much, you'll learn to love him, too. I cried when I married your father but now I can't imagine being with anyone else."

For days Father, Mohtaram, Taheri, and his sister, and sometimes Pari, too, discussed the wedding. Taheri wanted everything carried out in the old traditional way with its elaborate rituals.

"It's all so stifling," Pari said to me.

Pari didn't bring up Majid at all, and I left it up to her to do so, as I assumed at this stage it was very painful for her even to mention his name.

Pari had become a bit remote from me, partly because she was buried in all the expectations and planning. But I sensed she was upset that she hadn't kept her side of the promise that we would marry only for love. I wondered about Majid, if he was now going to ask his mother to look for another wife for him or if Pari had been unique to him, someone he truly loved, someone whose loss he would not get over for a long time.

Maryam and Aziz came for the occasion and planned to stay for two weeks. While Pari was busy with her wedding plans I spent a lot of time with them. Although I had drifted from their values, I still felt immense comfort in their presence. They had brought me presents. Maryam gave me a gold ring with a cornelian stone on it; she bought it in Karbala, Iraq, where she went to visit the shrine of Imam Hussein, the son of Ali and grandson of Prophet Mohammad. She planned to rent her rooms in Tehran and live in a rooming house near the shrine, at least for a year. "My home has never been the same since you were taken away from me," she told me. "Being by the shrine and praying there every day will help my soul."

Aziz gave me *sohoon* and *gaz,* sweets filled with honey and pistachios, treats unavailable in Ahvaz. She told me I didn't need to share them with Manijeh, about whom I had complained to her.

"She's just afraid you'll take her place in Mohtaram's heart," she said in a kind tone.

"But Mohtaram is cold to me, too."

"I'm sure you love Maryam more than her and she must sense that."

I contemplated her remarks, but caught as I was in my insecurities, they didn't help.

The day before the wedding Mohtaram took Pari to a woman to get her pubic hair removed. This was the custom for a girl about to get married. The woman applied an herbal concoction to Pari's pubic hair, then, after a half hour, removed the hair, which came off easily but still left a sting, Pari said.

On the day of the wedding Mohtaram took Pari to a beauty salon. When they came back Pari's hair was set in curls, her eyebrows plucked to narrow lines, her face made up with dark lipstick, rouge, and eyeliner. Now that she was about to become a married woman makeup was acceptable. Pari said it made her feel she was onstage, as the whole marriage did.

Then followed the two stages of a traditional Persian marriage, originating partly in Zoroastrianism, the religion of Iran before Islam. It could last for several days but Taheri wanted them both on the same day as he was in a rush to go on their honeymoon and then to Tehran as soon as possible.

The first part was *aghd,* the legal process of getting married. This took place in our house.

Mohtaram, with the help of Maryam, Aziz, Ali, and Fatemeh, a young maid who came in every few days, prepared the salon, putting bouquets of flowers in different spots and spreading the *sofreh-ye-aghd* on the floor.

The cloth used for the *sofreh* on this occasion was passed from mother to daughter. Mohtaram, who received it from Aziz, intended to use it in each daughter's wedding. It was made of a rich gold-embroidered cashmere fabric. On the *sofreh* they placed symbolic items: a mirror (for fate), two candles (representing brightness in the bride and groom's future together), a platter of seven multicolored herbs and spices (to break spells and witchcraft), a basket of decorated eggs (to symbolize fertility), a platter of pomegranates, "heavenly fruits" (to assure a joyous future), and a bowl of gold coins (symbolizing wealth and prosperity). A cup of rose water extracted from special Persian roses perfumed the air. Two hardened sugar cones were also there, to be crushed over the head of the bride.

A specially baked and decorated flatbread with *"Mobaarak-Baad"* written on it in powdered sugar and saffron blessed the wedding. In addition, an assortment of sweets were set on the *sofreh* for the guests to eat after the ceremony: honey, sugar-coated almond strips, baklava, mulberry-almond paste in the shape of mulberries, rice-flour cookies, chickpea-flour cookies, almond-flour cookies, and honey-roasted almonds.

A copy of the Koran, opened to the middle, was placed on the *sofreh,* too, symbolizing God's blessing for the couple. Taheri's sister had made sure it was there (it wasn't part of the Zoroastrian origin of the ceremony). Of course Maryam and Aziz were pleased about having the Koran there.

The bridegroom was the first to take his seat in the room at the head of the *sofreh-ye-aghd.* The bride came afterward and joined the bridegroom. An *aghound* and a notary came in to perform the legal part of the ceremony. After the preliminary blessings and a few words about the importance of the institution of marriage, the *aghound* conferred with the witnesses. Hassan, Taheri's uncle, a tall, hefty man with an upward-twisting mustache, was his witness, and Father was Pari's. Both said that they indeed wished to proceed with the ceremony and that there were no objections.

"Do you wish to enter this blessed marriage?" the *aghound* asked Taheri.

"It is my deepest wish," Taheri said.

Then the *aghound* asked Pari the same question.

Pari didn't answer immediately. It was proper for the bride not to show eagerness. To make the bridegroom wait for the bride's answer signified that it was the husband who sought the wife and was eager to have her and not the other way around. But again I could tell Pari wasn't playing a role here. Her hesitation about the marriage was still there and I could sense it.

The *aghound* asked the question three times and at the third time Pari said, "Yes." A simple yes. Then the *aghound* asked the groom if he understood that in case of, God forbid, a divorce initiated by him, he would have to pay the bride the full *mehrieh,* as was the law. Taheri said yes.

The *aghound,* Father, Hassan, the bridegroom, and the bride signed the documents and the *aghound* pronounced the couple husband and wife. "God bless this marriage," he said.

Then the bride and bridegroom placed the wedding bands on each other's fingers and fed each other honey.

Manijeh and I held a cloth over the bride's head, as we had been instructed, and Mohtaram held the two cones of sugar over the cloth and rubbed them together, to sweeten the marriage. The pieces of sugar fell like crystal onto the cloth. Then everyone in the room broke into clapping and congratulating the bride and groom, *"Aroosi Mobarak . . ."*

Pari was showered with gifts—mainly expensive jewelry that Taheri himself and his sisters, parents, and other family members had sent or brought. Maryam and Aziz also had brought presents, and relatives who weren't attending had sent them—a crocheted silk bedspread, a linen table-cloth and napkins, embroidered at their edges, a silver tea set, a samovar.

My parents gave Taheri a Rolex watch (it wasn't proper to give the groom more than one or two gifts).

Ali brought in tea in our best tea glasses, dainty, gold-rimmed, in fili-greed silver holders, and served it to everyone.

After a while everyone dispersed to get dressed for the reception that would be held two hours later at a garden restaurant. Maryam and Aziz de-clined to go to that part of the celebration—neither of them would be com-fortable at a large party where none of the women would be wearing the chador and alcohol would be served to men.

The garden was decorated with colored bulbs and lanterns strung be-tween trees. A fountain splashed colored water into a pool, making a rain-bow. The moon was full and its jewel-like brilliance was reflected in the water.

Pari was wearing a long white satin dress with embroidery at the neck-line. Her diamond engagement ring and wide gold wedding band sparkled on her finger. About two hundred guests—family friends, some with their children, Pari's friends—kept trying to get close to her and the groom.

As Father and Mohtaram had insisted, Manijeh and I were dressed iden-tically in rose-colored dresses and dark blue shoes. Manijeh had borrowed Mohtaram's ruby earrings and ruby-studded pendant. Mohtaram had on a blue satin dress and blue silk shoes. She didn't look much older than the bride.

Waiters walked around and served marinated whitefish, caviar, *doogh,* a drink made with yogurt, and *sharbat,* a drink made with fruit and cardamom, for women, and alcoholic drinks for men who requested it. Some men and women chose to sit at tables separated by gender. I took care not to sit with Manijeh, always aware of the thick cloud of tension between us, neither of us able, at this stage of our lives, to get beyond our irrational jealousies of each other. Young boys and girls looked at one another wistfully, not daring to go any further than that.

Waiters began to serve the dinner—roast lamb, sweet rice, dill and lima bean rice, broiled whitefish, pomegranate chicken, lamb and beef *kababs*, Shirazi salad, yogurt-and-cucumber salad.

Mrs. Alavi and Mrs. Davoodi, friends of my parents who frequently came to our house, were sitting at my table. Their husbands were at another table.

"Jaleh is getting a divorce," Mrs. Davoodi told Mrs. Alavi. "The judge granted it after we got a statement from a psychiatrist that her husband is manic-depressive. He couldn't perform his husbandly duty, even on the first night. Jaleh knew something was wrong from the beginning."

"Didn't you know that about him, I mean the mental state?" Mrs. Alavi asked.

"The few times we saw him before they got married he must have been under control by drugs. He seemed perfectly normal. He returned from America, where he was studying, and then his parents looked for an eligible girl. He's good-looking, educated, but sick in his mind."

"These days girls aren't the same as in our time," a woman sitting at an adjacent table said to another. "They don't have our tolerance. We were better off, we knew only one way of life."

"Hasn't Manijeh turned into a beautiful woman? She's going to be snapped up soon," a woman sitting behind me said to another woman.

I caught snatches of conversation from other tables.

"I'm going into my father's business as soon as I graduate," one boy said.

"I'll be going to the polytechnic university in Tehran," another boy remarked.

"You used to live with your aunt in Tehran?" a girl sitting next to me asked.

"Yes," I said.

"I wish I could live in Tehran. But my parents have someone in mind for me. He's an officer in the army."

Another strand of conversation reached me.

"He's in jail? No! For what? Such a nice young man."

"Maybe someone didn't like the way he dresses, or scratches his head."

"Let's not dwell on sad things. This is a wedding, two people uniting for life."

"It's all the Westoxication that creates turmoil," a man said, his voice rising above all others.

"Our view of America isn't all realistic." This was said by a man with a rigid posture and expression who was standing under a tree. "If you examine the country closely you see serious problems there. All the suicide, murder, violence. There's no soul."

"You're right," the man standing next to him said. "No closeness between people there, no sense of family. They are a lonely crowd, as one of their own sociologists said."

Lonely crowd. *Didn't these pompous men see the loneliness in our own country?* I thought. *Look at me. Look at Pari.* Pari, dressed in expensive clothes and jewelry and sitting next to her dark-suited husband, seemed to be a million miles away.

After dinner, two waiters brought out a gigantic cake with the blessing *"Aroosi Mobarak"* written on it with colorful sprinkles. They put it on a table in the middle. Everyone stood up and clapped and sang, starting with "The *aroosi* be blessed by God, *mobarak bashe.*" A few women spontaneously broke into group dancing among themselves, snapping their fingers and singing. When they were planning the reception, Father and Mohtaram and Behjat had discussed having dance music for those who wanted to dance but Behjat thought it was a bad idea to encourage dancing, since a few of her conservative relatives would be at the reception and wouldn't like boys and girls dancing together. So even the bride and groom didn't dance.

The waiters cut the cake and served it with tea and *sharbat,* and the women returned to their seats. A variety of pastries and ice cream were served along with the cake.

Musicians on a platform in the middle of the garden began to play the drum, tambourine, and violin.

At the end of the evening, after the guests had departed, Pari left with Taheri and his sister to stay in their home in Ahvaz for the night. The following day Pari and Taheri would be going on their honeymoon to Babolsar, a town on the Caspian Sea, and from there to Tehran, where the house was ready for them. Behjat was going to live with them until Pari learned how to run the household. Then Behjat would move in with her elderly parents.

I went over to Pari and we embraced tightly. "I'm going to miss you so much," I said.

"You know I will miss you, too," Pari said but her face reflected something I had never seen on it. It was as if she were on a river, floating away, without control. I had to push away the dark image that came to me, of her drowning. This was followed by intense loneliness. Soon Maryam and Aziz would leave, too, and I would be alone in this cold household.

Thirteen

D ays, weeks went by and there was no word from Pari—not a phone
call, not a letter. I wrote her a few long letters but got no response.

When I tried to call her, Father snatched the phone from my hand. "Let
her adjust to her new life," he said.

"I'm worried," I said. "She hasn't answered my letters."

"Do you think you care more about your sister than I do?" Father burst out.

"Don't create problems for your sister," Mohtaram said.

I sank back into the state I had been in when I was first torn away from
Maryam and forced into a home alien to me. I flared up easily and cried at
the slightest provocation.

It was particularly hard for me during the Norooz holidays that year
without Pari. Norooz, originating in Zoroastrian times, is the biggest secular holiday in Iran. Starting on March twenty-first and lasting for two
weeks, it marks the beginning of spring and celebrates the renewal of life.
Mohtaram planted seeds in trays so that they would sprout by the holidays.
On Norooz day Mohtaram set on a table the *Haft Siin,* seven items, each
starting with the letter *S*, representing rebirth, health, happiness, prosperity,
joy, patience, and beauty. As we gathered around the *Haft Siin* table Father
gave Manijeh and me money, the customary present.

On the thirteenth day of the holiday, "getting rid of thirteen," we went on a picnic in a park, as spending the day close to nature was supposed to be good luck. The park, on the outskirts of Ahvaz, was popular and many other families were there, too.

We sat on a rug we spread on the ground next to a stream and ate fish *kababs* cooked by Ali on a charcoal grill, and currant rice, and other dishes he had prepared earlier at the house. Ali sat under a tree, separate from us; as he ate he watched the pigeons pecking on the ground or flying. The air was filled with scents of spices and flowers in bloom. Children were jumping rope and swaying on swings hung from trees.

After we ate Father went for a walk by himself. Mohtaram, Manijeh, and I went to the stream while Ali stayed to guard the rug. Many other mothers and young girls were throwing plants they had grown for the occasion into the stream. The plants were supposed to have collected all the sickness, pain, and ill fate hiding in the paths of families throughout the coming year.

Before throwing her plant Mohtaram asked Manijeh and me to tie its thin leaves and then make our wishes, a ritual for young girls symbolizing the desire "to be tied" in a marriage during the following year.

Instead of obeying her I walked away to a secluded area of the park. Mohtaram, focused on Manijeh, didn't try to stop me. As I reached a quiet corner, I was startled to see Majid, Pari's love, standing by the water, holding a fishing rod. He was wearing American Levi's. A few brown curls hung over his high forehead. He looked sensitive, alive to the world; his large hazel eyes focused on me.

"How is your sister? Do you hear from her?" he asked.

I just shook my head, not knowing what to say.

"I have a favor to ask," he said. "It's confidential. Can you do that for your sister?"

"Yes."

"I want you to give her a letter from me. I knew you come to this park every year, so I brought it with me." He took out a folded envelope from his shirt pocket and gave it to me.

Suddenly I saw Father walking toward us with another man. Luckily he was so engrossed in conversation that he didn't notice me. I quickly slipped the envelope into my pocketbook, said good-bye to Majid, and hurried away.

Later that day, as soon as I was in my room, I read the letter. I knew Pari wouldn't mind my reading it. It was very brief but in it Majid declared his everlasting love for Pari, and urged her to leave her husband. Again he declared what had sounded like a fantasy, "We'll elope."

I tore up the letter and put the pieces inside my notebook to discard as soon as I went outside. I would have to tell Pari about the letter when I saw her. It was too dangerous to keep in the house.

Mahvash came to Nezam Vafa High School in the middle of the semester. Her father had been transferred to Ahvaz from Tehran, where he worked for the city. At recess I noticed her sitting on a bench under a canopy reading a monthly magazine *Setareh* that had one fiction piece per issue.

"I subscribe to *Setareh*," I said, sitting next to her.

"Did you read that they aren't going to run the rest of the novel by Ardavani?"

"Yes, I'm so disappointed."

Mahmood Ardavani was a slick, popular writer but I liked the segments of his novel I had read in *Setareh*, mainly because they were set in America, my obsession. In the story an Iranian man studying in America falls in love with an American girl. It is a dilemma for him since his parents want him to marry an Iranian girl. We wouldn't find out now what happens at the end.

"The note said the author requested that they stop running it for his own personal reasons. I wonder what they are," Mahvash said.

"Maybe the novel is autobiographical."

After that we sometimes walked to the Karoon River together and watched the activities on the other side—American girls riding bicycles, considered improper for Iranian girls, boys and girls walking together, holding hands.

She had a brother who was two years older than us. Father didn't like the idea of my visiting her because he thought people would start gossiping that I might be seeing her brother. So instead she visited me sometimes. We sat in my room and talked about our dreams the way I used to with Pari.

"I want to become a writer," I said.

"That's a hard battle. You know you'll be so restricted in what you can write about, particularly since you're a girl."

"I'll go to America, if I can get my father to send me."

"I'd like to get out of Iran, too, become a ballet dancer."

I took on a school-sponsored job, teaching illiterate adults twice a week. The students came from the poor, underprivileged segment of Ahvaz's population and I enjoyed their eagerness to learn. I also liked the independence of making money on my own. I was able to afford more things. I bought more books. I dropped into Tabatabai Bookstore weekly, sometimes more frequently, and asked for recommendations from Jalal, always making sure no one else was in the store.

"You know so much about books," I said to him once.

"I was going to Tehran University, studying literature," he said. His face became tinged with pain. "Then my father was arrested for distributing pamphlets. He died in jail, who knows of what. I stopped going to school. I couldn't bear it. I couldn't bear being in Tehran, either. I came here, and brought my mother. She has a sister in Ahvaz. I opened this bookstore. I like it even better than going to college. I read what I choose to read."

I asked Jalal to recommend a book for me to read to Ali. Ali was illiterate. The novel Jalal recommended was by an unknown Iranian writer. It described the adventures of an Iranian man traveling in the jungles of Africa and South America. The man encountered dangerous animals; he managed to calm them down and get away from them without ever harming them. Ali came to my room one or two evenings a week—he squatted on the floor and I sat at the edge of my bed—and I read to him. Ali was visibly excited at some scenes, getting up and sitting down again, waving his hands in the air.

Finally a letter came from Pari.

> . . . *I'm sorry I haven't been writing but my life has been full of turmoil, hard to be coherent about it. To sum up some aspects of it, I was wrong to believe Taheri wouldn't stop me from acting. In fact he's keeping me a virtual prisoner since he found out about the bit part in a play I managed to get. It was put on in Do Rang Theater, produced by a group of graduates of American universities. They show plays translated from other languages. It's a very small theater and they sell tickets by subscription only. I told Taheri about wanting to take on a part but he more or less ignored the issue. Then he became enraged when one of his coworkers saw me in it. He forced me to stop immediately. He said I had shamed him by going into a "disreputable" place. Actresses are immoral, he said, and these places are no more than brothels. His idea of disreputable is anything that has to do with entertainment, similar to Father's and so many other people's attitudes. I reminded him of his promising me I would be free to do what I wanted. He said he hadn't thought it through then and now he saw that people were talking behind our backs. When he's at work his sister comes to the house and watches over me like a prison guard. Don't refer to any of this when you write to me since she or Taheri might get to the mail before me. Did Mother or Father tell you that I called and complained? I was hoping after hearing me they would encourage me to come home, but Father said I just got married and I must give it a chance. Mohtaram got on the phone and said the same thing.*

I wanted to burst out and say something to Father and Mohtaram but she was pregnant. Both she and Father were totally absorbed in that. She became big and heavy and sluggish.

"At my age, having a baby again! I'm not young, I'm thirty-nine years old," she complained. "I've been giving birth since I was fourteen." She waddled around in loose print dresses, sweaty, irritable, miserable, her voice shrill. "I'm getting so big, you'd think I was pregnant with two."

I couldn't understand why she would let herself get pregnant again. But then I remembered how Father always said, "Birth control is preventing life." He didn't believe in abortion, either, which was illegal anyway. "It's killing, no difference."

Mohtaram went into labor late one afternoon. Father brought in an obstetrician—by then using midwives was no longer a common practice. After a few hours the obstetrician, a heavyset, somber-looking man, came out of the bedroom and spoke to Father, who was sitting on a chair on the porch, keeping vigil. "We ought to get her to a hospital quickly. She may need surgery."

They took Mohtaram to the hospital in town. When Father returned he told us that indeed Mohtaram had twins, two girls. Three days later Father brought Mohtaram and the twins home. Each baby was wrapped in a thin pink blanket. Father called Manijeh and me in to look at the babies. They had named them Farzaneh and Farzin. They weren't identical and in fact looked very different. Farzin was smaller, her face thinner, and she had lighter eyes, a grayish color, whereas Farzaneh's were dark brown. Mohtaram opened her blouse and put Farzin at one of her breasts and the baby began to suck.

"Two more girls to worry about," Father mumbled, shaking his head.

Mohtaram's friends came to the house to see the babies and bring gifts. I thought how sad it was that Mohtaram had so many children and Maryam didn't even have one. I was hoping Maryam would come to visit, but she was still in Karbala.

Once when Manijeh came out of Mohtaram's room, Ali was sitting on the porch. He turned to Manijeh and said, "Your mother now has two babies to look after."

That threw Manijeh into a fit. "All you do is stare at pigeons. And you're squinting. Are you blind? Be useful and get me some lemonade."

In fact Ali didn't see well. He had trachoma in one of his eyes and it couldn't be operated on. Sitting there, a small man with graying hair and a squint, he seemed vulnerable. Manijeh's attack made me angry.

"Leave him alone," I said. She and I barely interacted except in anger, even now that Pari was no longer at home. We lived in the same house like strangers.

"Didn't you hear me?" Manijeh said to Ali, ignoring me. Then she pressed her tongue between her teeth, her face becoming deep red.

Ali didn't move.

"You'll pay for this," Manijeh said before storming off.

Farzin was behind Farzaneh in her development. She didn't crawl yet, didn't smile or look at people the way Farzaneh did.

"I spoke to the obstetrician," Father told Mohtaram at breakfast one morning, just after I left the room. "He said most likely she didn't get enough oxygen at birth." He sounded depressed.

"Terrible, terrible, how could that happen?" Mohtaram's voice was urgent.

"They weren't prepared for twins. The poor child is going to have even more problems than most girls."

My heart began to ache for her. I had gotten attached to her and Farzaneh and played with them joyfully during my breaks from studying or reading or writing.

Mohtaram didn't have enough milk in her breasts to feed two babies, so they hired a wet nurse, Zeinab. She had an oblong, ruddy face and wore her hair in two thick braids. She was a small woman but her breasts were large and filled with milk. She came over every day, leaving her three children with her own mother. One day she brought them with her and they ran around or hovered over the twins, watching their mother nurse them. The youngest, a two-year-old girl, demanded to be fed, too, even though she had been weaned. Zeinab let her suck at her breasts and kissed her, saying, "My little sweet baby." After sucking for a while the little girl broke loose and joined her brothers. They playfully pulled one another's hair, embraced, kissed. Their faces were smeared with watermelon or cherry juice. When exhausted, the children lay next to one another on the ground and went to sleep. I envied the harmony between them.

Zeinab said about her own daughter, "Poor little girl, her father and brothers are nice to her now but as soon as she's older and shows any independence they're going to bully her. Men!"

"Men!" Mohtaram echoed. "When I got pregnant this time I squeezed my thighs, hoping the babies wouldn't come into this world. Didn't I have enough children already?"

"God who gives them to us will look after them," Zeinab said.

They each picked up a twin and hugged and kissed them.

Sometimes I sat with Zeinab and listened to her stories about people in her village. We would put the twins in a hammock hung from two palm trees in the courtyard and rock it as we talked.

"Poor child, you're treated badly by your mother," she said. "Mothers should be nice to their daughters. Girls have enough trouble." How could she help noticing that Mohtaram came to Manijeh's side every time she and I got into a fight? Zeinab gave me presents—a handkerchief she had embroidered, a potpourri with flowers she had dried in sunlight.

Once I overheard Zeinab and Mohtaram in the courtyard, pushing the babies in their carriage toward the outside door. Mohtaram complained to Zeinab about the responsibilities she had had all her life having given birth to so many children. It was the usual complaint. But this time she added, "Nahid treats me like an enemy."

I was shaken. Was it possible that I had started the pattern of coldness between us? Was it me who had rebuffed her that first day, years ago, when Father brought me home? I recalled an incident soon after one of Maryam's visits. I was sitting with Mohtaram at breakfast, eating silently, not looking at her, not saying a word. Suddenly she said, "Aren't I your mother, even a little?" I was so startled by her question that I remained silent. Then I got up and left. I felt, deep in my heart, that I would be betraying Maryam if I opened up to Mohtaram, even though Maryam never tried to turn me against her sister.

Fourteen

ome out, don't make me break the door!" I could hear Father's voice from the courtyard.

I hurried up the stairs to where Father was standing in front of Pari's old room.

"This is crazy," he shouted. "You leave your handsome, wealthy husband and come back home. What's the matter with you?" He walked away, shaking his head angrily.

"Pari, please let me in," I pleaded, my hand on the doorknob. She opened the door just enough so I could slide in. She threw herself on the bed and buried her face in her pillow. I cried out when I saw bloodstains on the pillow and sheets.

"What happened? You're bleeding," I gasped, putting my hand on her arm.

"I've been having nosebleeds."

Pari had neglected to latch the door and Mohtaram came in, carrying a washcloth and a glass of orange juice. She sat at the edge of the bed and wiped Pari's nose with the cloth.

"My dear daughter, didn't I tell you no marriage is good at the beginning?" she said. "You've been with him for only a little more than a year and you're already home complaining." She lifted Pari's head and put the glass of orange juice to her lips.

Farzin and Farzaneh began to cry loudly in the nursery, and Mohtaram left to attend to them.

"I told Father I wasn't going back. He started shouting at me, so I locked myself in here," Pari said.

The flower scents had faded from Pari's room but I could still feel Majid's presence there now that Pari had returned. "Pari," I whispered. "Majid gave me a letter for you, but I tore it up. I was afraid Father would find it." I told her about the encounter in the park and what he had said in the letter.

"I want a divorce," Pari said, flushing. "I can't bear living with Taheri another day."

It was pleasantly cool for October in Ahvaz, which usually had only two seasons, summer and winter. Throngs of people were out shopping, strolling, or sitting in cafés.

"Maybe if I had been allowed to marry Majid, I would've soon found faults with him," Pari said as we reached the river and started walking on the bridge. "But because he was forbidden to me I idealize him. Every morning I wake, my heart is filled with desire for him, and I am sad to find Taheri beside me in bed. But you know, Nahid, even if Majid didn't exist I would never warm up to Taheri. He's a liar. He went against all his promises to me. He goes out and gets drunk after he pretended to Father that he didn't drink. The slightest thing makes him angry and he throws tantrums." She said nothing for a few minutes. "I have to find a way to get out of the marriage."

"Pari, all I wish for myself now is to go to America to study. If you got a divorce you could aim for the same thing. We have to try to bend Father's will."

The bridge was becoming crowded with young people. Boys and girls strolled separately. The boys watched the girls and sighed loudly. Some leaned over the railing and stared at the water flowing below.

Suddenly I noticed Majid, alone, bent over the railing. Pari noticed him, too, and immediately flushed. He gave a start at seeing Pari and his face also became red. We stood next to him, long enough for him to whisper something to Pari.

Pari shook her head at something he said and we started walking back.

"He wants to meet me," she said finally. "I don't know if I can get away with it."

The streetlights flickered on one by one and we walked faster.

"Pari, you're a married woman and have come home without your husband," Father said when we got home. He was sitting on the porch, listening to the radio turned on high in the salon. "You shouldn't be walking on the streets. I don't want any cause for gossip. I want you to return to your husband as soon as possible."

Pari avoided Father's eyes and we headed to her room.

"Taheri keeps saying if I give him a son everything will be good between us," Pari said. "It's as if I have the power to produce a boy. Anyway, I don't want children, I don't want to become a baby machine like Mother. And I don't want a child from him."

I looked at the posters of actresses on the walls. She had left her room intact.

"It's terrible that he stops you from acting," I said.

Pari nodded. "I thought my home life was terrible with Father always telling us what to do and Mohtaram paying so much attention to Manijeh. But it is heaven compared to my life with Taheri. Father is never *deliberately* cruel. Taheri is a sadist. He put a lit cigarette on my arm."

She pulled up the sleeve of her blouse and showed me her arm. Little scars lined her arm. My heart sank at the sight. "Did you show it to Father?" I asked.

"I tried, but he ignored it. Taheri tortures me mentally, too, Nahid. He wants me to cook and iron his clothes in certain ways. Make his food the way his sister does. The slightest deviation throws him into a fit. His sister is there almost every day, and she criticizes me, too, for not knowing anything about domestic tasks."

In our household domestic tasks were taken care of by Ali and Fatemeh, with Mohtaram only supervising them. Our parents believed that their daughters didn't need to actually know how to perform household tasks as they expected we would marry men who could afford servants.

"What's the good of Taheri's wealth? We don't live in a good neighborhood. It's in a dreary section of the city and the house is drab and dark. Except for his sister, we don't have help. Taheri likes to keep his money invested, and of course none of the money is in my name. And the *mehrieh* is good only if he is the one who divorces me. We never entertain friends, only Taheri's huge number of relatives. They're dull, with no aspirations. They see me as someone from another planet—in their eyes I'm flighty, impractical."

"Pari, how did you manage to come here without him?"

"I didn't tell him I was coming. He's away in Karaj; he has a shop there, too. I just left him a note. He gives me a weekly allowance for 'incidental expenses,' and I saved it and that's how I was able to buy a plane ticket. I wish I could work, have some independence, but he's absolutely against it. He says if I work it'd be a bad comment on him, as a man and a breadwinner. And he doesn't like me to be exposed to people he doesn't know, that's how controlling he is. Nahid, I can't talk to him about anything. He isn't interested in movies or plays or books. I hate my life. Endless, mundane chores every day, the same dull rhythm."

Hours later I woke to sounds I thought were cicadas carrying on, but it was Pari weeping. I had fallen asleep on her floor. In the rays of moonlight streaming through the blinds I could see she was still asleep. I gently woke her. "Pari, are you having a nightmare?"

She slowly opened her eyes and sat up. "I dreamt I was pregnant but something was seriously wrong. In desperation I threw myself down a steep stairway."

I caressed her back. As if not quite awake yet, she lay down and closed her eyes.

"Your husband is coming to take you back," Father said to Pari the next morning at breakfast. "That only shows how much he cares about you. We had a talk on the phone."

"I'm not going back to him. I hate him," Pari said. "I want a divorce."

"You must give him a chance," he said coldly.

"I've given it enough time."

"Do you want to lose your *mehrieh*, millions of *toomans* we worked hard to negotiate? You know you won't get one *rial* of it if you're the one divorcing him. Besides, what are people going to say about us if you come back home? Do you want to disgrace us? Why do you hate a man who cares about you so much?"

"I don't want that money. I'm a slave to him because of it. He knows that I'd lose it and he keeps me a prisoner. He's crazy." Pari hid her head in her hands and started to cry.

"Father, Pari is miserable with him," I said.

"Pari doesn't need you to stand up for her." He turned his gaze toward me. His face was contorted. He turned back to Pari. "He's coming to Ahvaz, maybe tonight. Be ready to go back with him."

A loud knock on the outside door woke me out of a restless sleep. I tiptoed onto the porch.

"*Agha*, they're already in bed," Ali was saying to Taheri in the courtyard.

"I'm so sorry, Taheri, I admit my daughter is spoiled," said Father as he approached his son-in-law. "Bear with her. She'll grow up."

Father led him to the guest room, Cyrus's old room.

The next morning he called Pari into the salon, where Taheri was waiting. I watched as Pari walked into the room and closed the door behind her.

"Taheri knelt by me and apologized and begged me to go back," Pari told me later. "He made all sorts of promises. I'll give him one more chance."

By the end of the day she was gone again.

Fifteen

I found a letter from Parviz on the kitchen table.

Dear Father,

America is so vast, you can find whatever you wish for. Everything is grand, beautiful—buildings so high they seem to hit the sky, vast fertile lands, mountains, valleys full of meandering streams. When you travel, the landscape changes continually and startlingly. At night the streets glitter with bright lights. There's so much freedom, so many choices. It's hard to capture it all. In America you can go far if you're willing to work hard. You can become who you want, find the kind of people you want to be with and learn from.

Your loving son, Parviz

The idea of Father sending me, a daughter, to America was ridiculous. I knew that. But Parviz's letter inflamed me.

I began to study even harder, aiming to come first in my class, hoping that my academic success would make Father sympathetic to my cause. It wouldn't be hard to come first, as few girls took their studies seriously.

At the end of that school year I saw posted on the bulletin board in front of the principal's office that I was first in my class. At home I found Father, Mohtaram, and Manijeh in the salon. Mohtaram was embroidering another tapestry and Manijeh was sitting on a chair next to her, talking to her. Father sat in another corner, listening to the large radio, taking a break from his work.

"I'm first in my class," I announced.

"Very good. But I wish you didn't lock yourself up in your room and work and work," Father said. He turned to the radio to catch the end of the news, something about oil revenues rising in Iran.

Mohtaram and Manijeh ignored what I said. I tried to say to myself that they hadn't heard me but I didn't believe it. I left the room, went to my own, and cried.

I began writing letters to Parviz, asking for help.

"You're doing so well at school. I don't understand why Manijeh does so poorly," Mrs. Soleimani said when classes started in the new year.

"She isn't interested in studying." It was true. Manijeh, now seventeen, was focused on marriage. Mohtaram was already adding more and more items to her dowry, which she had begun to prepare as soon as Pari got married. She and Father hadn't committed yet to any of the suitors who had started asking for Manijeh's hand, but they expected that soon the right man would come along.

"A new radio station has just come on the air," Mrs. Soleimani said. "They're interested in stories by students. Why don't you give me the one about the mother and the blind child. I'll send it in."

Days later, the radio station accepted my story.

I wished I could share my good news with Maryam but she had been out of reach ever since she went to Karbala.

I wrote to Pari, and this time she wrote back promptly.

I'm so happy for you, you deserve it. . . . There is so much I want to tell you but it's hard right now. I'm still trying to make things work.

"You know that kind of story can get us into trouble," my father said, after he demanded to read it. "It's going to be interpreted as a social criticism. Your teacher and the radio station can get into trouble, too. You should have shown it to me before you sent it in. From now on you must show me everything."

One day my school notebooks were missing.

"Did you take my notebooks?" I asked Manijeh as we were rushing to our rooms from the porch. It was a cold December day, one of the two or three months of the year when temperatures in Ahvaz dropped sometimes to almost freezing. We had space heaters in all the rooms, taking over from the fans.

"Why would I?" she said.

"She took my notes, I know it," I said to Father, who wandered onto the porch before Manijeh and I reached our rooms.

"Don't make accusations without any basis," Mohtaram said, appearing out of nowhere. "Why do you hate your sister so?"

"I know she took them; she wants me to fail."

"Why don't we ever have a moment of peace around here?" Father said. "My sons are doing fine; it's the daughters who are always causing problems."

I ignored this. "I have exams in two days and my notes have vanished. They were on my desk." I turned to Manijeh. "I'm going to search your room."

"Don't you dare," she snarled. "I'm not a thief."

"Now stop this, both of you!" When arguments erupted between Manijeh and me, Father was careful not to take sides.

That evening, I saw the lights on in Father's office. It was hailing; large hailstones drummed against windows, treetops. I ran over and knocked on his door.

"Come in," he said. "What is it?" His head snapped up from his work.

I began to cough, the nervous cough that still attacked me at times.

"Stop that. What is it?"

Finally it stopped. "Father, I want to go to college in America like my brothers," I said.

"You already know the answer. No!"

I suddenly didn't care what his reaction would be. "You brought me back here, and Mohtaram hates me," I blurted out.

"You've been here all these years and you still call her Mohtaram instead of Mother," he said, his voice losing its sharp edge. "How do you think that makes her feel?"

"Manijeh hates me, too," I said, evading his question.

"Don't you know these things are always two-sided? I have work to do. Go to your room. And remember, don't ever write stories like that." He turned back to the thick legal book open on his desk.

A few days later I found my school notes torn up in the cistern under the old-fashioned toilet that had never been renovated, and which we never used.

Mahmood Ardavani, the writer whose novel was published in part in *Setareh*, was going to be visiting Ahvaz for business purposes. He was seeking advice from Father on legal matters and would stay at our house for one night. He and Father shared a mutual friend from their university years.

"Can I meet him?" I asked Father when he talked about Ardavani at breakfast.

"I suppose it won't hurt. He isn't a controversial writer."

"Can I invite my friend Mahvash?"

"Go ahead."

At school I looked for Mahvash immediately and told her about Arda-vani's visit. "That's so exciting," she said. "I can't believe he's actually going to be staying at your house."

"You'll be coming over and we'll meet him together."

After classes we went to Café du Park to have ice cream. We sat in the shade of a clump of trees to talk about Ardavani. He had just published a new novel and we wondered if it contained some of the themes of the novel we had read segments of in *Setareh*.

"We should get a copy each and have him autograph them for us," Mahvash suggested.

"Yes, we should get them soon, before his visit."

Several familiar figures came in—the boy who wore a yellow shirt and a black tie and waited at street corners for girls to pass by; another boy, tall and gaunt, who walked up and down in front of our school whenever the people in authority weren't around to chase him away. The boys had at times followed us from one winding street to another. We turned our backs to them and went on talking about Ardavani.

"I don't know what I'm going to say to him," Mahvash said.

"I can't imagine being face-to-face with him."

Finally we left the café and went our separate ways. At home I noticed Mohtaram was already preparing for Ardavani's arrival, which was a week away. With Ali's help she got the guest room ready for him to sleep in and planned menus for breakfast and dinner. "I don't understand why we have to entertain him. He could stay in a hotel," she complained to Ali.

On the day of Ardavani's arrival, Mahvash and I, before leaving school for my house, took off the gray uniforms we were wearing over our dresses. It was early fall and we both had on printed cotton dresses, mine with designs of bright butterflies, and Mahvash's with leaves. On the way we stopped at Tabatabai Bookstore and each bought a hardcover copy of Ar-davani's latest novel.

At home we went to my room and waited for Father to call us in to meet Ardavani. Shortly after we arrived Father came to the door.

"Don't you two ever get tired of chattering?" Father asked. "Come to the salon."

We followed, carrying the books.

Mahmood Ardavani was sitting alone on the sofa, holding a glass of *arak*. He looked just like the photograph of him on the jacket of his latest book—penetrating dark eyes and wild dark hair. He was wearing a bright yellow shirt with the top buttons open and casual khaki pants, a contrast to Father's suit. Father introduced us and Ardavani greeted us warmly.

We were silent. I felt a tremor inside from just being in his presence; the air around me felt charged. The words I had prepared to say—"I wish we knew what happened in the novel that was printed in . . ." or, "I'm pleased to be in the presence of a writer"—escaped me and I glanced toward the window.

"I'm so happy to meet you after reading your work," I finally managed to say.

"Thank you. I'm very flattered," he said. He looked at Mahvash.

"I'm pleased to meet you," Mahvash said, blushing.

I noticed they looked into each other's eyes for a long moment.

"You two are classmates?" Ardavani asked.

"Yes. We've always admired your work," I said.

"I am so pleased to know that lovely girls like you are my readers."

Mahvash raised the book she was holding so that he could see it.

He smiled. "I see you have a copy of the same book," he said to me. "Shall I autograph them for you?"

Mahvash and I nodded.

He took the books and thought for a moment. He wrote something in one book and then the other. He gave the books back to us. "Do me a favor. Don't read what I wrote for you now. Save them for later."

Mahvash and I nodded.

"Sit down. Tell me what other things you read."

We sat down.

"We read Hafiz and Saadi for school," Mahvash said.

"And we read the *Ahvaz Monthly* and *Setareh*," I said.

"Very good. I had no idea lovely girls like you have an interest in reading."

Father looked impatient. "Mr. Ardavani and I have business to discuss," he said. "I'm sorry to say we won't be eating here tonight. We have to meet someone."

Mahvash and I stood.

"I'm happy to have had the pleasure of meeting you," Ardavani said, smiling.

We watched them leave, then raced back to my room to read the inscriptions.

For me he had written:

One morning I woke and realized I was in love with a dark-eyed, dark-haired girl with a mole on her upper lip. Now every time I see a girl looking like that I recall that faraway love and fall in love again.

For Mahvash he had written:

Your ethereal beauty will always remain food for the imagination of the poet.

"He liked you better than me," Mahvash said.

"Yours sounds better to me, more grand."

"It's so impersonal."

"He kept his eyes on you almost the whole time," I said.

That night I couldn't sleep. I tossed and turned and finally got out of bed. I walked to the window. The night air was crisp and clear, the sky crowded with innumerable stars. I could see the light was on in Ardavani's room. I wondered if he was reading or had fallen asleep with the lamp on. I pondered tiptoeing over to his room, talking to him, having him all to myself.

At school the next morning, Mahvash was cool and distant. All day she kept to herself. Her eyes seemed focused on a view that I could no longer see.

Two weeks passed without the two of us speaking. Then I came across her standing on the Karoon River bridge, staring down at the water. She was wearing the dress she had on when we met Mahmood Ardavani. I walked over and stood next to her.

"Oh, you!" She grabbed my hand and then let go.

"Tell me, why have you been avoiding me?" I asked.

"Oh, no reason."

"Please tell me."

"You must know," Mahvash said after a long pause. "It was what happened with Ardavani, what he wrote for you coming spontaneously from him. I envied you so much for it. I just had to avoid you until the feelings passed." Her voice sounded hollow and far away. I felt a chill listening to a voice that was almost unrecognizable.

"Oh, that's so silly," I managed to say.

"When we were in the room with him, I wished so much for you to be out of the room—you and your father. I wanted so badly to be alone with Ardavani," Mahvash went on.

I thought how I had had similar feelings. "All that is in the past," I said.

The confession helped us resume our friendship. We never saw Ardavani again.

Sixteen

Javad Golestani lived in Abadan, an oil refinery town about two hours away from Ahvaz by car. He was a doctor, came from a good family—some of whom lived in Ahvaz and were the ones who had first noticed Manijeh—and he was handsome. He was tall, with olive skin and unusual purple-green eyes, as well as a hooked nose that actually enhanced his appearance.

Manijeh would have gone along with any man our parents approved of, having absolute trust in their judgment, but as it was she was in love with Javad from afar. And it wasn't just his good looks. Though she herself had never been studious, she admired him for being educated and for his erudite way of talking.

"He has everything," she told Mohtaram. "Good looks, education." Now, preoccupied with her impending marriage, she flunked all her courses at midyear exams. She was in her final year in high school but decided to drop out instead of repeating the exams. Father and Mohtaram thought she should finish now that she was so close to graduating, but Manijeh didn't see the point of it. She didn't like studying and her friends were dropping out one by one to get married. Manijeh now spent much of her time preening in front of the mirror.

But then I became aware of tension surrounding the marriage proposal. I overheard Mohtaram say to Father, "Javad's mother keeps changing the date of the engagement. She says one thing and then something else." I didn't hear Father's response. But on the same day Mohtaram told Father, "Manijeh is going to be so upset if Javad backs out."

There was tension in the air every time Javad's or his mother's name came up.

The thought of Manijeh getting married and being out of the house gave me a feeling of relief but at the same time of dread. I was next in line.

Manijeh

Again, I tried to talk to Father about sending me to America, telling him how well I had done at midterm and reminding him I had come in first in my class the year before. But he brushed me off.

I wrote more letters to Parviz, begging him to try to persuade Father to send me to America. I received no replies.

❁

I was standing on the riverbank by myself when a male voice shook me out of my reverie. "*Salaam, halet chetoreh.*"

It was a boy I often saw on the way to school. Our eyes sometimes locked as we passed. He had blue eyes and was clearly at least half foreign.

"Will you go on a boat ride with me?" he asked.

I accepted, not giving myself time to think beyond the moment, to allow the fear of doing something forbidden to take over me. He told me his name was James.

Rowboats for rent were moored on the bank. Except for the owners of the boats, mostly Arab boys, no one was around. James rented a boat, telling the boy that he wanted to row himself. Then he took my hand and helped me onto the boat. The water shimmered gold in the sunlight. I couldn't believe my own daring to get into a boat with this boy in broad daylight.

James's father was English, his mother Iranian, he said. His father worked for the oil company. "I'll be going back to England if I get into a film school there."

When we reached the other side of the river, he helped me out of the boat and tied it to a tree. He took my hand and we walked on a quiet, empty backstreet. It had cooled off somewhat after weeks of wretched heat, even though it was only April. The hot, damp wind blowing from Shatt-Al-Arab had finally ceased and was replaced by the cooler breeze from the Karoon River. American women were sitting on lawns in front of their Tudor-style houses, drinking from tall glasses. An American boy and girl passed by, both laughing in a carefree way.

Nahid by the Karoon River

After a few minutes we entered a park filled with palms and *khar zahreh* bushes. The spiky green leaves and bright red flowers of the plant supposedly killed mosquitoes and then devoured them. A few American children were playing catch in one corner. Others had gathered around an ice cream truck. James bought vanilla cones for both of us, then we wandered to a secluded corner. We sat on a bench, ate the ice cream, and talked. Rabbits darted out of the bushes and roamed around on the grass, then ran back to their hiding places. The air was fragrant with the scent of flowers, masking the smell of petroleum that at times permeated the air. "Do you live on this side?" I asked James.

"No, my mother likes the other side, so we live there."

After a moment of silence between us James reached over and kissed me, theatrically like the actors in American movies. Suddenly I understood what Pari meant when she spoke of being inflamed. James pulled back. I saw why—two Iranian men were coming in our direction.

"We should go back," I said, wanting to get home before dark.

James rowed us back, and after we landed he asked me to meet him at the same time the following week. He asked if I wanted to hear a concert at the Armenian church. I nodded faintly. How alluring he was.

Then we went in different directions. Pahlavi Avenue was crowded with traffic and people going in and out of shops or walking on sidewalks. The blind flute player was now sitting against a sooty wall next to a row of sad beggars, playing a soft romantic tune. A line had formed in front of Javani Cinema, which was showing *Casablanca*. Across the street a sermon from Friday Mosque, with its large gold dome, warned against sinful pleasures.

As I sped home I caught glimpses of my reflection in store windows. My reflection seemed unfamiliar. There was a glow on my face, as if something was about to open up for me. I felt light, as if flying in unison with the tiny circular balloon designs on my dress.

Around the corner from our house the owner of the barbershop was closing up his shop early. He gave us free haircuts in exchange for Father's free legal advice. I took advantage of their agreement when my money ran out. He stared at me in a strange way, making me worried that perhaps something was written on my face, giving away my secret.

A boy had climbed the tall palm tree on the sidewalk and was picking dates that had dried up in clusters between leaves. His eyes looking down on me produced the same anxiety in me. I tiptoed up the back stairway and went directly to my room.

The following week James was waiting for me near the boats. The concert was Western chamber music, unfamiliar to me. Afterward there was a reception and everyone, all foreign except for me, drank and talked and laughed. Then a man came in and announced that a turbulence was breaking out on the river and those who came by boat should leave as soon as possible. No one was concerned as they all seemed to live on that side, but James and I left hurriedly. The water was already a little agitated and our boat swayed back and forth, falling forward and backward.

"Can we meet again?" he asked as we landed. "I'll think of a private place next time."

"I'll try," I said.

Two days after that meeting with James, I was aware of cold, hostile glances from Mohtaram and Manijeh at the dinner table. Father wasn't there and Farzin and Farzaneh were sleeping.

"Pass the fish," Manijeh said, addressing no one in particular.

"She's asking you to pass the fish," Mohtaram said to me. "Is that too much for you?" She reached over, picked up the platter of fish, and put it before Manijeh. "I know you have no feeling for your sister or else why would you ruin her chances with her suitor? You've given us a bad name. And now Javad has backed away. This town is full of eyes."

"She hates me, she's always been jealous of me," Manijeh said and began to cry. She got up and dashed out of the room.

A few hours later Father came into my room.

"From now on Ali will take you back and forth to school." His eyes were bulging and his posture was stiff. He raised his hand, about to slap me, but then lowered it, turned around, and walked away.

For a few weeks Ali escorted me to school and picked me up every day. He and Fatemeh had married quietly in the village they both came from. She worked for us three days a week and he spent his one day a week off with her at her parents' home where she still lived. On our walks, he told me how he wished he and Fatemeh could have children and how hard it was under the circumstances. Fatemeh was much younger than him and very pretty, but she seemed to really like Ali, maybe because he was gentle and kind and projected intelligence, though, like her, he was illiterate.

Feeling that I was his friend because I read to him, Ali talked to me confidentially. He said he aimed to eventually quit being a servant and work at

Fatemeh's family orchard, but he didn't want my parents to know that yet. He told me Fatemeh believed that beneath her insolent front, Manijeh was shy and insecure. Manijeh had always been kind to Fatemeh, and even gave her a silver bracelet. I was as surprised as I had been when Mohtaram told Zeinab that I treated her like an enemy.

One day James was standing in a store doorway, and as I passed he slipped an envelope into my hand. If Ali saw he didn't acknowledge it, and I decided not to say anything. When I reached school I opened it. His letter said that he was leaving for England, where he had been accepted to a film school; could I see him before he left? But of course I couldn't, I was so closely watched.

Not long after that, I saw a photograph of him in the window of Dream Photography on Pahlavi Avenue. He was wearing a tweed jacket. His hair was parted on the side and he was smiling in a crooked, winning way. *He must already be in England,* I thought enviously.

❋

Manijeh was now wretched because Javad had backed out of the marriage. She refused to go back to school. I heard her tell Mohtaram that she would feel shame in front of other girls because of what had happened. There was gloom and an edgy atmosphere in the house.

I was more keenly aware than ever of Father watching me. Every footstep, every door opening, made me think he was approaching my room. If nothing happened I breathed with relief. If he came in to preach to me I exploded now, screaming, "I hate everything, this house, this town, I want to go away, send me away."

Once I awoke to noises in the middle of the night. Then I realized someone was crying intermittently on the balcony. I looked out the window. Manijeh was standing there, barefoot, in a long blue nightgown, her hair tumbling down her shoulders, just staring at the moon, round and full that night. In the bright light I could see, pinned to the neckline of her gown, the rose brooch Javad had given her as a present. She looked lovely, I had to admit. What was the real reason for Javad abandoning her? I wondered.

I don't know if she became aware of my presence at the window but she suddenly turned around and tiptoed back to her room.

What had she been doing on the empty balcony in the middle of the night? Did she expect Javad to miraculously drop from the moon? Was she sleepwalking? (Mohtaram had said once that Manijeh had sleepwalked a few times when she was a child. She attributed it to Manijeh's susceptibility to the slightest stress.) For the first time I could see the fragility in Manijeh, which so often prompted Mohtaram to say, "She's weak, needs help."

"Whore," she mumbled the next day as she passed me on the porch.

Manijeh's dowry—exquisite, carefully chosen—lay in the room, collecting dust.

Seventeen

Some weeks later, Manijeh's suitor inexplicably changed his mind and sent his mother and aunt to ask for forgiveness and to patch things up. Father was reluctant to accept the suitor again but Mohtaram, giving in to Manijeh's wishes, urged him to do so. "This man can't be trusted," Father protested. "He's unreliable." But finally Father gave in.

"Relax, breathe, and when you speak, exhale to allow for pauses between words," Mohtaram told Manijeh before the wedding.

"Stand straight, enunciate your words, and make eye contact with the guests but not with the groom.

"Don't apologize for anything. If you don't highlight your mistakes, no one will notice them."

Neither my brothers nor Pari attended the wedding. Cyrus and Parviz were still in America, and Pari was in Turkey with Taheri, where he was showing his carpets to merchants.

The reception was in the same garden restaurant as Pari's had been. Javad had asked the musicians to play classical Persian music and the singer to sing old songs. As the musicians played violin, *tar*, and *santur*, the singer, a woman with long hair and arched eyebrows, sang one old song after another. One was a loose translation of a Hafiz poem:

With its fragrance, the morning breeze will unlock those beautiful locks.
The curl of those dark ringlets has shredded many hearts to mere strips.
Trust in this traveler who knows of many paths.
Don't be afraid of the dark midnight, turbulent waves, and the
whirlpool.
I know the path of love . . .

I thought it was ironic and sad that Javad's taste and his manner were what Pari would have liked in a husband. In fact, he reminded me a little of Majid.

At the end of the evening Manijeh and Javad left for a hotel. The next day they would go on a weeklong honeymoon to Shiraz. After that they would settle in Abadan, where Javad had his practice and was affiliated with the oil refinery's hospital. They would live in a modern apartment in a modern area, where many of the American employees of the hospital and oil refinery lived as well.

"Next is your turn," Father said to me at breakfast. His smile was hesitant, as if he was unsure if he wanted to be gentle with me.

"I don't want to get married."

"Do you want to be an old maid?"

"I want to go to a university in America," I said.

As if my not wanting to give in to marriage signaled other kinds of trouble from me he replied, "Are you careful about what you say in public? SAVAK is tightening its grip. The Shah is afraid of the mullahs. He can't count on the CIA again if he's forced out."

Though Father was preaching at me I was flattered that he was talking to me the way he used to with my brothers. Was he seeing me differently? Would he soon change his mind and let me go and join my brothers?

That flicker of hope was rudely extinguished a few days later. I was sitting in a shady corner of the courtyard, reading the novel *Mother*, by Maxim Gorky, another white-jacket book I had bought from the Tabatabai Bookstore. I was usually careful to do my reading alone, but because Father wasn't home, I was sitting in the open with it. I saw a shadow pass behind me, then Father was standing over my shoulder, looking at the book.

"Let me see that," he said. I handed it to him. "Where did you get this communistic book?"

"I found it in an empty classroom," I said, not wanting to give away the bookstore man. I had been drawn to it because of its title, preoccupied as I was by the issue of motherhood.

"Don't you know Communism is outlawed?" he said. "Your brothers never gave me trouble like you do." His voice escalated as he said, "If I'm caught with that book in my home I'll lose my license and be sent to jail. Three years for owning that book." Like an interrogator investigating a crime, he asked, "What else have you been reading?" Without waiting for an answer he began to pull out the pages from the book and tear them into pieces. He was in a frenzy. He collected the pieces that fell to the ground and walked away with them. I remained frozen in the same spot where I'd been when he appeared.

In 1962–1963 the Shah launched his White Revolution. The White Revolution ("white" as opposed to the "black" revolution of the religious conservatives, or the "red" revolution of Marxism) consisted of a package that included land reform, profit-sharing for industrial workers in private-sector enterprises, nationalization of forests and pastureland, sale of government factories to finance land reform, and establishment of a "literacy corps" made up of high school graduates sent to teach in villages instead of serving in the army. In addition to these reforms the Shah also announced that he was extending the right to vote to women.

"Father, do you like all the changes the Shah is making?" I asked him at breakfast.

"None of it should concern you."

"Women can vote now," I said.

"Girls wouldn't know whom to vote for," he said scornfully. "It's better if they didn't."

Criticism of the White Revolution leaked out in spite of widespread censorship. Almost everyone had a family member or a friend in a country with a free press; then there were newspapers and radio stations that reported such news before they were forced to shut down.

Some newspapers and stations criticized the Shah and said his White Revolution wasn't doing much—that most of the oil money was still going into the pockets of the royal family and the "One Thousand" (families connected to the Shah) while the majority of Iranians were poor. That the Shah had his suits made by the best tailors abroad and that they cost six thousand dollars each, millions in *toomans*. His office and his palaces were decorated with solid gold and jewel-studded panoramic mirrors and rugs woven with gold threads. He owned luxury homes in European countries. His assets totaled more than a billion dollars, which were valued as trillions in *toomans*. His court was described as lavish and, worse, depraved. He and Shahbanoo Farah, his third wife, took a private plane to Italy and France each week to dine in the most expensive restaurants, get a haircut, shop, or go to St. Moritz to ski.

One article maintained that while on the surface the White Revolution seemed as if it would be beneficial to people, it came with traditional colonial trappings. Thousands of American technicians, support staff, and military men flooded Iran. Furthermore the U.S. army personnel and their staff and family members had been given diplomatic immunity in Iran. In the Majlis (parliament), which was usually tame, one outspoken deputy had asked why an American refrigerator repairman should have the same legal immunity as Iran's ambassadors abroad.

Another article complained that the Shah allowed companies to pay Americans and the English several times more than Iranians employed in the same jobs. They bitterly condemned the brutality of SAVAK, which hadn't changed since the White Revolution, as well as the United States for helping the Shah to form the police force and keep it going. Now SAVAK directly controlled all facets of political life in Iran. Its main task was to suppress opposition to the Shah's government and to keep people's political and social knowledge as minimal as possible. SAVAK had become a law unto itself, having legal authority to arrest, detain, interrogate, and torture suspects. SAVAK operated its own prisons in Tehran, the notorious Evin prison among them. Many of these activities were carried out without any institutional checks.

Jalal carried in his bookstore an underground newspaper, *Bidar Sho* (*Wake Up*). It came out weekly and I read it cover to cover and then discarded it before Father could find it. One week the issue was full of articles that debated the pros and cons of the Shah's White Revolution.

One article said the White Revolution had lifted Khomeini, an ayatollah (the title, meaning "sign of God," was given to major Shiite clerics), to national prominence. He had taken a leading role in opposing the Shah. He said that the Shah's reforms were there only to satisfy his American allies. He criticized the Shah's catering to American values—allowing liquor to be sold in stores and consumed in public, allowing women to walk around without being covered. He also criticized the Shah for giving immunity from prosecution to Americans living in Iran.

In his sermons Khomeini said, ominously, "If the Shah should run over an American dog, he would be called to account. But if an American cook should run over the Shah, no one would have any claim over him. If the men of religion had any influence, it would be impossible for the nation to be at one moment the prisoner of England, the next of America."

In 1963 Khomeini issued a fatwa against the Shah's reforms. In response, the government-owned radio station began a campaign designed to ridicule the clergy. On the radio the Shah announced that his reforms would take Iran into the "jet age," whereas the mullahs wanted to remain in the "donkey age." This comment led to demonstrations by theology students and clergy. The Shah cracked down on the dissent.

Then, in the holy city of Qom, theology students who were demonstrating against the scheduled opening of liquor stores there were attacked by the Shah's paratroopers and SAVAK. The violence only led to more demonstrations, not just in Qom but in Tabriz, as well. Government forces killed hundreds of people. Khomeini publicly attacked the Shah's rule, calling it tyrannical. He called the Shah "Yazid," who, according to Shiites, was a dissolute leader who had ordered the assassination of Hussein. Yazid was condemned and ridiculed in the passion plays Maryam used to take me to.

"What do you think of Khomeini?" I asked Jalal in his bookstore.

"I don't want the clergy to take over, but Khomeini does have a point about the Shah catering to America," Jalal said vehemently. "The Shah's reforms are superficial. Look how we live. It's no better than a jail cell."

I was confused. I hated the Shah's tyranny and all the power he allowed the SAVAK. But I liked his modernization ideas. The same was true of my feelings about America—I didn't like their having helped create the SAVAK, but I yearned for the personal freedom I would be allowed in that country.

At school Mrs. Soleimani told us that the Shah's recent amendment to the voting laws, allowing women the right to vote, wasn't really enforced, since men told their wives, daughters, and sisters not to vote, or dictated to them whom to vote for. Anyway, she continued passionately, how could anyone vote meaningfully, since so much about the candidates was hidden from us?

The class fell into silence. These weren't issues anyone talked about in public. But I was stirred up by what she said and nodded my approval. Indeed, news of the new law had barely reached girls. No one I knew talked about it or acted on it.

At school a few days later I spotted Mahvash talking with two other girls. Their heads were bent together, their voices hushed. I joined them.

"Mrs. Soleimani has been given warnings by the principal," Soroor said. "I overheard a conversation between them."

"What kind of warnings?" I asked, my heart sinking.

"A SAVAK agent told the principal that Mrs. Soleimani was brainwashing the young girls."

Tooran joined us. She was a nervous girl who kept to herself most of the time and I was surprised that she approached us. She had arrived in the middle of the year because her father, who worked at the Educational Ministry in Isfahan, had been transferred to Ahvaz.

Suddenly she started to cry. She said that police had come to their house, searched all their books and every document and paper, and arrested her father. She had no idea where they had taken him. This was her last day at school. She and her mother were going to Tehran to see if they could do something to track his whereabouts. He could be in Evin Prison.

The bell rang and everyone scattered to classes but Tooran said good-bye and left the school.

On my way home that afternoon, I came across a demonstration in Pahlavi Square. A crowd, all men, were holding banners demanding improvement in their lives: "Workers Break Your Chains," "Fight for Equality," "Americans and British Are Stealing Our Oil."

As I walked past them, I could hear their voices over a loudspeaker. Government employees demanded higher salaries. Others protested rising prices, which were controlled by the government. Some wanted subsidized housing. They were zealous, desperate, risking arrest.

At home the radio in the salon was on and Father was sitting next to it, concentrating on every word. As soon as he saw me he gestured to me to come to him.

"Nahid, I'm telling you now very firmly, you have got to watch what you say, what you read. Do you understand?"

I nodded and went to my room, the sound of the radio broadcast fading away.

Eighteen

One day Mrs. Soleimani was gone. She had been forced to resign and no one knew where she was. The school's atmosphere was more somber than ever and I mourned her absence.

Then there was the day, not long after Mrs. Soleimani disappeared, when I went to Tabatabai Bookstore to talk to Jalal and find new material to read. It was a dusty October day with no breeze blowing and no sign of rain, which hadn't come yet that year. The air smelled of petroleum. I gave a start at the sight of the bookstore. One window was boarded up and another window-pane was shattered, its pieces on the ground. Though the pane was broken, there was no way to see inside the store because thick cardboard covered the break. I felt personally assaulted. I sat on the step of an old abandoned house across from the store and wept uncontrollably. I could only imagine what had happened to Jalal. Most likely he had suffered the same fate as his father. I didn't know his last name or where he lived, even though we had had so many conversations. I had no way of even inquiring about him.

What was happening in Ahvaz was only a fragment of what was happening across the country. Then Khomeini was arrested. After being imprisoned for two months, he was put under house arrest in an isolated suburb of Tehran.

❋

At lunchtime Father was waiting for me outside my school. "Come with me, I need to talk to you," he commanded.

My heart began to pound. He led me to the restaurant in Melli Park. After he ordered he said suddenly, "I'm going to let you go to college in America. Parviz advised me to do that."

I stared at him, incredulous. So Parviz had been influenced by all the letters I wrote to him and was coming to my aid.

"He knows a women's college not far from his medical school in St. Louis," Father said. "They offer a few scholarships each year to foreign students. You've performed well at school, so you have a chance." As if my going to the college was already finalized, he went on to say, "You must promise you won't try to imitate American girls, their ways. And under no circumstances should you get ideas in your head about American men. You'll come back. There are men here who like educated women."

As I walked back to school, I tried to understand what was happening. Father was afraid of the kind of books I read, the stories I wrote, of the fact that I broke rules. He knew I would put up a bigger fight than Pari if he tried to marry me to someone he and Mohtaram selected.

Soon after that talk he gave me application forms. As I filled them out, I was confident I would get into the college and with a scholarship. But my situation had changed so suddenly that I couldn't quite trust it. I was excited one moment and despairing the next that Father might change his mind about sending me there. My future shone in colors that changed continually as if refracting light through a prism.

A few months after I mailed the applications Father came into my room and handed me two letters. I read both of them quickly. The first letter from Lindengrove College said:

. . . *We are happy to inform you that you have been accepted* . . .

The second one said:

. . . You have been awarded a scholarship, covering room, board, and tuition . . .

I looked up at Father and noticed a faint smile on his face. Perhaps in spite of everything he was secretly proud of my being a good student. He went on to outline the steps I would take. He was getting the necessary papers together for me and by the end of the summer they would be ready and I would then leave for America.

Mahvash was my only friend who understood my desire to go to America. She herself was going to Tehran to study at the university and then maybe also find a way to pursue her interest in ballet. She would live with her older married brother and attend classes.

I had had no contact with anyone who spoke English. Oddly, foreign languages weren't a part of the curriculum in the high school. Except for some words I had absorbed watching American movies, I had no knowledge of the English language. I started taking the English course offered after the regular class hours at my school. I bought a Farsi-English dictionary and looked up words.

Soon Maryam and Aziz came to visit. Maryam had finally returned from Karbala to take care of some affairs connected to her house and to see her family.

"I have a suitor; he's young and well educated. I don't know what he wants from a widow like me," Maryam said as she sat with Aziz, Mohtaram, and me in the salon.

"Some men like widows, value them for being experienced," Mohtaram said to her sister. "Can he afford to take care of you?"

"I don't need his money," Maryam said.

"You're a widow, in a vulnerable position," Aziz said to her. "It's good to have someone to look after you."

"There was no joy in my life when Fatollah was alive," Maryam said.

"Still, it's better to be married. All your sisters are married," Aziz said. Turning to Mohtaram she added, "Your brother Ahmad knows Rahbar well enough and praised him highly."

"Rahbar would take me to Dubai," Maryam said, softening. "He works for a caviar export company and has been transferred there. He wants to have a wife to take along."

"I'd be so happy for you to get married," Mohtaram said.

"Honestly, my life is more peaceful without a man."

But Maryam's face was glowing, and I could sense a stirring in her heart for this man.

"I'm so glad you're going to university. I never had that chance," Maryam told me when we were alone. "I know you're a good student, always were. I remember the day you came home with a crown on your head." After a pause she added, "But I hope you'll return. When you have your own home and are independent we'll be able to see a lot of each other."

I nodded and said nothing. I was thinking that I would never come back to Iran if I could help it. Then I felt sad as that would separate me further from Maryam.

At the end of the visit Aziz embraced me tightly and said, "You're going so far away, God be with you."

Maryam and I cried as we kissed, knowing this was good-bye for a long time to come.

Pari managed to come home to say good-bye to me.

Perhaps she didn't want to complain too much, so as not to ruin this happy occasion for me. It was as if she had finally resigned herself to Taheri.

"I've struck a bargain with Taheri," she said. "I promised I won't resist getting pregnant and he promised to let me take courses in theater and cinema at the School of Dramatic Arts and be in their productions. Their plays and movies have only a certain kind of audience who wouldn't overlap with the people Taheri knows."

As for Majid, Pari said she had heard from a friend that he moved out of Ahvaz. That was all she knew. She still thought about him, but she was trying to stop.

"Nahid," Pari said softly. "Remember how Taheri threatened suicide if I didn't marry him? Sometimes he turns that around. Once he told me if I leave him, I'd be in serious trouble."

"Pari . . ."

"It's all a bluff, as his threatening suicide was," she said, reverting to a more cheerful tone. "I've made some friends at the school. That helps a lot."

We parted in the same tearful way as I had with Maryam. In spite of Pari's more optimistic manner and tone, I couldn't help feeling upset for her. I was getting out and she was still in her prison.

I never said good-bye to Manijeh. When she visited she stayed close to Mohtaram as usual, never interacting with me directly. More often, Mohtaram went and visited her at her new home. But now that I was leaving, our mutual hostility was like a crevasse I wished I could somehow bridge.

A few days before I was to leave, Father sent me to his friend Mr. Boroojerdi, a pharmacist who also exchanged currency. He was going to give me the best rates from *toomans* to dollars. Father was giving me some money to take along; after I arrived, he would send me pocket money through Parviz, who was going to meet me at the St. Louis airport.

On the way to Mr. Boroojerdi's office I came across another demonstration. Hundreds of men and, to my surprise, some women, too, were shouting, "You can't silence us forever." "Open the jail doors and free our sisters and brothers." They looked angry, determined.

When I arrived at the pharmacy Mr. Boroojerdi pulled two chairs together and we sat across from each other.

"I'm very glad that your father is sending you to university," he said. He was about Father's age, had a pile of gray hair and an erect posture. His manner, in contrast to Father's, was mild and congenial. "My own daughter studied in London for a few years. Then she returned, wanted to be with us. But this is a terrible place for an ambitious and outspoken girl."

The demonstrators passed the pharmacy, their voices drowning out ours. "The American Shah is hoarding the oil money." "Americans, the oil eaters, must leave," they shouted daringly.

"Americans have been exploiting us and giving the Shah too much power, but still America has a lot to offer a young girl like you," Mr. Boroojerdi said.

"It's been my dream to go there."

As I packed on my last day, rapid, tropical rain poured down. I placed the clothes I liked well enough and the photographs I had collected of family and friends in a large navy vinyl suitcase. For the first time in years I felt lighthearted. A tightly sealed door had started to open and I was finally walking out.

Before I left for the airport, Father came into my room and said, "It's good for you to go to university." Then, as if his kind remark had to be followed with a harsh one, he said, "Go, go, you've been causing so much worry, trouble." His face looked haggard and his usually erect shoulders were stooping.

His cold words hit me like pieces of hail. I leaned my head against the wall so that he wouldn't see my tears.

"I can't take you to the airport, I have work I must do," he said. Then I heard his footsteps receding.

Mohtaram started shouting from the other room, "Go pick up Farzin, she's crying so. I'm exhausted." I picked up Farzin and, leaning her on my shoulder, rocked her until she calmed down.

I didn't hear Mohtaram coming in. She startled me with an avalanche of words.

"Each time I became pregnant your father and I searched for names, fantasized about the baby. Would it be a boy or a girl? What would it look like? I prepared a room, set up the crib. Then labor, giving birth, nursing, watching the baby grow. Each child was so different from the others, unique. Life was snuffed out of three of them. Hoveida with his light curly hair, Asghar with slanted eyes like an Oriental, Mina with dimples in her cheeks."

As she talked the row of thin gold bracelets she always wore jingled on her wrist. "One day Mina became yellow, her face, arms, and legs stick thin. She knew she was going to die. She said, 'Mother, I'm going to go to another world.'"

"You gave me away." The words just flew out of me.

In the deep silence that followed I could hear Farzin gurgling, the echo of the music from a movie at the Sahara Cinema.

"My dear sister craved a child. And she felt she wasn't a woman unless she had one. Her husband was so old, maybe it was his fault. But everyone blames the woman when she doesn't get pregnant. . . . How quickly children grow. You look away for a moment and look back and they've grown." Then, for the first time in the years that I had lived there, she pulled me to her. Holding me tightly, Mohtaram kissed me.

When we pulled apart, I looked at her face. I had a feeling I was seeing only fluctuating reflections of her—who she was, what her true feelings were. I wanted to ask her questions but I was so full of contradictory emotions that I couldn't talk. I left the room. In a few moments I saw her leave the house, taking Farzin and Farzaneh with her.

In my room I pulled out a photograph of Mohtaram and me that I had packed. I stared at it, riveted. I had been told that the photograph was taken just before my grandmother took me away. In the photograph Mohtaram is holding me, an infant, on her lap. She looks pretty with her hair cut neatly to the nape of her neck, wearing a white dress with a low neck, and white high-heeled shoes. Was Mohtaram painfully disengaging herself from me then or had she always, for some reason, been detached from this one child?

If she had fallen in love with me in those early months of my life, would she have changed her mind and not given me to her sister?

Ali accompanied me to the airport in a taxi. The rain had stopped and sunlight glittered at the treetops and on the surface of buildings and houses. I was leaving this home and going where I deeply wished to be. *Free, free, free,* I sang to myself.

PART TWO

America

Nineteen

I stood by the window of my room in Green Hall, one of the five dormitories that accommodated Lindengrove College's four hundred students. It was as if years, not just a day, had gone by since I left Iran and only hours since Parviz picked me up from the St. Louis Airport and dropped me off on the campus in St. James. I was so remote now from my family and Ahvaz. The campus, with its colonial and Greek Revival architecture, wide old shady trees, flowers in bloom in rectangular beds, and sets of swing chairs in different spots, looked glorious in the pale, late-afternoon sunlight. I watched with fascination the girls walking about the campus or sitting on the swings. They reminded me of the women I had seen in American movies with Pari, or on the other side of the river. One girl with curly short hair and dimples was an older version of Shirley Temple. Another, with pale blond hair, the color of straw, and milk-white skin, reminded me of Marilyn Monroe. I couldn't wait to write to Pari and tell her all about them.

I pulled out a photograph of Pari from my suitcase and put it on the desk. Then I spread the paradise tapestry, which I had brought without its frame, on the back of a chair until I could frame it and hang it on the wall. I didn't have a good photograph of Maryam—only a small one with her hair covered in a black chador, only her eyes showing. After taking a shower in the common bathroom, I sat in bed and wrote a long letter to Pari and one to Maryam. I went to bed early, exhausted from the eighteen-hour flight from Iran. I fell into a dreamless sleep.

I woke late the next morning and made my way to the college dining room. It was nearly empty. I took some food from the buffet and sat at a table with two other girls. I asked one of them, in broken English, what I had put on my plate.

She stared at me for a moment. "Grits," she said, pointing to a white lump. Then pointing to a hunk of bread, she said, "Corn bread."

In a moment they got up and left. I lingered in the large room by myself.

I registered for as many courses that didn't require fluent English as possible—piano, swimming, home economics. In home economics, the professor taught us how to set a table and seat guests. She also taught us "charm"—not much different from *taarof* in the Iranian culture. We should always say, "Yes, ma'am," she said, when addressing a woman older than ourselves; we should write a thank-you note to our hostess and it should be phrased in a certain way. At the required introduction to English literature, I could absorb only some of the lecture. The one English course I had taken in high school hadn't prepared me adequately. Between classes I sat in my room or on a swing chair and tried to understand the assignments and make sense of my notes, poring over my Farsi-English dictionary.

After dinner I went to my room, leaving the door half open to create a draft with the breeze coming through the window. As the evening wore on other students began to come back, holding Cokes or instant coffee, cellophane-wrapped crackers, cheese, and cookies. Some of them stood in the hall in clusters and talked. When the weekend came most of the girls went out together or on dates with boys from nearby colleges. I stayed in the dormitory, studying.

My isolation felt like freedom at first. But soon the reality of the college and my separation from the other students began to hit me.

Beauty contests, mixers with boys the school invited from colleges in the area, sermons in the Presbyterian chapel at which attendance was required

no matter what your religion—all just floated around me without meaning. The ideal young girl, one whom the staff and parents approved of and
promoted, was a good Christian who dressed properly and was agreeable
and sociable. If a student didn't go on frequent dates with boys she was
"antisocial" or "a loser." If a student had plans with a female friend and then
a boy called and asked her out at the same time, she would automatically
accept the date and cancel plans with the girlfriend. If a student dated a boy
from outside her religion it created problems. Smiling was compulsory. One
girl in my dormitory said, "Smile," every time we passed in the hall.

The pocket money Father sent me through Parviz shrank when converted from *tooman*s to dollars. The other girls flew home often for family
gatherings or to reunite with a high school sweetheart. They had their hair
done in expensive beauty salons in St. Louis, then went shopping and returned with packages of hats, gloves, blouses, shoes. They often skipped
dormitory meals to buy their own food. The girls who didn't have cars took
taxis everywhere, rather than buses, which ran infrequently on limited
routes. They decorated their rooms with their own personal furniture.

I was out of the prison of my home, but I was here all alone. I didn't have
easy access to my brothers. I didn't know a single other person.

❊

One day toward the end of the semester I found a note from the dean in my
mailbox inviting me, along with the three other foreign students on campus, to participate in Parents' Day. She asked that I stop by her office. The
dean was wearing a linen suit, her blond hair set in neat short curls. She
greeted me with a warm smile. "I'm telling this to all the foreign students on
campus," she said. "You should wear your native costumes on Parents' Day."

I was silent, feeling awkward. I had no costume. She was waiting.

"In Iran, some women cover themselves in chadors, but they wear them
on top of regular clothes, similar to what people wear here," I said.

"Then wear a chador," she said.

My awkwardness only increased.

"I never wore one in Iran," I said finally, my voice drowned in the sound of laughter and conversation in the hall.

"I still want you to wear it for this occasion, to show a little of your culture to us," she said, smiling cheerfully.

To me the chador had come to mean a kind of bondage, as religion had. It felt ridiculous to wear it in this American college. "Maybe I can think of something else to wear," I mumbled.

"No, no, the idea of the chador is excellent. I've seen pictures of women in Islamic countries wearing them. It fascinates me. What is the point?"

"Well, in Islam, exposed hair and skin is considered to be seductive to men."

"I wish I felt my hair and skin were so seductive that I had to cover them up," she said with a chuckle. But her attempt at humor only made me more insecure in this unexpectedly alien environment. I was realizing quickly how different this place was from my expectation of America.

That afternoon after classes I walked to St. Louis's Main Street to buy fabric for the chador. On one side of the street was a pharmacy, a post office, a small department store, a small supermarket, and a diner. Several residential streets branched off it and led to the Mississippi River, a muddy and turbulent body of water, with traffic racing on the wide street running alongside it. I thought of standing on the bank of the Karoon River and looking at the Americans on the other side. Here I was among them and feeling cut off and insecure.

In the department store I looked at stacks of fabric in one corner. I wondered what to buy, a lightweight bright fabric like Maryam and other women wore around the house when a man was there, or the more somber black material they wore outside. Finally I decided on a few yards in blue with floral designs in paler blue. I also bought thread, scissors, and a needle.

Back in my room, I spread the fabric on the floor, cut it in the shape of a chador, and hemmed the edges. It was hard to cut it right; I went very slowly. Maryam used to have hers made by a seamstress. As a child, I chose not to wear the chador. Now cutting one felt almost like making a shroud, as I had seen Maryam and her tenants doing. My mind went to my grandmother telling me that Reza Shah, the father of the present Shah, had forbidden women to wear the chador. The police used to pull it off the heads of women who wore it outdoors. He wanted the world to see Iran as modern. Then the present Shah, who had the same idea of modernizing Iran, as a compromise to please the clergy made wearing it optional. Women like Maryam, who were totally observant, wore it; some, who were less religious, wore head scarves; more Westernized women like Mohtaram didn't cover their heads. The whole notion of the chador was very strange to Americans; I could tell by the dean's reaction, yet she wanted me to wear it.

On Parents' Day I put the chador on and looked at myself in the mirror. I was reminded of the times I wore it to passion plays and to a mosque Maryam took me to. I didn't connect to the chador and the realization had made me sad—at one time Maryam and I were so much alike. Now, here I was in this land of freedom and more or less forced to wear it. I tried to brush off my thoughts, to not be so easily dissatisfied.

I went to the room where the reception was taking place. Framed photographs of various benefactors hung on the walls. As I stood with Margarita, from Greece, who was wearing a full embroidered skirt and blouse; Rachel, from Turkey, in something similar; and Bharti, from India, in a sari, everyone's eyes focused mainly on me.

"Isn't that pretty," one young mother said, with a Southern drawl. "But it must be difficult to move around in."

"Does everyone dress like that in Iran?" another woman asked.

"No," I said, "it's optional; only about half the women wear it."

"I can't imagine wearing it."

Though I didn't accept the chador, I felt insulted, thinking of Maryam always enclosed in one, by choice.

After enduring more questions from mothers, the foreign students and I left together. Outside, sitting on facing swings, we talked among ourselves.

Maryam

Margarita, dark-haired and plump, was a sophomore; she said she disliked the college and planned to return home as soon as the year was over. Rachel, red-haired and pale, with a quiet manner, said she was happy enough so far, this being her first year. On the plane ride to the United States she had met a man from her own country who attended a nearby college; the two of them spent a lot of time together. And Bharti, thin and dark and serious, was unhappy but intended to stay on until she graduated. I told her I also intended to finish, although I was beginning to feel the college wasn't the right place for me and wasn't what I had imagined it to be like.

"I think they gave us single rooms because we're foreign," Bharti said. "Everyone else shares rooms. They didn't think anyone would want to room with us. I get strange glances from everyone when I say I'm a Hindu."

"They're narrow and bigoted," Margarita said.

"No one has tried to befriend me," Rachel said.

"I feel the same way," I said. "But maybe it's an illusion."

Rachel shrugged her shoulders.

"My mother asked me to ask you if you're a Catholic." Judy Conrad was a pretty blonde who lived on my floor. She had stopped me in the bathroom.

I shook my head no.

"But my mother said you were wearing a habit."

"That wasn't a habit, it was a chador. Good Muslims wear them."

"Are Muslims Catholics?"

"No, it's a different religion."

"Are you a good Muslim?"

I just stared at her. When I didn't answer she put her hand on her hip. "Well, in this college we're all Christians," she said coolly and walked away.

Twenty

I was feeling hot and stifled by the sermon in the chapel. The preacher was a stout, gray-haired man. He talked monotonously about passages in the Bible, interpreting them. I kept staring at the stained glass, my mind going to happier childhood days when multicolored light poured into my room through stained glass. Though Maryam's household had been filled with talk of religion and religious practice, I never felt pressure from her to believe or to practice religion. Here in this college I felt a pressure to believe in Christianity, and going to the chapel was compulsory.

I was sitting next to Janet, a girl from my hall. She frowned at me as I kept shifting in my seat. I got up and left before the sermon was over and sat under a tree in a meadow that stretched beyond the campus.

When I returned to my dormitory later that day, the housemother, Cynthia, approached me in the lobby and asked me to come to her room on the first floor. According to rumors, she had been married to a Lindengrove professor and he left her for one of his students. He had been fired and the student expelled, but Cynthia had stayed on.

"It's sacrilegious to leave the sermon halfway through," she said the moment we reached her room.

"I'm sorry," I stammered.

"Anyway, you keep to yourself too much. Try to mingle more, make friends. To start with I want you to go to the mixer next week."

I had no idea what a mixer was and was embarrassed to ask. So I just looked at her.

"We invite boys from the surrounding colleges. We play dance music. We have mixers a few times a year. The girls love them."

I nodded noncommittally.

"You must go, be more sociable. There may be a few foreign boys there from the Missouri School of Mines. The engineering school attracts foreign boys."

"I don't know how to dance. I only learned a little from my brother," I said.

A clock on the wall chimed, interrupting us.

"You can just follow the steps," she said and got up. I assumed that meant it was time for me to leave. So I got up, too, and left.

Before the party on Saturday night, the bathrooms on my floor were filled with girls checking their makeup, spraying perfume on their necks and arms, fluffing up their hair, and examining their dresses one more time. I put on a pale yellow dress I had made in my home economics course and low-heeled shoes I brought with me from Iran. The shoes were handmade with good leather but had an old-fashioned, un-party-like look. The other girls wore dresses with low-cut necklines and high heels. They wore rouge, lipstick, eye shadow. I wore no makeup as I was not used to it.

As soon as I arrived at the mixer I regretted coming. Girls stood around the room with smiles glued on their faces. None of the other foreign students was there, and neither were there any foreign boys, from what I could tell. The boys scrutinized us superciliously. A few asked some of the girls to dance. The girls who weren't asked began to talk among themselves and laugh in an artificially cheerful way.

Since I was neither asked to dance nor pulled into conversation by other girls, I left and sat on a swing in the far corner of the campus. A full moon was shining in the sky. I thought of Pari and me standing on the terrace at night talking, with the same moon dangling in the sky. Now we were so far away from each other.

As I trudged through my days in a place where I didn't fit in, I tried to focus on my future. I would go somewhere in America where I could blend in more, though I had no idea yet where that was or how I would get there. I thought about what Maryam had said to me, "As soon as a baby comes into the world an angel writes its destiny on the baby's forehead." I hadn't accepted that as a child, and now, too, I believed that it was my own sheer determination that had enabled me to come to America. I should be able to determine what I would do next.

I reminded myself of the luxury of being able to read and write what I wanted without Father's vigilant eyes on me, or the fear of SAVAK in my heart.

Late at night I turned to my writing, my long-lasting friend. I wrote in English now, though I had to constantly look up words in the dictionary. Writing in English gave me a freedom I didn't feel writing in Farsi. Yet everything I wrote had to do with people I knew growing up. Though Iran and people in it were out of reach at the college, as if from a different lifetime, they occupied my deepest emotions.

I wrote a sketch about reading to Ali, with some changes from real life.

. . . On my visits home I read to Ali. He would sit before me with his head bent, his back hunched, while I read from Amir-Al-Salaam, a long heroic tale of a brave man in pursuit of his beloved. The book was very old and had been bound many times. As I read he would gasp or thrust his body forward at the hero's mishaps or smile triumphantly, revealing his small teeth, at the hero's good fortune. I read to him very loudly and distinctly because he was hard of hearing. Because he had round eyes and a very small stature, sometimes I would imagine him to be a child and me his mother. He would never tire of my reading, and when I put the book aside he would thank me profusely and shake his head up and down, still tantalized by the book's flowery language and Amir's adventures. Then he would take the book from me very gently and mark the page with a pigeon feather.

On a warm, starry night I was sitting in the courtyard, watching green frogs jump in and out of the round pool, bats travel back and forth in straight lines under a canopy, when I suddenly became aware of Ali standing in his room near the doorway. In the light of a kerosene lamp in his room I could see him bending and straightening up, his hands gesticulating widely. Then I saw the glimmer of a knife he was holding. I got up and walked toward his room. I coughed and made noise with my wooden slippers but he did not seem to hear me.

He threw the knife on the floor with an élan uncharacteristic of him and knelt before an imaginary figure. "I'm Amir, Amir the fearless, the brave," he chanted, his voice shaking. "I'm here to free you."

I walked away, suddenly wary of being seen by him. After that night, throughout the rest of my visit, he did not ask me to read to him. I had glimpses of him while he washed clothes in a pail or prepared meals. His face was very tense with thought, his gestures had acquired grandeur. He never was aware of anyone even when they came near him, and he often whispered unintelligible words.

After completing the sketch I burst into tears, recalling Mrs. Soleimani, mourning her disappearance all over again. I decided, after some hesitation, to hand it in as my composition assignment. I had the same bland response from the students at Lindengrove as from those at my high school.

"Can't Ali read?" Mrs. Smith, the teacher, a young, vivacious woman with a Southern accent asked.

"Ali was our servant. He was illiterate."

"I guess in Third World countries many people are illiterate." She thought about it. "Isn't Iran Westernized? The Shah is a very modern man. I've seen pictures of him."

"His attempts haven't gone very far yet."

The students had started talking among themselves, bored with the conversation. We went to the next piece. I had no idea what Mrs. Smith thought about the sketch.

I had a desire to talk to her and went to her office one day. But in spite of her friendly manner, she was not open to questions and conversation. She intimidated me, in this place I couldn't understand. So I got up after a moment.

"You have talent," she said as I was leaving.

I built a cradle of dreams for myself; as I lay in bed at night I imagined having an impact on the world through my writing. I rocked myself in that cradle every night to put myself to sleep.

Linda Chesterton had a large room to herself because her roommate had left to live at home and attend a local college. She was a thoughtful girl; she spent a lot of time alone, staying in the dormitory even on most Friday and Saturday nights. Tall, with large green eyes and chestnut brown hair that she wore pulled back, Linda was a sophomore who planned to major in art. She knocked on my door one Friday night when the dorm was practically empty and invited me to her room.

"I know you have sorrow in your heart," she told me.

I was startled by her remark. Did it show on my face? The aftereffects of my losses seemed to have followed me like shadows. Then I began to pour out to her about my childhood, how Pari had lifted me out of utter loneliness and desolation when I was abducted by my father from Maryam, and how now I was so far away from them both.

"When I was twelve years old I injured my spine jumping off a tree in our backyard," Linda said. "I was in bed for weeks. All I did was read and think about things."

She made a deal with me to help me with my English and edit my papers, in return for Farsi lessons. Linda had read Omar Khayyám's poetry and had become interested in ancient Iran and the Farsi language. She intended to use Farsi letters in her paintings. "I want to juxtapose something mystical with the ordinary," she explained.

I took it that she was referring to me as well as the language when she used the word "mystical." Coming from Linda, it was a compliment.

We began to spend a lot of time together. We were an odd couple on campus: she was tall and thin, I was short and suddenly a little overweight from the high-calorie food in the school's dining room.

During the Christmas holidays Linda invited me to her home in Dallas.

"Don't be put off by my parents," she warned me before we left. "They're very provincial."

We reached her house at dinnertime, having taken an early bus from St. Louis. Linda's mother, Shirley, kissed her.

"Welcome," Shirley said to me but with a scrutinizing gaze that immediately made me uncomfortable. Linda showed me the guest room and then we went to dinner. The house was furnished with ornate, imitation European items, the way my parents' house was. But the ranch-style architecture and the quietness surrounding it were vastly different.

Linda's father was already sitting at the table. He nodded to me and said, "Sit down, Nadia."

"Nahid," Linda corrected.

"Nahad, how do you like our country so far? Isn't it lucky you came here?"

I was blushing, uncomfortable with him.

"Let's eat," Shirley said. The table was already set with food similar to meals at school—corn bread, deep-fried chicken, and grits. Shirley bent her head and began to say grace, and we all bent our heads, too. In a moment she raised her head and said, "Amen," and we all repeated, "Amen." I had participated in the ritual on different occasions in the college.

Shirley began to pass around the food.

"What do you eat in Iran?" she asked me.

"The most common dishes are fish and lamb and chicken *kababs* and stews."

"Do you have houses in Iran?" was Shirley's next question.

"Yes, definitely," I said.

"You're so much more refined than other foreigners," she said.

Linda's father was quiet throughout, listening to the hum of the TV turned low in the corner.

After dinner Linda and I withdrew to our rooms. Before going to bed I had to use the bathroom and I passed Linda's room. Her mother was inside talking to her.

"Why don't you ever do things like everyone else, the normal way? First you go out with an Egyptian and now your best friend is Eyeranian. Before we know it you're going to announce you're engaged to a Negro."

"Mom, stop it," Linda shouted. "I don't want to hear any of this!"

I couldn't hear them after I went into the bathroom. Later Linda joined me in my room and shut the door. I was sitting in bed, reading the *The Dallas Morning News*, which I had picked up in the living room.

I hid my head in the newspaper.

"My parents share the herd mentality of the people around here," she said, assuming I had overheard the conversation. "Sometimes I lie in the dark and think about how disappointed they are in me. I don't date much, I'm not in a hurry to catch the right husband. I'll never be a typical house-wife and mother. They sent me to Lindengrove to groom me for the right kind of husband. The college is just a finishing school."

I thought of the home economics course that was immensely popular at school. The homecoming queen was a home economics major.

When we returned to St. James, Linda seemed more restless than ever and began cutting classes. One afternoon she came to my room and an-nounced, "I'm not staying for the rest of the semester. I'm going to New York to enroll in art school. All I want to do is paint."

"You're quitting in the middle of the semester?"

"I can't bear it here," she said. "You could come to New York, too. Maybe we'll room together."

"I can't quit," I said. "I'm on a student visa. I have to be at school. And I wouldn't be able to support myself anyway. I need the full scholarship."

After Linda dropped out I tried to get away from the campus as much as possible. One day I looked for a bookstore in town but discovered there were none. A drugstore had a rack with some paperbacks and magazines on it. As I was browsing through the books with their shiny covers, my mind was totally on Jalal and his bookstore. I missed him, and my fears for him returned. Was he in jail, dead, alive? None of the books interested me and I bought a copy of *Time* magazine. I decided to treat myself to a meal out, something I rarely did for lack of money. I sat in a diner and read the magazine as I ate.

This was 1965 and there was a reference to Khomeini in a brief article. He had been released from house arrest and sent into exile in Turkey. He was sending messages to Iranians, demanding that they openly criticize the Shah. But, the article said, the upheaval that had beset Iranian cities had diminished over the last several weeks and there was no real threat to the Shah.

I noticed a young man sitting alone, staring at me.

"Hello," he said, catching my eye. He had blue eyes and short-cropped blond hair, like most of the boys in the area. "Can I sit with you?" he asked.

"Yes, please," I said.

He joined me. "I'm Bill Owen. And you?"

"Nahid Mehramy."

He repeated my name a couple of times and asked, "Where are you from?"

"Iran."

"A modern Shah and queen and all the oil," he said. "Everyone must be rich there. Is your father rich?"

"Yes."

"Did you live near oil fields?"

"Right in the middle of them."

He said he sold electronic equipment and occasionally passed through

St. James. After we finished eating he got the check and paid for my lunch, too. "I'll take you for a ride," he said. "That's my car right there."

I hesitated. Not that I was afraid of being seen with the man, as I had been when I went for the boat ride with James, but because I was afraid of who Bill Owen might be, where he would take me. In the dormitory students talked about rape and murder. But I was terribly lonely and wanted to make a connection. So I got into his car. He drove to a quiet spot just a few minutes out of the town. He put the car in park, then took my face in his hands and kissed me. I felt nothing. It was as if I were asleep or my flesh was numb. I was used to being wooed by a boy before anything could happen. Before I got onto the boat with James, I had seen him around town, our eyes had locked, we had smiled at each other. I had just met Bill. His hand touched my breast and I began to resist.

"Why not?" he whispered, breathing fast.

I didn't know what to say to this stranger, so I said nothing.

Bill put his head on the steering wheel and gave an exasperated sigh. Then he began to drive me to the college.

"Let me know if you're in town again," I said, as he dropped me off.

"I will," he said and quickly drove away.

I stood by the school's gate as if I had been thrown out of his car. I thought of how persistent the boys in Ahvaz were—day after day standing on the sidewalk waiting for us girls to pass by. This encounter seemed to be part of an American code I didn't quite comprehend.

But for weeks, I missed this man I had met only once.

※

It was helpful to see how my brothers had adjusted to the culture. Cyrus, who lived in Ohio now, was visiting Parviz in his apartment in St. Louis. Both my brothers had assumed the more informal American appearance and manner. They were immersed in the culture and even had American girlfriends, who joined us for dinner. Cyrus's girlfriend, Mildred, grew up on a farm in Ohio and was blond and Christian. Parviz's girlfriend, Shirley, was from Tennessee and also Christian, and had light brown hair and brown eyes. In certain ways my brothers had fulfilled our parents' expectations. Parviz was doing well in his field of medicine, having gotten an internship at a prestigious hospital, and Cyrus was getting a Ph.D. in mathematics, after completing his engineering degree. Neither had returned home for visits, even though they could now afford it. They both explained that it was difficult for them psychologically. It had taken a long time to understand the cues of this new culture and to finally become a part of it. It would be jarring to go back and forth.

Twenty-one

Throughout the year, I had written Pari several letters. I never received a reply. But finally one came in my second semester.

I'm so happy to get your letters and have a glimpse of the way you live. I didn't write back sooner because I have so little to say about my life that you don't already know. As you might expect, Taheri went against his promise again and when I got a part in a play he stopped me from being in it. He's a caricature of the romantic man he presented himself as. I'm passing time by doing what he approves of—renovating the house.

There's a dark hollow space between me and my husband. I feel this is a good time to get out of the marriage, before I have a child. I wrote letters home to see if Father and Mother would help me get a divorce. As expected, they said no. You know how impossible it would be for me to do it alone, without their help. How would I make a living? I would be penniless without the mehrieh, which I would surely lose. I don't even have access to most of my jewelry. Taheri put most of the valuable ones in a bank safe. He says I don't have enough sense and will lose them and also there are home robberies at times. Jobs wouldn't come easily to a young divorced woman here and the same with trying to rent a place and liv-

ing alone, even if I could afford it. It's easier for a woman who's widowed to live alone than a divorced woman, even in the most modern sections. A divorced woman living alone practically has the status of a prostitute. I don't want to give up hope but I can't help despairing at times. You were stronger than me. . . .

I remained in my chair, almost paralyzed with sadness. Finally I put the letter in a cardboard box where I kept an antique tortoiseshell comb and brush set that Pari had given to me when we were in Ahvaz. The lid was decorated with designs of a willowy girl sitting by a stream. I had written "Pari" on it.

A few months later, another letter arrived.

Nahid, I am pregnant, two months. I was hoping I wouldn't get pregnant but here I am with a baby growing inside me. My dear sister, I can tell you honestly that I'm not happy about it. It kills the hope of my somehow getting out of the marriage. In spite of his possessiveness of me, I'm sure Taheri goes to prostitutes. I smell different perfumes on him. I couldn't hold myself back and I confronted him. He vehemently denied it. Then, as usual, he tried to comfort me with lavish gifts.

One good thing in my life is having Azar Mirshahi as a friend. She lives in a house across the street. She's about my age, is married to a businessman working for a caviar cannery, and they have three small children. I go to her house and we have tea and talk. Yesterday she said something that upsets me terribly. She asked me if I knew anything about Taheri's past. I assumed she was referring to his going to prostitutes but she said no, there were things about him that I should know but I had to find out on my own, as she had been sworn to secrecy. It makes me apprehensive what it could be. I'm going to try to pry it out of her.

At the bottom of the letter Pari had copied a poem, "The Wind-up Doll," by the famous Iranian poet Furugh Farrukhzad. Farrukhzad, who lived in

Ahvaz for a period of time, was both admired and attacked by people for her outspokenness on issues having to do with women's private desires, so suppressed in Iran.

With a frozen gaze like that of the dead
you stare at the smoke drifting from a cigarette
at a cup
at a fading epigraph on the wall
With stiff fingers you push aside the drapery on the window
you stand there motionless and like a wind-up doll,
you see the world with glass eyes
you watch the rain falling in the alley
a child standing in a doorway, flying colorful kites
At night in bed, enveloped in a man's domineering arms
you cry out with a voice that is false and remote, "I love . . ."
You sleep for years in lace and tinsel, your body stuffed with straw
Rise up and seek your freedom, my sister
Why are you quiet?
Seek your rights, my sister
You must tear apart from those who seat you in a corner of the house
so that your life will be free.

Now from an even farther distance than that between Ahvaz and Tehran, I was haunted by Pari's state in life, in the hands of her despotic husband. She had hoped that in Tehran she would find freedom. She had been naive to believe Taheri would let her pursue what she wanted. She had pulled a veil of self-deception over her face in order to bear marrying him.

I had an urgent desire to talk to Pari, hear her voice. I decided to use the public phone in the dorm lobby. It was ten o'clock in the morning in St. James; it would be nine o'clock in the evening in Tehran. The international lines were busy for a long time. When I finally got through, Pari's phone rang and rang and no one picked up. The same thing happened on the following days. Each time I failed to reach her I was filled with a bottomless sense of foreboding.

I thought about visiting her. I would need a permission letter from Father again to be able to get out of Iran and return to school. What if, for some reason, he decided to keep me there and force me to marry? Besides, I didn't have the money for travel and I knew he wouldn't pay for the trip since he had never sent money to my brothers to visit. The unfavorable exchange rate from *toomans* to dollars made the tickets exorbitantly expensive. Pari couldn't visit me because Taheri would never allow her to come all the way to America; now that she was married, Iranian law stipulated that he (rather than Father) was the one from whom she needed a permission letter to travel.

I began to dream about Pari. In one dream I was in Maryam's house. Pari was there, too, and the three of us were sitting in her large living room around a *sofreh*, eating. Mellow green, yellow, and amber lights seeped into the room. Maryam suddenly frowned and said, "That isn't Pari, she only looks like her. And that isn't really my courtyard." I looked at Pari and I could see there were certain obvious differences. And the courtyard was filled with paper flowers, not real ones.

I woke, covered in sweat.

The next night in my dream I was sitting in the hollow trunk of the old plane tree in Maryam's courtyard. It was a very clear day and everything around me was vividly delineated. Then the air suddenly changed; a hard wind began to blow and it quickly turned into a hurricane. Someone was walking toward me in the darkened air, calling my name, asking for help. I jumped out of the tree and ran toward the figure, whose voice became more desperate. It was a tiny, featureless figure with hands stretched out toward me, trying to move forward but not able to. I realized that the figure was Pari, only smaller and younger. She sank into the ground before I could reach her.

Pari gave birth in the modern and well-equipped Russian Hospital in Tehran. After she came out of anesthesia, she found Taheri sitting on a chair by her bed, looking at her with loving eyes. He kissed her and said, "You gave us a lovely son." But Pari knew this new behavior would not last; beneath his congenial and adoring manner lurked the desire to control, the dark possessiveness. It would return. A nurse examined Pari's breasts to see if she had enough milk to breast-feed. She did but it hurt when she fed Bijan, so much that Pari couldn't help but cry. Pari considered bottle-feeding Bijan, as some modern Tehrani mothers did, but Taheri didn't like the idea.

After two days in the maternity hospital Taheri took Pari home. His three sisters were waiting for them there. Taheri's elderly parents visited for a week. Other family members, hordes of them, some of whom Pari hadn't met before, visited daily. Many of Taheri's relatives were ultraconservative Muslims who were hoping Taheri would give Bijan a name like Mohammad or Hussein. They insisted that he and Pari, too, start praying daily to set a good example for their child. Taheri prayed while they were there and forced Pari to do the same. Pari pretended. Mohtaram and Father didn't visit as they were saddled with responsibilities at home. Farzin was having seizures that were hard to control with drugs. She couldn't speak and threw tantrums in frustration. She couldn't attend school, and they had hired tutors for her.

Twenty-two

That fall, the foreign student adviser called me into her office. "What is your major going to be?" she asked.

"I want to be a writer."

"You know we don't have a writing major," she said, frowning. "Besides, writing isn't practical. How are you going to support yourself? Are you engaged to a rich man or are your parents willing to support you through the struggle?"

I shook my head.

"Why don't you major in psychology? It's a practical field and it is about people, like writing. After you get your degree here, you can apply to graduate schools."

I liked her suggestions, though I wasn't sure how I would manage to go to graduate school. I became fascinated by mother-child relationships. I devoured literature about teenage girls, how during teen and preteen years girls often rebel against their mothers, even hate them. They think of their mothers as being too restrictive and are sensitive to the slightest criticism. In turn they are critical of anything their mothers do: their clothing, way of speaking, hairstyle. It reminded me of my attitude toward Mohtaram, with whom I had lived only during those typically rebellious years.

I began studying anything that had to do with mother-child issues, including the rights of a biological parent as opposed to an adoptive parent, and the fierce fights often put up by each. Most of the time a child was given away for adoption by his or her mother because of financial or psychological problems. Mohtaram didn't have either of those problems.

Once I was watching a TV program in the lounge about a mother who had spent several years trying to regain custody of the child she gave up for adoption. Tears collected in my eyes and streamed down my face. Janis, who lived on my floor, was doing homework on the sofa. She asked, "What's wrong?"

"My mother has cancer," I said and got up. I went to my room and cried some more.

Parviz found me a job for the summer as an assistant to a psychiatrist at the hospital in St. Louis where he did his internship. Parviz himself was leaving St. Louis for another state to do his medical residency. He'd assured Father, "Don't worry, I'll still check on Nahid."

I lived in St. Louis with a roommate, Amy, whom I hardly ever saw. One afternoon, while I was waiting for a bus, a young man came over to me and asked, "Are you a singer?" He was carrying a guitar case.

Perhaps it was the way I was dressed, in a red T-shirt with a picture of a pair of darker red lips on it, a full white linen skirt, and large, dark sunglasses (my attempt to cultivate a style).

"Have you ever been to Leopard's Jazz Club?"

"No," I said.

"I thought I saw you there," he said. "I play the guitar there." His hair, long and disheveled, hung in curls over his shoulders. He couldn't have been more different from the clean-cut boys who came to our college to pick up their dates. He said his name was Jack Bruhel. By the time the bus came he had invited me to the jazz club that evening and offered to pick me up at my apartment.

That evening I tried on different outfits, put my hair up in different styles, applied different lipsticks, anxious about my first date in America.

Jack drove me to the club in his silver, somewhat banged-up convertible sports car. He took me to a table and ordered me a beer before joining a group of musicians on the stage.

A young woman came onstage from a back room and stood behind the microphone. The proprietor introduced her as Martha. She was very tall, with wheat-colored hair and large blue eyes. After the applause died down, she began to sing in a soft, melodic voice:

Am I blue, am I blue, ain't there tears in my eyes telling you . . .

At intermission Jack came over holding a beer. "What do you think of Martha?" he asked.

"She's very good."

"I may as well be honest with you. She and I have been going out—well, on and off. We've had a lot of ups and downs. We're in a down period right now." He played with his beer bottle, turning it around on the table.

I was confused. Why was he telling me this?

It was after midnight when we started for my apartment in his car. In the living room, Jack kissed me.

"You have such a nice complexion and hair," he whispered, his lips close to my ear.

In my room, he started to undress me. My heart beat wildly with yearning.

But again, as with Bill, in spite of my desire to open up, I became stiff. "Not tonight," I mumbled.

"What's the matter?"

"I can't," I said.

"Don't play games with me."

"I'm sorry. Another time."

He squeezed my breast hard with a surge of irritation and got up. He left, slamming the door behind him.

I lay there, hearing all the negative remarks and warnings about sex in Iran, expressed by Maryam and her neighbors as well as the more modern people like my parents and people at school. "Sex is only for procreation," one of Maryam's neighbors said to her daughter. "Men are nice to you until they fulfill their lust and then they abandon you," my high school principal lectured. It was amazing that I had tried to model myself after American women in movies and books but I was crippled by the voices of my own past. *Here I am,* I thought, *in the land of freedom, and yet I am so unfree in my own life.* In spite of my rebelliousness, the deep fear of losing my virginity was still with me. Kissing James that afternoon in Ahvaz, so daring in that repressive town, was still all I was able to allow myself. If I were an American girl, raised in America, would I have given in? Was this what Father meant when he warned me not to become like American girls? I was overwhelmed by confusion about who I was. I wanted to have new experiences, to experiment, but alas, most of the time I felt as if I were in a precarious situation and had to be cautious.

That summer I received a letter from Maryam. She had married Rahbar and was living with him in Dubai. She didn't provide a return address. She said they moved frequently because of his job, which took them to different cities in the Middle East. I recalled the glow on her face when she talked about him, and was happy she had him in her life.

Twenty-three

Back in Tehran, Pari had joined a group of women, arranged by her friend Azar. Pari attended meetings while Behjat, Taheri's sister, babysat.

In the meetings they talked about how to improve laws for women. Shirin, Azar's sister, had worked as a secretary in a law office and had studied all the laws relevant to women; she believed they were unfair. There were five women in the group: Pari, Azar Mirshahi, her sister Shirin Tavalodi, Zohreh Nadjoumi, and Latifeh Ahkami. Shirin was married but thinking of getting a divorce. Latifeh, who was unmarried, lived with her mother, who suffered from bouts of depression; she believed that her late husband had poisoned her and that the poison was still in her system. Latifeh thought there was some truth to her mother's fears; her father had been violent and abusive. Now her mother slept most of the day in a back room in the house. Latifeh herself didn't see joy in marriage and didn't see the point of bringing children into a miserable world. Zohreh had been married for a short time, before her husband had left the country without a trace. She lived with her aunt and worked in a travel agency, and knew a lot about world affairs. The group always met in Zohreh's house because her old aunt kept to herself in a room on the other side of the courtyard.

After discussing various issues, they wound down by reading poetry. If the weather was nice they sat in the courtyard under a clump of trees next to the pool. Some read poems they wrote themselves. Writing poems was something many women did, most of the time with no intention of publishing them. At one meeting, Pari recited one of the poems Farrukhzad wrote before she left her husband:

More and more I am thinking that
I will suddenly spread my wings.
And fly out of this prison, laughing at my jailor.

In a letter, Pari revealed to me what it was in Taheri's past that Azar had once hinted at.

"Azar thinks it's fair that I should tell you what I know about Taheri's past," Shirin said to Pari after one of their meetings.

"Please, what is it?" Pari stared at her, waiting breathlessly.

"Did you know he was in jail for a year? Nine, ten years ago."

"No, I had no idea. For what?"

"He was riding his motor scooter recklessly and he ran over a woman. If he had sought help for the woman immediately she'd have survived. But he sped away from the site, leaving her on the ground bleeding. She went into a coma and died in a week. Taheri was sentenced to ten years in prison. His father bribed people and got him out after a year. My cousin works in the lamp shop on the street where your husband ran over the woman. He also knows the woman's family intimately. Please, please don't tell your husband I told you all this."

Pari thought about what a reckless driver Taheri was, always full of freefloating anger and the conviction that he had the right of way. When he wanted to emphasize a point he clenched his fist so tightly that his knuckles became white and then he would pick up a vase or a plate and throw it against the wall. Leaving the shattered pieces on the floor, he would zoom out of the house. True, he was regretful later for his behavior—he would get on his knees, ask for forgiveness, cry, and declare his love for her. But what good did any of that do? She had come to hate even his presents because they made him feel he had paid penance. After she and Shirin went their separate ways, Pari walked rapidly, propelled by anxiety, disgust, and fear. She almost stumbled into a *joob*.

Then a thought came to her—if she found the evidence that Taheri had been in jail and for what crime, maybe the information would enable her to get a divorce without losing custody of her son and the right to her *mehrieh*. If there were any documents in the house, pointing to Taheri's guilt, they would be in the black filing cabinet in the basement that was always locked. Not long before, she had gone into the cluttered basement and sorted out all the unnecessary stuff stored in boxes—old clothes, chipped dishes and utensils, broken chandeliers, dented samovars. She had hired someone to come and take them away. Another day she had looked through the folders stored in the cabinets set against the wall. They contained documents that had to do with old family affairs and she left them alone. One of the cabinets was locked. She had asked Taheri what was in it. He said it contained documents having to do with important business matters and she should leave them alone.

As soon as she got home she went directly to the basement and tried to open the lock with a knife and scissors, but neither worked. She thought of getting a locksmith to open it but was afraid he might talk. She left the basement and called Shirin, who would get her cousin to open the lock.

In the morning Shirin and her cousin Ebrahim came over and Pari led them to the locked cabinet. After Ebrahim opened the lock they found only two folders inside. Sitting on an old sofa Pari hadn't discarded, they went through every piece of paper in the folders. And there it was—a yellowish document drawn up by a lawyer, asking a judge to reduce the jail sentence. Pari kept the document and put the folders back in the cabinet. Then Ebrahim fixed the lock. Taheri would never know.

Taheri's parents and sisters treat him like God, Pari wrote. *But he's inexplicably depressed, deeply so. It could be because he hates the weakness, the needfulness in himself. And he might have deep guilt locked inside him. The depression turns outward at times, making him violent. He goes from a gentle, weeping man to a terrifying one and then back again.*

Pari had decided that she would go home and show Father the document. Taheri planned to go on a business trip in two weeks and that would be a good time for her to leave. With what she had discovered about Taheri, surely Father would understand why she wanted to leave him. And perhaps this time Mohtaram would be on her side.

That evening at dinner, Pari noticed Taheri was tense and uneasy, as if he somehow sensed what she had found out about him. Was she giving out subtle cues? It was true that when looking at him, she kept thinking, *he killed an innocent woman.*

Pari slept in the guest room that night, telling Taheri that she had a terrible headache and wanted to be alone in bed. Now Pari was waiting only for Taheri to go on the trip and then she would take Bijan and go home. Her biggest fear was that if indeed Taheri was vaguely aware that she knew something, he would cancel his trip and stay home to keep an eye on her.

In the letter she included another poem by Furugh Farrukhzad.

If one day I try to fly out of this prison,
how will I explain it to my weeping child?

Outside my dorm room, I heard the footsteps of the other girls, whispers, giggles. I sat in my room, all alone except for Pari's letter.

Pari's next letter came from Ahvaz. Before taking Bijan and starting on her journey, she had removed her wedding ring and put it on the dining table. She left no note. When she arrived home Father and Mohtaram took turns holding Bijan, cooing to him, kissing him, murmuring, "My only grandchild," or, "My beautiful little boy."

Then, Pari showed the document to Father.

"The woman would have lived if Taheri hadn't driven away from her," she said to him. "Wouldn't the court grant me the divorce and let me keep Bijan, and my *mehrieh*, too, if you show them this document?"

Father read the document carefully and said, "This doesn't say anything about his running away from the scene, and he was let out of jail after a short time. Pari, you have this wonderful son now, you shouldn't be contemplating leaving your husband."

"My friend's cousin was on the scene and saw everything. Maybe he knows others who were there, too."

"I've been in law for years," Father said. "Witnesses aren't given much weight, particularly years after the incident."

"Father, please, please try. I can't bear living with this man. I'm afraid of him."

"I'll think about it," he said, turning to leave.

In the morning, Father looked at Pari. His face was clouded by concern. "Imagine how we will all be stigmatized if you get a divorce."

"Aren't I entitled to some individual happiness?" Pari said.

"Pari, you're under the influence of those American movies. Their idea of individual happiness is selfish and it has hurt their sense of family life. That's why so many Americans are miserable, lonely, killing themselves with drugs and alcohol. What we have is superior; each person should think of the happiness of the whole."

"Look at this wonderful child," Mohtaram said, holding Bijan in her lap. "You may never see him again if you get a divorce. The court will let Taheri keep him because he's two years old and doesn't need your milk. That's the law. The most you'll get is visitation rights. Taheri lives far away from here, and anyway, he'll make sure to keep Bijan from you." They fell silent.

"You want to be in the same situation as those poor, lonely women who aren't able to find husbands?" Mohtaram asked after a moment.

"But I've been married already."

"You'll be unmarried again if you pursue this kind of attitude."

Taheri's sisters informed him that Pari had taken Bijan and most likely gone home, so he cut his trip short and came directly to Ahvaz. When Taheri arrived, Pari was in the courtyard with Bijan. He picked up Bijan. "Pack and let's get going, or else I'm taking my son without you."

Father walked into the courtyard from the street and tried to pry Bijan out of Taheri's arms.

"He's my son and he's going with me," Taheri shouted. "You've spoiled your daughter! She isn't suitable to be a wife or a mother. You need to work on her." Taheri walked out of the courtyard with a crying Bijan in his arms.

Father didn't run after him, he didn't see the point. He told Pari she should go back to her husband and child. Pari stayed, even though our parents weren't welcoming and she missed Bijan terribly. Both Father and Mohtaram criticized her for leaving her husband in the first place. Father would concede only that Taheri was "below our family in intellect and culture."

Majid was married and living in Isfahan, where he was teaching and working as an assistant director in a film studio. His mother had selected his bride, Pari had heard from her friend Golnaz. Golnaz also told her that Majid found his wife to be "too common," not someone he could talk to or share ideas with. Majid's expectation for a wife was different from most men's, Golnaz said. Pari hoped that Majid would hear about her being in Ahvaz and come to look for her, put a letter in her hand, send her flowers as he used to. She still had the dried flower petals in her bureau drawers. But in her darker moods she tortured herself with images of Majid and his wife sharing the same space, exchanging intimate words, touches.

She could not stop thinking of those stolen meetings she had with

Majid—their breathing stilled and then revived by the tempo of desire. She had hoped to induce those kinds of feelings in her marriage but of course it didn't work.

Manijeh came home frequently, without her husband, and stayed for a few days at a time. Manijeh hadn't been on my mind for a long time and just seeing her name in Pari's letter brought back all the unresolved tension between us. There was a change in her, Pari said. Perhaps Pari herself had changed, too, and could see Manijeh in a more sympathetic light. Now Manijeh confided in Pari, telling her that she was convinced her husband was in love with someone else. She longed for closeness with him, wanted to have children, but Javad wasn't open to her. Most evenings he came home late and left early in the morning. When she questioned him he claimed he was swamped with work at the refinery hospital. On the few occasions when they went out with other couples, Manijeh noticed continuous glances between Javad and Shahla, a nurse at the same hospital. Manijeh had seen them holding hands surreptitiously under the table. Javad, who spoke disdainfully about most women, was always complimentary of Shahla. Strange, Manijeh thought, since other people criticized Shahla, saying that she had bad manners, that her family wasn't reputable, that her father had once been arrested for smuggling drugs into the country from Dubai. Manijeh had come to believe that Javad really wanted to marry Shahla but married her instead for the sake of appearances and because of pressure from his mother. He never told Manijeh that he loved her.

Mohtaram couldn't believe that Javad, or any man, would ignore Manijeh, her angel. She thought perhaps it was Manijeh who was keeping herself aloof from him. She advised, "Show him how much you care for him." "Wait and see, he'll be dazzled by you once he starts really looking at you."

Mohtaram said Javad's mother was self-satisfied and arrogant, or she would try to discuss the matter with her. When Mrs. Golestani had come to ask for Manijeh's hand for her son, she had spoken very little, as if she didn't want to waste any words with her, Mohtaram said.

To Pari's astonishment Manijeh blamed Mohtaram for not preparing her for real life, for keeping her in a padded, soft, cocoon-like space. Manijeh, whose slightest headache prompted Mohtaram to take her to a doctor, whose mere frown filled Mohtaram with self-recrimination, now expected Mohtaram to fix her life for her. Still, Manijeh didn't intend to ask for a divorce. She hoped that Javad would turn around and begin to love her. Moreover she liked the idea of being married. She wanted Ali and others who came to visit to address her as Mrs. Golestani. She held her hand so that her wedding and engagement rings caught the light.

"The problem lies in you girls," Father told Pari and Manijeh. "Expecting too much and being too spoiled."

Mohtaram and Father were also concerned about Farzin's future. Who would marry her, when she reached that age? Mohtaram consoled herself saying, "She has a delightful disposition and those beautiful gray eyes." She added, with rare humor, "After all, intellect in a woman isn't the first priority with men."

One day Pari saw Father standing on the balcony, crying.

Twenty-four

F ather said he'd send you a plane ticket when you graduate," Parviz informed me in a letter.

My senior year, 1968–1969, Iran continued in turmoil, with tension and
threat in the air, as in my high school years. Since the late 1960s, increases
in the price of oil had brought billions of dollars into the Iranian economy.
But most of that money, people believed, was going straight into the pockets of the Shah and his close circle, or spent on the military. From his exile
in Iraq, having left Turkey, Khomeini was sending messages to Iranians, ad-
vocating a democratic Islamic regime in place of corrupt rule by the Shah
and his alliance with the United States. He provoked people to go to the
streets to show their sympathy with him; that led to widespread arrests of
demonstrators.

Added to the political situation in Iran was my painful family situation.
In spite of ups and downs in America, I wanted to stay on. But unless I
could continue as a student, my visa would expire six months after graduation. In my sophomore and junior years my grades had improved consid-
erably along with my English, but I had to solve the problem of how I
would support myself while in graduate school. There was no point in asking Father for help.

I contacted Linda, my friend who had moved to New York City. She told me about the New School, a university there that allowed students to attend part-time and work part-time. No formal application was necessary. She was moving out of New York in a few weeks—she and her painter boyfriend were going to Taos so they could save money and devote themselves to painting. If I went to New York without telling Father or anyone else, I thought, he would have a hard time tracking me down; he wasn't going to drop everything in his complicated life and come look for me.

On graduation day linden trees were in bloom on campus. Wearing a cap and gown and standing with other girls on the campus lawn, I was the only one without any family members attending the ceremony.

After the ceremony, while the air was still filled with congratulatory remarks and cheers, I wandered back to my room to pack. I planned to take a bus to New York the following day. I wrote a letter to Father that night, telling him that I had decided to go to graduate school and work part-time, that I wouldn't be returning home. I gave no information about my intention to go to New York. Putting that letter in the mailbox was more painful, even frightening, than I had anticipated. It was as if I had been dangling from a rope Father held and had just been cut loose.

The Greyhound bus pulled into New York's Port Authority terminal at six in the morning. Groggy and disoriented, I sat in a restaurant in the Port Authority to have breakfast, trying to think, to pull my mind together. I had made no advance plans about where to stay, and I didn't have a job.

"Do you know of any safe, inexpensive hotels in New York?" I asked a woman sitting at the table next to mine.

"There's nothing inexpensive in this city," she said, looking up from her newspaper.

I had one suitcase and $755 to my name. Outside the bus terminal, so many people were roaming the streets, so many cars, that my knees became weak.

I began to walk slowly toward lower street numbers, stopping every few blocks to put down the heavy suitcase and rest. I wandered into the lobby of a modern hotel.

"Do you have a single room for tonight?" I asked the woman behind the counter. She consulted a large notebook, then said, "Yes," and handed me a rate sheet. Rooms started at $100 a night.

I left and started walking again. When I reached streets in the twenties I noticed a hotel with a plaque next to the door saying that it was a residence for women. The lobby was small and dingy, with stained walls and bouquets of artificial flowers set in different spots.

"What are your rates for a single room?" I asked the woman at the front desk.

"We have a minimum stay of one week," she said. "Rates start at $350 per week."

"Do you have any rooms available at the $350 rate starting tonight?"

She nodded and asked for proof that I was over eighteen. I showed her my passport. I gave her $350 in cash and she handed me a receipt and a key.

After resting for a while in the small, dark room, I went outside for a walk.

As I ate a sandwich at a nearby diner, I looked at the want ads in a newspaper. There were pages and pages of jobs, but most required higher education, experience, and, at the very least, good typing skills. I circled a few, went to a public phone, and started making calls.

Twenty-five

In New York, I managed to get a job babysitting in exchange for room and board. Natasha was the eight-year-old daughter of Greenwich Village artists. After putting the little girl to bed each night, I'd steal a few minutes to write.

I wrote a story about the time Ardavani visited my father. I gave it a different, darker ending.

> . . . Mina walked over very quietly and, standing behind her, whispered, "Simin."
>
> Simin turned around and looked at her dreamily for an instant. "Oh, you!" She grabbed Mina's hand instinctively and then let go.
>
> "I'm so glad to find you here. I've been bored all day," Mina said.
>
> "Where's your family?"
>
> "Over there."
>
> "Mine are on that side. That's why we didn't run into each other before." Simin raised the rod, lifting the hook from the water, and abandoned it on the ground. "I have to sit down. I'm tired."
>
> She sat on the grassy bank of the stream and Mina sat next to her. Mos-

quitoes buzzed in the trees that stood sparsely around them. The air had a slight rotting smell.

"Tell me, why have you been avoiding me?" Mina asked after a few moments of silence.

"Oh, no reason."

"Please tell me."

Simin, holding her head so that all Mina could see was her profile, said, "You must know. It was what happened that day with Ardavani, what he wrote for you coming spontaneously from him. I envied you so much for it. I just had to avoid you until the feelings passed." Her voice sounded hollow and far away. Mina felt a chill listening to that voice that was almost unrecognizable.

"Oh, that's so silly," she managed to say.

"When we were in the room with him, I wished so much for you to be out of the room—you and your father. I wanted so badly to be alone with Ardavani," Simin went on.

Mina recalled that she had had similar thoughts when she stood in the room and felt ignored by Ardavani. But the thoughts had quickly vanished, like sparks. She lowered her head so that Simin could not see the tears that had come into her eyes.

"All that is past now," she said after a moment. She was hopeful for an instant, but the next moment she could see that the gap that had begun to open between them was only deepening. The confession had made it worse instead of better. A grayness, denser than ever before, enveloped her.

One day, I watched as Natasha's mother picked her daughter up and cooed to her, "You're the prettiest, the most perfect little girl. You're the love of my life," and I knew I had to leave. I had been only a year older than Natasha that day in the school courtyard. A wound inside me opened up. I couldn't even bear to look at Natasha anymore.

After brief stints as a waitress and a hospital aide and living in rooming houses, I wandered into Judson House, a student residence in Greenwich Village, subsidized by an adjacent church. I had just registered for three courses at the New School, two in psychology and one in English literature, for the fall semester.

"Though we're affiliated with a church, we don't discriminate on the basis of religion or have any kind of quota," the manager said as we sat in his small office overlooking a tree-lined street. "We have Jews, Christians, one Buddhist."

"I come from a Muslim background."

"And now a Muslim," he said.

I immediately felt at ease in the place. Though not luxurious, it was pleasant, with coffee always brewing in the kitchen and music in the background as someone played the old piano in the dining room. At breakfast, which was included in the rate, I talked to some of the residents, students from nearby universities. The women were very different from those at Lindengrove. One was studying to become a film director, another an anthropologist, another a physician, another a business manager. Most of them weren't New York natives. Many had come to the big city to escape the confinement of small towns or a history of family difficulties.

After a few weeks there, I began to feel that not letting Father know where I was (which also meant I had no access to Pari) was more unbearable than letting him know, so I tore out a sheet from a notebook and wrote him a brief letter, giving him my address and assuring him that I was in a good, safe place and would be pursuing my education. In the morning, as I stood by a mailbox on the street with Father's letter in my hand, I hesitated. I tried to tell myself that even if he came after me, he would have no power to force me back to Iran, that I was living in a different country with different rules now. Finally I dropped the letter in.

That evening in my room, as I was writing a letter to Pari, the sky darkened and the air grew chill. From the adjacent room, I could hear Judy Garland singing "Over the Rainbow" on a record player.

Somewhere over the rainbow
Bluebirds fly
Birds fly over the rainbow
Why then, oh why can't I?

I burst out crying, a long deep sob that shook my whole body.

With a second part-time job, in the admissions office at the New School, my subsidized housing at Judson House, a student loan, and frugal living, I was getting by. I was at ease, not just in Judson House but in the whole city, with all its ethnic variety and different languages. I didn't stand out as "foreign" in New York the way I had in Lindengrove.

I didn't hear from Father. He had never written to me before, but I had expected him to respond this time.

Twenty-six

One day, I pulled a letter from Pari out of my mailbox and read it as I stood in the small mailroom.

She had finally managed, with Father's reluctant help, to get a divorce. But her freedom from Taheri came at the expense of her *mehrieh* and her son. She had visitation rights to Bijan, but so far hadn't succeeded in seeing him. As Mohtaram had warned, the long distances and the difficulties of arranging things with Taheri made it impossible. Father had gone to Tehran several times and tried to use his influence with a judge he knew from law school, to see if he could get his grandson to live with them but the judge said it wasn't in his power to change the laws. Father mentioned Taheri's crime but, as he originally suspected, too much time had passed, and they didn't have evidence of what had really caused the woman's death. Father came back, despairing and then angry at Pari for wanting the divorce to begin with. Both Father and Mohtaram were shamed that Pari had gone through with the divorce.

Their criticism only adds to my self-blame. Have I done the wrong thing not to have tolerated Bijan's father so that I could be with him? I miss my little sweet boy so much. I hear his voice calling me, asking me ques-

tions. I have qualms that he will be influenced by Taheri and become like him. I feel a dread in my stomach just thinking about that happening.

Dearest sister, it's so lonely here without you to talk to, to share hopes and dreams with, but for your sake I'm glad you are far away from home. It's so tense and gloomy here. Except for Miss Partovi and Golnaz, I don't have any friends left in Ahvaz. All my previous friends disapprove of me for leaving my husband at the expense of being separated from my son. They can't conceive of contemplating divorce themselves, even if unhappy with their husbands. They would remain married to save face for their families and to keep their children.

At home I help out with the twins, play with them. Two afternoons a week I go to the high school and help with future school productions. Miss Partovi and I read through plays, discuss them, and select the ones that we think might be approved. I get paid for that but it's very little, just pocket money. Now that I'm divorced it's in Father's hands to send me to America. I thought of asking him but I know it would be futile. I did ask if I could go there for a short visit and his response was a blunt no. It's still expensive, as you know, with the unfavorable money exchange, but more, he pointed out that if I leave even for a short time, I may lose Bijan altogether. He's still trying to get a judge to let Bijan live with us. Sometimes I'm hopeful, at others I feel I'm standing behind a thick glass door, knocking and knocking and no one is opening it. On the other side of the door are Bijan, my acting, and Majid.

Through the mailroom window I could see a hard wind blowing and traffic going by in a continuous stream. Residents of Judson House were rushing in and out. I stood still, clutching the letter.

Twenty-seven

In my second semester at the New School, I noticed a man with a lot of dark hair and blue eyes in my psychology class. Every class he'd pause in the doorway and look around the room before taking the empty seat beside me.

After one class, he followed me outside and asked me to have dinner with him if I hadn't eaten yet. When I hesitated, he said, "I'll treat you." It was more than not being able to afford eating out. I was wary of a date, several of them having ended badly.

It was raining and we went to a Chinese restaurant around the corner.

Howie was four years older than me and had a degree in mechanical engineering from Cooper Union. He had worked as an engineer for a year, but gave it up because he found the field dull. He was put off by having to wear suits and work nine to six in an office. He had begun graduate studies in philosophy at Columbia University, but after a year dropped out of that, too. Now he was getting a degree in psychology. I told him I was studying psychology to be practical and that my real dream was to become a writer.

His last relationship with a girl had ended several months ago, he said.

"She was a good Jewish girl. My mother would have been happy if it had worked."

"My family would like me to marry someone from Iran and a Muslim."

"They wouldn't like you going out with me then, an American Jew."

I nodded. "If you were Christian it'd be the same."

"Are you religious?" Howie asked.

I shook my head.

It was after midnight when he walked me back to Judson House. The rain had stopped and the moon was visible in the sky. He kissed me quickly and I went inside.

After that we met whenever our schedules could be squeezed to match—five minutes in the lobby of the graduate school building, twenty minutes in the cafeteria, an hour in the evening in a restaurant near the school for something quick to eat. Or just sitting in the library doing work. With Howie I felt freer than with other boys; perhaps it was because I felt sparks of attraction immediately and trusted them, or just that I felt compatible with him. Although from different backgrounds, we could talk for hours, exchange views, or be quiet and just read and do our work together. I took him to a Persian restaurant. He bought a bunch of roses for me from a vendor who wandered in, taking my mind to Pari and Majid.

After dinner near the New School one night, I spent the night with him in his apartment. Although the apartment was small, it had the luxury of abundant light pouring in. Shelves around the rooms were filled with books and records.

In the morning, when we had to go to our different appointments, parting was difficult for both of us.

Then everything between us moved quickly.

"I want to introduce you to my parents," he said after he proposed marriage in a candlelit restaurant and I said yes without pause. "Don't worry, there's nothing they can say or do that would have any effect on us."

Howie and I drove to his parents' apartment in Yonkers.

"How can a Jew and a Muslim mingle?" Howie's mother, Gussie, asked.

I looked at the plates of roast beef, potato pancakes, and coleslaw and tried to think of an answer to the question.

"I'm not sentimental about religion, you know that," Howie said to his mother.

"Aren't you going to miss home and want to take our son there, too?" Irving, Howie's father, asked me. "He has no place in your country."

"I don't plan to live there," I said shyly.

"I know the Shah is friendly with Israel but Jews are just a small minority there."

"In Iran Jews are respected. They have prestigious jobs; some of them are close to the Shah," Howie said.

We left quickly after dessert.

"Are you upset?" I asked Howie as we drove home.

"What?"

"About us?"

"Of course not. I love my parents but I don't share their values." He put his arm around me to reassure me.

I watched the scenery move past me as we drove toward Manhattan, thinking how strange it was that this man from a different culture and religion had met and fallen in love with me, an Iranian Muslim.

What Maryam had told me about destiny all those years ago came to me, as it often did at crucial turns in my life. Would she, despite her belief in predestination, be hurt that I was marrying someone outside her religion? Her beliefs and feelings were often at odds. I recalled her telling her sisters that Jews were recognized as sharing a common lineage with Islam, that the Koran venerated the Bible as one of its sources, and that Christians and Jews were called "People of the Book."

We got married at City Hall. My parents were in Iran. Cyrus, who had married his girlfriend Mildred, couldn't attend because his wife was in the last days of pregnancy. Parviz was in Iran, having accepted a one-year appointment at a hospital in Karaj, a village in serious need of qualified doctors. Howie's parents didn't come.

I was happy that there were no vigilant eyes on me; no one was going to inspect my sheets the next morning, looking for virginal blood.

Twenty-eight

I finally wrote to my parents and Pari with news of my marriage. Only Pari wrote back to congratulate me and added:

> *Father brings up your name and shakes his head in anger and disappointment. But I think at some level he's happy that you aren't here to add to his problems.*

There were also new developments in Pari's life. She had a suitor, named Mansour Behbehami, and she was thinking of marrying him. Mansour had been in Ahvaz for a few months for work (sent there by his boss at the National Iranian Petrochemical Company in Tehran to assist with a job). He was staying at the Hotel Pahlavi near our house and had noticed Pari passing by. He inquired about our family, then wrote a note to Pari to express his interest and slipped it into her hand once as she was passing his hotel.

> *I wake every day with the hope that I would be accepted by you, a beautiful woman and from an excellent family. It's hard to capture in words the feeling that comes over me at the mere sight of you. Ever since*

I laid eyes on you, flowers started to bloom in the salt-sand that my soul has turned into as a result of my tragedies and losses. I can detect some sorrow in you too and hope that a union between kindred spirits will create a fertile soil and our souls will be nourished. God has taken an interest in me by allowing my path to cross with yours. I feel an urgency to be united with you and for us to be each other's guardians until death. I do believe marriage should give equal responsibility to husband and wife.

The man's flowery language at first amused Pari and then made her wary. He reminded her of Taheri and the way he acted when he first began wooing her.

Mansour didn't wait for Pari's response. Soon after writing the letter, he came to our house and asked for her hand. (He came himself because he had no relatives in Ahvaz.) He wasn't wealthy like Taheri, and wasn't better educated, either, but Father thought, as a divorced woman, Pari should consider herself lucky that a nice man from a respectable family was interested in her. Father also appreciated the fact that Mansour was willing to accept Pari with a very small dowry, this being her second marriage.

Pari hoped Mansour would take her to Tehran—she still wanted to pursue acting, but her main desire was to be in the same city as her son. Mansour seemed like a compassionate man and he told her he would welcome Bijan and treat him as his own son.

From the picture Pari drew for me, Mansour seemed to belong in the category of men we used to classify as "different," not tyrannical. Mansour resembled Majid a little, with the same widely spaced eyes and high forehead and cheekbones, Pari said, but he didn't have Majid's magnetism. A sadness seemed to hang about him.

He had been married once, but his wife had died of leukemia while she was pregnant with their second child. Then his five-year-old son had died in a school bus crash. He quietly gave in to Pari's ideas of the life they should lead together, with an almost submissive affection.

Pari hardly knew Mansour—her contact with him had been confined to a few private hours together in the salon. Yet they married.

In another letter a few weeks later, Pari wrote that she and Mansour were looking for a different house; the one Mansour had been living in with his late wife and son, he quickly realized, reminded him too much of his tragedies.

My communication with Pari came to a halt that year, 1971, when the Shah had his extravagant 2,500th anniversary celebration of Cyrus the Great in Persepolis, a city on the outskirts of Shiraz. Iran was in turmoil. Letters disappeared in transit.

The amount of money spent on the celebration highlighted the monarchy's extravagant existence while many people were living in poverty. In speeches the Shah referred to himself as the latest heir in a 2,500-year-old monarchy stretching back to Cyrus the Great, the very first of the world's empires. To impress foreign dignitaries, he spent nearly two billion dollars on the celebration.

For six months the Imperial Iranian Air Force made repeated trips between Shiraz and Europe, bringing in air-conditioned tents, Baccarat crystal, Limoges china, Porthault linens, an exclusive Robert Haviland cup-and-saucer service, as well as five thousand bottles of wine. These items were carefully loaded into army trucks for transport to Persepolis.

Each month, supplies were driven down the desert highway in full loads. Tents were decorated differently in classical and modern styles. The walls of the banquet rooms were of velvet, sewn in France. The Shah hired teams of workers to get rid of thousands of poisonous snakes and scorpions that populated the desert where the tents were set up, to build decorative water fountains near the tents, new roads planted with acres of small pine trees. The National Iranian Oil Company set up torches fueled by oil barrels. Hundreds of thousands of posters, stamps, and coins were made to mark the occasion. Teams of bulldozers demolished a few old village houses in the area and the whole town of Shiraz was cleaned, shop facades and houses repainted. Elizabeth Arden created a new line of cosmetics and named it Farah, after Queen Farah. Maxim's of Paris led the team of chefs and caterers. Except for Iranian caviar, served in quail eggs, all the food and wine were flown in from Paris. Foreign dancers were hired to perform. Orson Welles made the film *Flames of Persia* for the occasion.

As the celebrations were taking place, several students were arrested for writing anti-Shah graffiti: "Thief Shah is stealing from the starving people," they wrote. Khomeini, still in exile in Iraq, called the Shah's celebration the "evil celebration." The liberal press in Iran now openly criticized the Shah. "Lavish at the Expense of Starving People," read the headlines, or, "An Insult to Our Culture to Serve French Food."

Terrorists attacked a number of banks, assassinated police officials, and blew up cinemas. Guerrillas threatened to drown the Persepolis events in a bloodbath. SAVAK detained at least 1,500 suspects, but more sprouted up. After the celebration, the Iranian consulate in San Francisco was bombed; the Federation of Iranian Students claimed responsibility.

Twenty-nine

We had moved to Cambridge when Howie got into Harvard's psychology doctoral program. I worked as a medical pamphlet writer at a local hospital by day, and wrote at night. We wanted to wait until we were more comfortable financially before starting a family. But a desire to have a child was growing in me so intensely that we decided to go ahead and try.

I knew I was pregnant even before I took the test. I was sitting on a bench in a little park not far from where I worked.

Then I was dreaming. I was in Maryam's house and my aunts and Mohtaram were sitting in her large living room, eating pastries and talking. Maryam suddenly smiled at me and said, "Now we're together."

It was so unusual for me to fall asleep in the morning that I knew something was happening. I did not have an easy pregnancy. Much of the time I had morning sickness, and afternoon sickness, as well, so I quit my part-time job and stayed home.

Howie and I talked about names. Leila was both a Persian name and similar to Lena, Howie's grandmother's name. Cyrus, too, was a Persian name and similar to Howie's grandfather's name, Charles. Evidently neither of us was completely detached from our backgrounds.

I had contractions in the middle of one night and woke Howie. It was a cold December night and there was already snow on the ground as he drove me to the hospital.

The baby was big for my small size, eight and a half pounds. She had bright blue eyes (like her father's), which were open and looking around with curiosity. She had a pile of curly brown hair already. How would I raise my child? I couldn't look at Mohtaram as a role model. I wanted to be like Maryam, lenient and full of praise.

Leila was a good baby and very quickly began sleeping through the night. She didn't cry much and she smiled a lot. I watched with fascination all the changes she went through and the surprises she brought. The way she turned her head to look at something or someone, the smile of recognition that lit up her face, her first word, the first steps she took without falling.

Then came stretches of melancholy. I thought of my mother drawing milk from her breasts to give to my grandmother for me for the long trip to Tehran. I thought again and again of Maryam, of her taking me to a mosque where she worshipped occasionally. She held my hand as we climbed the steps to the entrance. She had on her black chador and I a scarf I had borrowed from my cousin for the occasion. A fine rain was falling, though it was sunny. I looked at her through the shiny veil of the drizzle and I thought I saw tears in her eyes as she said, "I pray to God every day that you won't be taken away from me." Inside, the chamber was lit by the flames of hundreds of candles in candelabras. She picked up a candle from a brass tray on a table, lit it with an already burning one, and put it in one of the candelabras that wasn't already full. She closed her eyes and after a moment of silence, prayed aloud.

When my husband's mother became a part of our life, accepting our marriage because of our child, I felt guilty that Maryam wasn't the one sharing Leila with us. As Leila would run to me to ask questions or get a hug and a kiss I thought of how I used to run to Maryam.

Then, one day, I received an unexpected letter from Maryam. The political climate in Iran was in a quiet period and the letter reached me without delay.

She had divorced Rahbar and was now back in her house in Tehran. She didn't explain in the letter what had led to the divorce, only that she was able to get a temporary visitor's visa for a month to come and see me. Being unmarried and fatherless, she didn't need a permission letter from anyone to leave Iran. Luckily, one of her neighbors had a teenage son who had been accepted at a university in the United States, and he would accompany Maryam all the way to my apartment in Cambridge—something that Maryam couldn't do alone because she didn't speak English.

We prepared a bed for her in the living room. Knowing she ate meat only if the animal was slaughtered in a halal way, I called a Middle Eastern restaurant I found in the Yellow Pages and asked the chef if he knew a halal butcher. He gave me the phone number of one in Boston; I ordered chicken and lamb.

I opened the door to Maryam and Bahman late one afternoon, and Maryam and I embraced and kissed, breathless with excitement. Bahman said he had to leave immediately and so we spoke only long enough for me to thank him for bringing Maryam.

"Nahid *joonam,* I've been sleepless at the thought of seeing you," Maryam said as I led her into the living room. "I thank God to have enabled me to live long enough to have the pleasure of seeing you in your new home."

"I've been so looking forward to this," I said.

Howie came in from our bedroom, where we had our desks, and greeted Maryam.

I translated the exchange between them.

"Welcome. Nahid has so been excited about your visit," Howie said.

"Please forgive me for the inconvenience I'm creating coming here," she said.

After a few moments Howie went back to the bedroom so that Maryam could take her chador off and we could speak freely in Farsi.

It was hard to believe she was inside my apartment in Cambridge. At fifty, Maryam looked youthful. She had covered the few strands of gray in her hair with henna, giving highlights to her lustrous wavy hair. Her face was nearly wrinkle free and her figure in good shape. She was wearing a navy dress with colored leaf designs, and she smelled of rose water.

I brought Leila from her small room adjacent to our bedroom. Maryam put my two-year-old little girl on her lap and hugged and kissed her with tears in her eyes. "Angels have been kind to you to give you this child," she said to me.

After Leila wandered back to her room, Maryam and I slowly tried to catch up with each other's lives.

As dusk approached, Maryam found the direction of Mecca, spread her prayer rug on the living room floor, and prayed.

For dinner I served the halal dishes I had bought.

"Bahman told me they use pork fat in cooking in America," Maryam said, looking a little embarrassed for mentioning it.

I assured her that everything I was serving was halal.

"I'm sorry for the trouble I'm causing," she said.

"It's no trouble," I said. Howie smiled, getting the meaning of our conversation.

After dinner Maryam went to sleep early to recover from the long flight.

Every day Maryam woke at dawn, prayed, and had breakfast. After lunch she prayed, took naps, had supper, and prayed again. She held Leila on her lap and said endearing things to her. After a few days she took on the task of cooking for us—*kuku, khoresh, kababs*, a variety of rices, and Shirazi salad.

Parviz, who had returned from Iran, and his wife, Bahijeh, were passing through Boston and dropped by for a visit. He had met Bahijeh in Ahvaz while visiting our parents from Karaj. His marrying an Iranian girl introduced to him by our parents was a surprising turn, considering how Americanized he had become.

Parviz and Howie began to drink beer in the living room.

"What's wrong?" I asked Maryam in a whisper, noticing that she looked tense.

She glanced at the men and then back at me. I understood what she meant.

"Sorry, Aunt Maryam," Parviz said to her, noticing the exchange. "We didn't mean to be disrespectful." He and Howie went into another room to finish their beer.

Bahijeh, who had studied abroad and came from a very modern family, seemed uncomfortable with Maryam's strict adherence to Islamic rules. She went to join the men in the other room.

"It's a treat to see you after all these years," Parviz said to Maryam, as he and Bahijeh were leaving.

"It's wonderful to see you, so grown up and with a wife," Maryam said.

As soon as Parviz and Bahijeh were out the door, Maryam began to cry. "I'm so sorry, I spoiled things," she said.

Her soft, gentle face was so sad that I felt tears coming into my own eyes; I was caught in this conflict.

"Don't worry, Mother, it didn't matter," I said. "Parviz had to leave anyway."

"I wish we could live near each other, but it isn't our destiny," Maryam said, as we strolled with Leila.

"Do you remember that day when Father came to my school and took me away?" I asked Maryam.

"How can I possibly forget?" she replied. "I had some hint that it might happen; he sent a message to your aunt Roghieh's husband that he was coming to Tehran around that time. And then Roghieh's husband sent another message on the day your father took you away from your school. It was as if God had forsaken me."

"Were you angry at Mohtaram for not sending me back to you?"

"I knew I shouldn't be," Maryam said. "She was under your father's control."

As we walked, several people gaped at Maryam, who was wearing a long, black chador.

She told me about her life during the years away from Iran, her marriage and divorce. She praised Rahbar eloquently; he was gentle and sensitive. It was clear she'd been in love with him, though she never said so.

"What went wrong?" I asked.

She sighed. "He started to come home with one young boy after another, going into a room and spending the night with them. He always said, 'He's my cousin,' or 'He's my nephew.' Finally I caught on. I told him I wanted a divorce and he knew why. No fights, no confrontations. It was easy enough for me to get a divorce after I let the judge know what was going on."

I was speechless. "Oh, this is unbelievable," I finally murmured. "I guess you knew little about him when you married him."

She nodded. "I'm going back to live in the same rooming house by the shrine of Imam Hussein in Karbala. I feel peace just being near the shrine. And I have good friends among the women living in that area."

Again I was aware how close Maryam and I were in our emotions and how far apart in our way of life.

"Your mother sent a ring with your grandmother when she brought you to me," she said after a few moments. "I was supposed to give it to you when you got married but I lost track of it during all those years of moving around. I'll keep looking."

"Really? A ring? You never mentioned it."

"I was waiting for when you got married."

So Mohtaram had expected me to stay with Maryam until I got married. It was something I'd never considered before.

On her last day Maryam promised to visit again. She and Howie had gotten along well and liked each other, and she was so happy to be with Leila. But it was clear she didn't feel comfortable in America. There were all her dietary restrictions. She didn't know a word of English and it would take years for her to become fluent enough to communicate with others. She couldn't read or watch TV or listen to the radio. There weren't that many Iranians in the area, no community for Maryam to get involved in. Other Asians—Japanese, Chinese, Indian—had more of a sense of community; their cultures had become more a part of America, with restaurants and ethnic neighborhoods.

As Howie and I were driving home after dropping Maryam at the airport, I already missed her presence in my life. It was an echo of the way it used to be when she left after a visit to Ahvaz.

Thirty

What Maryam had told me about the ring from Mohtaram lingered with me long after she left. I thought of the jeweler Pari had told me about so many years ago.

At first, when they passed each other on the streets, she and the man exchanged glances.

Could it be that the jeweler gave her the ring?

Then another version of that story came to me. In it, there is a child from the romance with the jeweler. And the child is me. Terrified that Father would detect something just looking at me, Mohtaram gives me to her sister. Maybe this was why she'd always been cold to me.

I imagined Mohtaram pushing the infant—me—in a stroller down a long narrow lane with high walls. She hears her name being called from behind. She turns around and sees the man approaching her. He asks her about the baby, tells her he loves her. He is talking in a whisper. He gives her a box containing the ring and quickly turns around and vanishes into an alley. Mohtaram is alone on the lane again with her little baby and the ring, unable to fully understand the meaning of the encounter. Was it a final good-bye or was he inviting her to start a new life with him?

"You always write about the past," Howie said one evening. "Write something about what goes on around you now." He was convinced that my preoccupation with my past—with Maryam and Pari—had to do, at least to some extent, with my not being engaged enough in my present life.

It wasn't just Howie who thought that. "Nahid, you're so obsessed, I feel bad for you," my friend Irene told me one day.

"I know you're right," I said.

So I started writing a novella about our neighbors in the building, with whom we shared a backyard. But it was flat, dead words on a page, and I abandoned it.

I drifted to Iran again, evoking the scenes and characters that had been part of my past.

After many years I went back to Tehran for a visit. I was sitting in Aunt Maryam's living room (she, not my mother, raised me), and she was drawing vivid pictures of people I had known growing up.

"Do you know Batul has twelve children now? Her youngest son drowned in the pool and the poor girl has been fainting several times a day ever since. Everyone says her child drowned because she didn't give alms." Or, "Remember Hassan? The truck he was driving turned over and he died instantly. He was such a mean man, no wonder."

In her stories she tried to leave nothing to chance. Yet all the elusiveness of my growing up echoed through her words. I thought of the starry nights I had lain beside her on the roof and the morning I had been frightened by my own shadow, the heavy silence of midafternoons when everyone was asleep and the pigeons stood drowsily in their cages, the inexplicable excitement as I lay beside my cousin under a blanket, listening to him talk about the other boys in the neighborhood. The picture of the tenants occupying the rooms around the courtyard came back to me—the woman who hid in our room to escape from her abusive husband; the young girl who mysteriously died in her bed. Then I thought of Sultaneh, a tall, slender woman with thick black hair, braided in several strands. I recalled her soft touch as she ·

handed me things—a dish or a bouquet of flowers. I recalled whispers about her not being married.

"She finally got married to a man of her own choice—a young man working in an office," Maryam said. "He took all her money away and then he began to take on other wives. But he must have had a spell on her. With all the pain he inflicted on her she pined after him when he just vanished. She searched for him everywhere. She went on trips to where she thought his business might take him. One day she came back and never mentioned his name again. But she was changed. Once she tried to drown herself in a tank of water. Another time she almost jumped from the roof. One night she began to curse and throw her belongings out into the street. They put her in a sanitarium for a while and when she was released she was put in chains. She lives in the basement, tied to a pole. She has a niece who comes in once a day and attends to her."

That evening I was standing at the edge of the roof, looking down into the courtyard of the adjacent house with its ancient plane trees and gables filled with pigeons when I had a glimpse of Sultaneh. Her hands were tied behind her with a chain, the end of which was held by a young girl I assumed was her niece. She was stooped, like a hunchback, and her chin protruded so far that it almost touched her long nose. The strands of her black hair were now replaced by a mass of unkempt gray, and she carried herself with caution, like one who has received many blows and expects new ones. Only in her dark, pensive eyes could I see her as she had once been but even they seemed puzzled, crazed. I watched the girl tie the chain to a column on the porch and I moved away when Sultaneh began to shriek as if she were being whipped.

I pressed my brain for a lesson that might be learned from Sultaneh's downfall but I could not honestly accept any of what came to my mind.

I put this sketch together with two others with similar themes I had written over the years—one about the woman with a blind child, one about reading to Ali. After making some changes, I sent them to a few literary magazines.

My first acceptance came a few weeks later. The old feeling returned in a rush, the one I'd felt years before when the radio station had chosen to air my story.

I received a letter from a Lindengrove girl, Judy Conrad, who had read my story in the magazine. I mentioned the name of the college I went to in the biographical information published with the story.

I don't know if you remember me. I used to live two doors down the hall from you. What stopped us from being friends? We were from different religions, countries. But should any of that have mattered? I know now it shouldn't have. . . . Life has dealt me a few blows. I married as soon as I graduated and that marriage finally has ended, thank God. We were truly incompatible. . . . As you see by the address, I live in Chicago, a big city. I meet people from all over the world here. . . .

I remembered Judy. She was the girl who had put her hand on her hip and said to me, "Well, in this college we're all Christians." Though the letter was apologetic, it brought back the ambivalent feelings that had plagued me over the years in America, being neither here nor there.

Then I met an Iranian woman named Nayereh in the supermarket. After a few minutes of conversation, she invited me to lunch at her house. She was married to an Iranian doctor. Her parents had arranged her marriage to the son of a family friend who had emigrated to America. Her house was large and fancy. The floors were covered with the most expensive silk Persian rugs, and there was marble everywhere. Nayereh wore a large diamond engagement ring and a large sapphire ring on her other hand; sapphire earrings dangled from her ears. She served Persian food, *fesengoon*, chicken and pomegranate sauce and crushed walnuts, saffron rice, and Shirazi chopped salad, which a maid prepared.

"I hope you don't mind me asking," she said as we sipped tea, "but isn't it difficult to live with a man from a different culture and religion?"

"I'm not so much a part of my own culture," I said.

"But . . . someone who doesn't speak your language, doesn't understand where you come from?"

I couldn't think of a response, and although the conversation drifted to other topics, her pointed question stayed with me. She stirred up the same feelings as the letter from Judy did. I had gone against many Iranian traditions, and was even now an American citizen, but I didn't feel like an American. I had an accent. I didn't look American. There was a lot I didn't understand about the culture. I had finally found freedom in America, but there was a hole inside me, a lack. I didn't feel either Iranian or American.

I started to devote my free time to writing a novel that captured those feelings. In the novel, *Foreigner,* I tried to channel that state of mind—feeling foreign in both Iran and America, into the female narrator. The protagonist, Feri, is a young Iranian girl who comes to the United States after high school to go to college. She marries an American and stays on. At one point a restlessness for her past begins to set in. After many years she goes to Iran for a visit. At first she feels like a foreigner there but then she gets involved in searching for her mother, whom she had lost as a child. She finds her, then begins to question her happiness in the United States. By the end of the book she is not sure if she wants to go back to America.

I suddenly yearned to go back to Iran and put myself in touch with the sights and sounds and people who were haunting me. I knew part of my obsession with the past had to do with my lack of contact.

But alas, turbulence had erupted in Iran again and was only getting worse. Political parties were formed and outlawed by the Shah in swift succession. The youth movement, consisting mainly of male students, was growing larger by the day. They sent out messages to people in Iran and abroad through newsletters in which they talked about corruption in the royal family, reported on the torture and execution of thousands of political prisoners, the suppression of dissent, and heavy censorship of books, radio and TV programs, newspapers, and speech. They displayed graphic photographs of men and women being tortured in Iranian jails. They described the methods of torture—hanging prisoners, male or female, upside down, stuffing urine-soaked cloths into their mouths, making them walk on nails.

They dared to shout, "SAVAK must be defeated," and they held demonstrations daily, not only in Iran but in America, too—in front of the Iranian Embassy, the UN, and on university campuses, accusing America of betraying Iran's trust and blaming America for manipulating the political system.

Once, passing through Harvard Square, I came across a group of demonstrators shouting that they wanted human rights, equality, and democracy. A young man was holding a pile of newsletters and handing them out to passersby. I took one and read as I walked on. The article reported arbitrary arrests, torture, and summary executions in Iran.

Since it was impossible to identify all the Iranians abroad who were actively opposed to the Shah's rule, any young Iranian who went back to Iran was taken into a room upon landing at the airport and questioned for hours. Many of them were detained, their passports confiscated. They were thrown in jail and some were executed.

One day I was reading a newsletter a young Iranian man had handed to me in Harvard Square. I looked at the photographs of two people who had been executed. My stomach dropped. One was the nephew of Ezat Sadaat, the sweet, gentle woman who used to rent rooms from Maryam when I was a child. A few weeks later I read in a similar newsletter that my beloved composition teacher, Mrs. Soleimani, had been killed by a truck while driving to visit her mother. The article maintained that witnesses had seen the truck driver turn aggressively into Mrs. Soleimani's car, driving it off the road. The article concluded that the driver had to be a SAVAK member. I recalled her sensitive face, her sympathetic voice talking to us in class, encouraging us young girls to develop our minds.

Thirty-one

In 1977 *Foreigner* was accepted by Norton. Simultaneously, the story I had written years ago about Ardavani's visit was published in *Redbook*. Pari wrote from Tehran.

I'm ecstatic for you. A dream come true. I can still see the two of us in my room and you reading one of your stories to me and me acting out the parts.

As for me, I'm not thinking of acting that much right now. I'm strug-gling to gain custody of Bijan and that absorbs almost all of my atten-tion. So far Taheri has managed to prevent Bijan from seeing me. Complaints to the authorities haven't gotten anywhere yet. The 1967 Family Protection Law that the Shah introduced to improve women's rights isn't enforced. . . . I wake in the middle of the night calling Bijan, Bijan. It wakes up Mansour, then he becomes sorrowful about losing his own son. . . . Sometimes I feel I'm always running after unattainable dreams—to be an actress, to share a life with . . . Yes, Majid is still with me . . . to have my son with me . . . It's like I'm losing my sense of self in-side a body I don't recognize. I wish we could talk like the old days, sit to-gether by a pool. . . .

That year, the Shah released 357 political prisoners. He promised that Iranians could come and go without questioning as long as they had valid passports and visas. This new approach was the result of international pressure. Amnesty International had reported that SAVAK's history of torture in jail was "beyond belief." President Jimmy Carter told the Shah that if he didn't improve his human rights record, U.S. aid to Iran, including military assistance, would be terminated. Carter had begun to believe that Iranian anger at America was due to the brutality of SAVAK, which had been created and supported by America. Indeed, anger at America was fierce and escalating by the day. An opposition group had bombed several international offices in Iran, including the Association of Iran-U.S. Relations, the U.S. Information Office, and the offices of Pepsi-Cola, American Airlines, and Shell. Several American employees were killed by those bombs.

Still, I thought it might be a good time to go to Iran for a visit. Perhaps now the risks weren't as serious as they were before. Iranians were going back and forth. But then the news of *Foreigner* not passing censorship in Iran gave me second thoughts about visiting.

Several months before *Foreigner* was to be published in America, I received a call from a young Iranian man who had read excerpts of the novel in *Redbook*. He wanted to translate the book into Farsi. I agreed, enlivened by the possibility that Pari might be able to read my novel.

One Iranian publisher was interested. The censorship authorities sent the translator a list of words and sentences to be deleted: words such as "red," which symbolized Communism, and "black night" and "high walls," symbolizing repression and prison respectively. I reluctantly made the changes.

A few weeks later, however, I learned that the censors had forbidden the book's publication. Though by the end of *Foreigner* the protagonist is won over by her own culture, the censors considered the tone of the book "uncomplimentary to Iran." It depicted a hotel bed with a bug on it, they said, and a dirty street. Such details might indicate that the Shah's attempts at beautification had failed.

My mind went to Ardavani, the writer whose visit to our house in Ahvaz I had woven into a story. Father had said he stayed on safe ground. I wondered what had happened to him, if he kept publishing or if even his mild books had gotten him into trouble at some point.

I thought of another, older writer, Sadegh Hedayat, I used to read in Ahvaz. He wrote interesting, surrealistic novels and short stories, some allegorical. His books were forbidden at some point because they realistically captured the suffocating atmosphere and the desperation of many of the citizens; I could find them only at Tabatabai Bookstore.

One of his stories, about a stray dog, outraged the regime because they interpreted it as expressing the brutality of SAVAK.

... Now his whole life had narrowed to the permanent quest for food, which he got by rummaging fearfully in garbage piles, and to being beaten throughout the day. Howls and whimpering had become his sole means of expression. . . . Once upon a time he had been brave, fearless, clean and full of life, but now he had become a yellow timid scapegoat. . . . He had become a bag of nerves: if he heard a voice, or something near him moved, he would nearly jump out of his skin and shiver. . . . Something in him had died, had burnt out. . . . Suddenly he went numb, remembering when he was a tiny thing sucking that warm invigorating liquid from his mother's breasts while his mother licked him clean with her strong tongue. . . .

I was in a cavernous, cement room with a lamp hanging from the ceiling bathing the space in eerie yellow light. I was standing in the middle of the room and a fire was streaming in through a window. A man who sounded like Howie but whom I couldn't see said, "Jump out the window in the back!" I ran toward the window, but it kept receding . . .

I woke with a start, my heart pounding. Howie put his arms around me, trying to calm me. "You're having a nightmare," he said.

PART THREE

Land of Jewels

Thirty-two

Twelve years after I left Iran, my father sent me his first letter. The mere sight of it in the mailbox shook me. He hadn't communicated with me since that strange and contradictory good-bye in Ahvaz.

Nahid, I'm getting on in age and I'm able to find forgiveness in my heart for my headstrong daughter. It's about time for you to come home and bring your husband and your child for a visit. It's a good time as the Shah is giving guarantee of safe return to Iranians abroad.

I stood there, sunk in a pool of emotions. So Father had been angry at me all this time. And now he wasn't. I hadn't thought about him for a long time, and now I was suddenly forced into it.

Perhaps the risks of going to Iran weren't as serious and I had fallen victim to my own fears. Iranians were going back and forth now and only a small number got into serious trouble. I called the Iranian Consulate in New York, where we were living now, and an official confirmed that the Shah was indeed guaranteeing safe return to Iranians abroad. He said, judging by the description I gave him, my novel wouldn't get me into trouble, even though it had been censored. What about the fact that I had become an American citizen? Though America accepted dual citizenship, Iran didn't. He said that the rule wasn't enforced, and many Iranians who went back and forth had dual citizenship. He informed me that I needed a permission letter from my husband to enter and leave Iran, unless my husband was accompanying me. He added ruefully, "Needing a permission letter for a woman to travel is certainly an outdated law; parliament argued against it, but it's still in place." My husband thought it would be healthy for me to connect with my family, since he saw his own regularly now.

But what finally persuaded me to go was an urgent letter from Pari. She said she needed to talk to me in person. Howie and I scheduled the trip for October. Father and Mohtaram would travel to Tehran and stay for two weeks. Father had a legal matter to attend to in Tehran during that period. We would stay with Pari.

At some point we decided not to take Leila. The separation anxiety we expected from her was counteracted by fear of complications in Iran, which wasn't completely alleviated by all the assurances. We thought if this trip went smoothly we would take her on subsequent ones. Our friends in Cambridge, Irene and David, invited Leila to stay at their home and Leila was excited about spending that time with their daughter Susie.

The night before leaving for Iran I slept in fits and starts. Sleeping was as bad as being awake, filled as it was with anxious dreams.

❋

When we landed at Mehrabad Airport, the official at the passport-check booth scrutinized the photographs on our passports, looked at our faces, and then at the sheets of paper spread in front of him to make sure we weren't on any lists of anti-government suspects. It was only after we picked up our luggage and headed toward the waiting area that I was able to breathe freely. Hundreds of people stood behind a glass partition, waiting to welcome their families and friends. I spotted Pari, Mohtaram, and Father standing in the crowd, waving to us.

As we entered the waiting area Father took me in his arms and kissed me. Mohtaram wrapped her arms around me as if there had been no history of trouble between us. Then Pari and I embraced and kissed with tears of excitement filling our eyes. None of us said anything; we only looked at each other as if a shyness had settled on us. Father shook hands with Howie and said, "Welcome," a word he must have learned for the occasion. He had more gray in his hair but Mohtaram looked almost the same as years ago. Pari's good looks hadn't diminished but I immediately noticed that her face had lost some of the vibrancy that used to illuminate it. Farzin and Farzaneh had stayed behind, as had Manijeh. Ali had remained with Farzin and Farzaneh.

Father had rented a limousine and we all piled in. As we headed to Pari's house, we passed the Tower of Freedom, a tall limestone arch that flared out at the sides. It was built in 1971 for the 2,500th anniversary of the founding of the Iranian kingdom. As the driver zigzagged through the heavy Tehran traffic I looked out the window at women walking by in fashionable clothes—some in miniskirts—side by side with women wearing chadors. Ads for Pepsi-Cola and Disney were everywhere. There were discotheques and boutiques selling imported clothes; skyscrapers loomed everywhere. Red Mercedes taxis, red-and-white double-decker buses, almost every variety of foreign cars, raced by alongside Iranian-made Peykans. The snow-capped Alborz Mountains surrounding the city created a serene contrast to the jumbled and hectic atmosphere. Father tried to communicate with Howie in French (French had been a required language when Father attended law school in Tehran and Howie had studied it in high school).

In a short time, we were at Pari's house. Mansour opened the door and greeted us warmly, using the *taarof:* "It's an honor to have you here in our modest abode. It's below your level but please make it your home. I'm here at your service." He had an earnest, welcoming face.

There was an absence of symmetry in Pari's house, which I liked. Not only was each room a different size, they were different shapes, as well— one oval, one rectangular, one L-shaped. Each was painted a different color.

The large windows in every room provided a view of the mountains. The pool in the courtyard shimmered in the sunlight. An ornate turquoise minaret and the dome of a mosque rose beyond the courtyard wall.

Pari had a private room on the second floor that was kept shut. "I keep it closed because Mansour thinks it looks childish," she said. "I suppose it is."

Inside it was almost a duplicate of her room at home in Ahvaz, with posters of actors and actresses covering the walls. The movie stars were no longer Judy Garland and Elizabeth Taylor but Meryl Streep, Jane Fonda, Warren Beatty. A pile of *Movie Star* and *Cinema News* magazines lay on a table. Next to them was the large red-covered album of movie star photographs from years ago, some of which we had bought together from the shop on Pahlavi Avenue. A pile of *Zane Rooz* (*Today's Woman*) magazines lay on another table. The covers showed photographs of Queen Farah or Googoosh, a famous singer, or other women celebrities.

"Pari, I still remember the first time you showed me that album. It was so exciting."

"Oh, dear sister, it's such a treat you're here with me and we can talk like the old days."

I picked up a framed photograph of a young boy with dark brown hair and eyes and a gentle, appealing face.

"He's three years old there," Pari said. "Eleven now."

"He looks a lot like you."

"He belongs to me. I want him back. I'm still trying and nothing yet after all these years. I dread that he's being raised by that lunatic father."

"Have you not had Bijan with you even for visits?"

She shook her head. "Taheri took him away from Tehran, and no one can track their address; it keeps changing. Even my lawyer, who is very good in his field, hasn't been able to force Taheri to come to court. I can't give up hope. . . ."

Next to Bijan's photograph stood a photograph of me, not a recent one but one from Ahvaz. I was standing by the Karoon River and my hair was blowing around my head.

"Remember those walks on the bridge and all the dreams we shared?" Pari said.

Mansour called us into the living room. We joined him and the others to have pastries and *sharbat* with orange petals floating in it.

Father clearly wanted the visit to go smoothly and to show his foreign son-in-law what a good family he had married into. It was hard to tell what he really thought about my marrying a man from another country and religion, whom I had met on my own. If Father had any reservations he did not reveal them. He smiled a lot and spoke about history and politics, as he used to with my brothers. He described Iran as being on the verge of a nervous breakdown. The Shah was pulled and pushed between the clergy and America, each demanding something different. Competing with the loud pulse of modernity was the equally loud pulse of opposition, not only from the religious segment of society but from intellectuals, too. Father admitted he himself was caught in the same ambivalence: he wanted to maintain traditional values and at the same time was won over by some aspects of modernity. He went on to say how in spite of SAVAK's close watch on people, corruption was rampant in Iran. It wasn't unusual for someone to sell the same piece of land to two people and get away with it; lawsuits took many years to settle and usually the person who paid the higher bribe won.

After an hour Mansour left to go to work, from which he had taken time off in the morning. He said he would stay in his office and work through siesta time. Father invited us to lunch at the restaurant of the Tehran Hilton Hotel, where he and Mohtaram were staying.

The restaurant was filled mainly with Americans, but the menu featured a number of Iranian dishes. Howie and I ordered lemon chicken and cherry rice, *gormeh sabsi,* and *joojeh kabab.* For dessert we had *gaz* and tea, which tasted like sweet, hot perfume.

I looked at Father across the table. He seemed softer somehow. Perhaps he really had forgiven me. If I had gone my own way, at least I hadn't gotten him into trouble. And although Mohtaram didn't address me directly, she smiled faintly when she looked at me, as if trying to reconcile with me, a daughter whom she had more or less abandoned. After I left home, I never heard from her: no letters, no packages like the ones other girls in college received from their mothers, no acknowledgment of my marriage or even my baby. It had all been incomprehensible to me for so long, yet I could see a frailty about her; she wasn't the cold, agitated mother I recalled. She seemed even more enveloped in my father's shadow than during those years when I lived with them.

"I didn't always predict my children's future," Father said suddenly. "My sons now live in America." He stopped short. After a pause, he began instead to talk about the advantages of Tehran.

Thirty-three

A few days into the visit, Mansour said, jokingly, "Your sister is cut off from reality." I didn't know what he meant, so I didn't respond, but I had noticed a remoteness about Pari in the company of others. Mansour was domestic—he supervised the household, told Pari what to prepare for meals, brought home large bags of produce and dairy products, and helped her with the cooking.

Once my uncle Ahmad took the afternoon off to show Howie around. He was eager to meet and practice his English with Howie. (Ahmad was a clerk in the Petroleum Ministry and hoped to be promoted. Since many of the employees at the ministry were Americans, being fluent in English was very important.) The American Embassy was near his office and he dropped in there every day to pick up free English-language newsletters. He was a lively, attractive man; when I lived with Maryam he often visited and entertained my cousins and me with jokes and card tricks and marbles. Like Father, he had married a nine-year-old girl—in his case eighteen years younger than himself. His wife, Mahtab, was blond and blue-eyed, from the north of Iran bordering on Russia, and she had some Russian blood. Mahtab sometimes visited Maryam by herself and complained that Ahmad stayed out late every night. Maryam told her, "He has you, a young, beautiful wife. Isn't that enough?"

I liked Uncle Ahmad in spite of his faults because he was full of dreams. He played the violin well and with emotion. He looked romantic as he held it on his shoulder, his eyes focused on something far away. He regularly went to the zoor Khaneh (House of Strength), where men exercised ritualistically, with classical Iranian music playing in the background. He even kept a photograph of himself showing off his muscles.

That night, Howie told me he liked my uncle but felt bad for him: he was an ambitious man searching for something that he didn't seem to find in the Iranian culture.

"Your uncle told me Pari is depressed and miserable about many things in her life," Howie said, looking concerned.

"I know she's upset about her son, and the custody battle that has been going on for years. Was there anything else?"

"Your uncle didn't elaborate. He said it in the context that he thought Pari should have gone to America, too, like you did."

The fact that Pari had confided in Uncle Ahmad shook me up, made me feel she was overflowing with unhappiness.

One afternoon everyone went out, leaving me alone with Pari.

"Pari, we haven't been alone together for years. I've been yearning for it," I said as we sat on the living-room sofa.

"Yes, and there's so much I want to talk to you about, it's hard to know where to start," she said. She told me she was still struggling for personal and artistic identity in Tehran with its fierce double standard and sexism. The whole city was the same tension-inducing amalgam as Ahvaz. True, in some of the ultramodern sections of Tehran, girls mingled freely with boys at parties, drank alcoholic drinks, danced to Western music blaring from sophisticated sound systems—what we used to crave when we were teenagers. But now she realized those were only superficial elements in the context of a larger lack of freedom for women, and men in certain areas.

There was all the censorship and oppression that kept down both men and women. And then there were all the limitations for women. Even though the government supported some official opportunities for women, the situation hadn't improved much because of the prevailing paternalistic attitude. Only a very small segment of the female population was employed. When a woman achieved success or prominence in the public arena, it was often due to her relationship to an influential man—as his mother, wife, sister, or daughter, or because of governmental tokenism. There had been a female senator, but she was never allowed a real voice. Her proposal to abolish the rule that a wife must have permission from her husband to travel to another country was rejected with no reason given. Angry and frustrated, she resigned from her post.

The few women who managed to succeed in the arts—such as the popular singers Googoosh and Hayedeh, the actress Aghdashloo, and the poet Furugh Farrukhzad—were referred to as "promiscuous" or "pushy."

The notion of progress was a matter of pride for educated and professional Iranians, yet they were merely paying lip service when it came to their attitudes toward women. The women who were walking around all made up, in miniskirts, still had to obey their fathers or husbands. So did the intellectual women who sat in cafés and argued about Descartes and Hegel and Marx. Like Pari, women were forced to leave their children with their husbands if they initiated divorce. The 1975 amendment to the Family Protection Law gave women equal rights in divorce, custody of children, and marriage settlements, but these reforms weren't actually put into practice; in court women almost always lost.

Before Taheri took their son and left for other cities, Pari used to stand in doorways or behind a tree near their house in Tehran just to get a glimpse of Bijan. Once she knocked on the door and asked Behjat, Taheri's sister, if she would let her have her son for a few hours. Behjat refused. Pari then went to Bijan's school, introduced herself to his teacher, and asked permission to see him. Bijan was brought to her, but when she tried to pick him up and kiss him, he broke away and ran back to his classroom.

"It all starts at the top," Pari said. "The Shah's conflicting values apply to his attitude toward women, too. With all these claims of improving women's situations, the Shah is totally sexist. When a monarch condones something, it trickles all the way down to every man. Did you read that interview by the Italian journalist Oriana Fallaci? A section of it was translated into Farsi and printed in a magazine, which was then quickly closed down because of it."

I had read Fallaci's *Interview with History,* translated into English. In one section the Shah said:

> Women are important in a man's life only if they're beautiful and charming and keep their femininity. . . . This business of feminism for instance. What do these feminists want? You say equality. Oh! I don't want to seem rude, but . . . You're equal in the eyes of the law but not, excuse my saying so, in ability. . . . You've never produced a Michelangelo or a Bach. You've never produced a great chef. . . . Have you ever lacked the opportunity to give history a great chef? You've produced nothing great, nothing. . . .

Not long ago, the Shah had repeated the same comments to Barbara Walters in an interview.

I recalled from my childhood the Shah's wedding to Farah Diba, a woman nineteen years younger than him. She was indeed beautiful, graceful, and feminine.

Pari said it made her happy that I left Iran and was able to fulfill my dream of becoming a published writer. We began to reminisce, the things half forgotten by one and fully recalled by the other. That magical afternoon when the little boy handed Pari a rose. That evening on the Karoon River bridge when boys followed us, whispering endearments. Me reading to Pari the stories I wrote. Her playing Laura onstage. It was as if nothing that had happened since equaled in intensity and excitement those moments Pari and I had shared.

Pari and I left the house and walked to Café Miami, where she sometimes met with friends.

At the café, tables were set on a platform over a stream. The air was clear, and from our table we could see the mountains against an azure sky. Also in our view was the Moulin Rouge cinema showing *The Castle of Fu Manchu*; teenage boys were lined up in front of it. Next to us a group of Iranian men smoked water pipes and sipped tea.

"You used to love ice cream with vanilla pieces in it," Pari said. We ordered two.

As soon as the waiter left, I poured out my problems in America. "I had many dark years before I found some peace," I said. "I was so lonely in the provincial college. In New York, at first, I was penniless. And now I'm not quite American or Iranian. It pains me to think that I've drifted away so much from Maryam's way of life, her beliefs. I wish so much that she, and you of course, were a part of my life."

The voice of a woman singing reached us from a radio inside the restaurant, mingling with the murmur of water flowing in the stream. The song was based on a Furugh Farrukhzad poem dedicated to her son:

On a parched summer dusk I am composing this poem for you.
This is my final lullaby as I sit at the foot of your cradle.
Against a shut door I rest my forehead in hope.
When your innocent eyes glance at the confused book,
you will see a lasting rebellion in the heart of every song.
A day will come when you will search for me in my words
and tell yourself: my mother, that is who she was.

We listened to the song for a few moments.

"I don't think Furugh's car crash was an accident," Pari said. "You know that she was killed driving her car in Tehran. It was years ago, but I still remember all the talk and speculation that it was self-inflicted or murder by the SAVAK. I'm convinced it was suicide. The public praising and condemning her at the same time must have been so hard to take. And then there was her losing custody of her son."

"Pari, I read that Mrs. Soleimani was killed in a car crash, too, that it was really not an accident but murder by the SAVAK."

"Yes, I heard that, and in her case there was evidence that someone ran into her car deliberately. I was upset for days."

"So was I."

"Didn't I write to you about it?"

I shook my head.

"Letters weren't getting to places they were meant to all the time." After a contemplative pause, Pari added, "The way Furugh died, running her car into a tree . . . It wasn't murder by the SAVAK for a change; it was her own doing." A sheen of sadness spread over Pari's face. "So often I wish I could smash my life into pieces and put them back together in a different way. It's the putting back that's hard, when you have so few choices."

"Maybe you and Mansour could emigrate to America and live there. I'd love for my little girl to get to know you, to be close to you."

"I'd love to see dear Leila, too. But there are so many obstacles. In America Mansour could never get the kind of work he has here. Anyway, he loves Iran. But more than anything, Nahid, I can't bear leaving the country until I know I've done everything to get Bijan back. But then if I do get him back it will be only part-time and I have to remain in Iran. No judge would allow me to live out of the country and deprive a boy of his father for long stretches of time. It has been so many years without any results but I keep hoping, hoping. I can't live without that hope."

"Did you think of having another child, with Mansour?"

"I tried to get pregnant but I couldn't. Something about the temperature in my womb. But having a child wouldn't make the loss of Bijan any easier to bear. Mansour, having lost one son, feels the same way, luckily."

Pari became lost in her own thoughts for a moment and then said, "It's amazing that he didn't show anger at me over not getting pregnant, because he's traditional in many ways. He really discouraged me from acting, so much so that I stopped auditioning. I just didn't want the constant arguments. There are many things I want to tell you." But instead she sank inward again.

We walked back through Elizabeth Boulevard, one of the in-town natural recreational places with a creek and well-cultivated grounds. In a corner a young man was playing the *tar* and a crowd had gathered around him. We continued through Mellat Park, which was patterned after an English park. It was filled with tall, old trees, flower beds, and vast lawns. It had a glimmering lake with boats for rent, cascading falls, sport facilities, a zoo. Children were bouncing around, feeding the animals. At that moment, missing Leila, I acutely felt Pari's yearning for Bijan.

"Manijeh is in some kind of trouble but no one is telling me about it," Pari said, as we headed back to the house. "She and I haven't been in contact, and Mohtaram and Father don't mention her in front of me. But I know something is wrong. At this point, Nahid, I hold no grudges. Her life has been hard, too, ever since she left home."

"Yes, it must be hard for her to deal with problems without Mohtaram's supervision. Anyway, I've been away from her for so long . . ."

"But I still can't forgive Mohtaram," Pari said. "That she didn't exert herself and come to my side when I first resisted Taheri, and then when I left him and came home."

"I don't know how I feel about Mohtaram. . . . It's a kind of detachment, more than anything, now that I'm not dependent on her."

After we left the park we passed the civil courthouse. "I've been there so many times to face the judges," Pari said offhandedly.

As dusk began to set we took a taxi back to her house. In the courtyard sparrows were swarming around the trees and the sky was streaked with red.

Thirty-four

That evening I suggested to Pari that we go and hear Googoosh sing. The room was suddenly flooded with tension. Pari and Mansour exchanged glances across the room, and then fell into silence.

"You remember what happened last time?" Mansour finally said to Pari. Pari blushed but didn't say anything.

"Is there something else we could do instead?" I asked.

Pari turned to Mansour. "Let's go hear Googoosh, if we can get tickets at the last minute." She explained to me, "Last time I felt overwhelmed by her songs, thought I was going to faint, so we left halfway through. It doesn't mean it will happen this time."

The hall was packed with young boys and girls accompanied by their parents. A star from the age of fifteen, Googoosh was an idol to the country's youth. We found a table in a corner.

The orchestra began to play, and Googoosh came onstage wearing a striped white-and-red dress with glittery threads woven through it, a low neckline, and shoulder straps. She wore long dangling gold-and-emerald earrings. Her hair was dark blond, cut in a pixie style. After the applause

died down, she began to sing, her eyes closed, her voice and her face reso-
nant with emotion.

I'm that same woman who wanted to become an ocean
I wanted to become the greatest ocean in the world.
Oh God, I'm as lifeless as a desert, Desert
tell the clouds to rain, I want to live again.
For I am the season of raining leaves
Deprived of gardens, flowers, and dew drops
I'm like a tree that is barren and lifeless
Caught in the tunnels of a hailstorm.
Don't tell me I've grown up
Don't tell me it's bitter
Don't tell me crying no longer suits me
Just take me in your arms and embrace me
What I desire is nonstop affection.

We left before the concert ended; Mansour said he had to get up early for
work, but I could tell he was uncomfortable. Tension still lingered between
him and Pari. When we returned home, Pari and Mansour disappeared
into their bedroom and I joined Howie in the guest room. He was already
asleep.

After hours of tossing and turning, I got out of bed and went to the window. I was startled to see Pari in the courtyard, shivering. For a moment
that scene of Manijeh standing on the balcony in the moonlight flashed in
my mind. I wanted to tiptoe out and talk to Pari, but just then she got up
and went back inside.

I said nothing about it to her the next day.

"Nahid, I saw Majid," Pari told me. "And not just once." We entered a
narrow street shaded by tall sycamore trees tangled at the top.

"Oh, Pari."

"He comes to Tehran frequently, mainly for work. That night when Mansour took me to hear Googoosh sing, Majid was there, too, and I recognized him after so many years. Even stranger was that I immediately knew I was still in love with him. My feelings for him have never left me. It shook me up, being in the same space with Majid and Mansour, and I told Mansour I felt dizzy and that we should leave. As he held my arm and led me out to the car, I felt so dissociated from him, from the touch of his hand. He could sense something else was wrong with me, but I never confessed to it. Majid recognized me, too. Just like those times in Ahvaz, he sent me flowers the next day. A little boy came to my door and gave them to me. There was a note with the bouquet, asking me if I would meet him at an address he gave. I was tempted to go but stopped myself. What would be the point? I'm married and so is he. That evening, having dinner with Mansour, the scent of the flowers I had put on the dining table dragged me down with confusion. It was as if a whirlpool was pulling me into dark waters. And then Majid sent me more flowers and notes. Oh, Nahid, I finally gave in."

Near the square was a bazaar, and carts heaped with fruit. We continued to a bakery and sat at a table in a secluded corner and we ordered honey-glazed pastry and tea.

"At our first meeting, in a studio apartment that belonged to a friend of his, Majid told me he came to Tehran periodically to see publishers, hoping to interest one in several nineteenth-century French poets he had translated into Farsi. Some of their poems dealing with decadence wouldn't pass censorship but some were delicate, full of interesting imagery. He particularly liked a poem by Mallarmé, about the wandering thoughts of a faun on a drowsy summer afternoon. It reminded him of those days in Ahvaz. We talked about literature, poetry, theater, movies. I was in heaven with him."

"Pari, I feel so good that you met him, had that pleasure."

"Yes, it was an amazing experience, at first. I realized even more clearly then that what I had with Mansour was what actresses feel toward the actors they kiss in movies—only pretend. We saw each other for a few months, then everything ended." Pari looked caught in a dream. "Nahid, it's such a long story. It's painful to tell it all."

"Pari *joon,* you don't have to talk about it if it's so upsetting."

But Pari went on. "I was in conflict, both for betraying Mansour and for taking Majid away from his wife for even those few hours. Worse, I hated all the hiding and the lies that went with it. I suggested to Majid that we tell everything to our spouses and face the consequences. He said he needed time to think about it."

A group of women and children rushed into the bakery, talking about a movie they had just seen. They sat at tables around us, filling the small bakery with their laughter. As the women talked, the children ran around the tables, playing among themselves.

Pari and I paid and started walking home on a long, winding street behind the bakery.

"Once Majid fell asleep while we were in the apartment together," Pari said. "I noticed a letter on the desk in the corner. It was addressed to his wife at her parents' home in Tabriz. Majid had told me she was visiting there and he was spending more time in Tehran. He must have taken the letter out of his pocket and absently put it there. The envelope wasn't sealed. I couldn't stop myself. I took out the letter. What I read was so upsetting. He told his wife that I was just a passing person in his life and that his love for her was far deeper because she was the mother of their two sons. I wondered if he left that envelope there intentionally. I confronted him. He actually began to cry. He said he loved me and he wrote that to his wife out of guilt because she had found out he was seeing me. Someone told her."

"Who do you think told her?" I asked.

"I'm almost sure Taheri is behind it. He stalks me when he's in Tehran. He follows me in his red Mercedes.

"We saw each other only once after that," Pari said after a long silence. "At our last meeting, Majid told me he had thought a lot about us and realized he could never leave his wife."

My mind went back to that Norooz picnic in Ahvaz when Majid gave me a letter for Pari, encouraging her to leave her husband. I reminded Pari of that.

"He claimed it was because of his children that he didn't want to break up his marriage. I even detected a touch of criticism in his tone that I left Taheri at the expense of giving up my son. You know, Nahid, what happened with Majid has weakened me. The fact that he was disapproving that I gave up my son brought out all my self-blame, more so than any other person's criticism. I really thought he would understand what I did. Here I was, face-to-face with a man I had loved so deeply and for so long, who had never left my heart, and he turned out to be not much different from all the others. The bright light of my romantic love for him died. It fell into the dark realm where my hope for being an actress is. All I yearn for now is re-uniting with Bijan."

It was as if Pari were lost in one of those endless staircases in an Escher drawing that lead nowhere. I could almost hear the bells of pain ringing loudly inside her and yet I didn't know what words of comfort I could of-fer. What she told me next hit me like cold, sharp-edged hailstones.

"Not long after my relationship with Majid ended, Mansour committed me to a mental hospital. It was a terrifying experience. Two orderlies came over, tied me up in a stretcher, and took me to Pahlavi Sanitarium. A doc-tor came in and gave me an injection to knock me out because I was screaming."

"Why didn't you ever tell me?"

"I didn't want to upset you long-distance. I didn't tell Father and Mother because of their attitude toward me, always thinking of me as a little insane because I left Taheri. You're the only one I'm telling about it now. Remember that movie *The Snake Pit* with Olivia de Havilland?"

"Yes, very well."

"I was so afraid they'd do things like that to me. But my main doctor, a Dutchman, told Mansour there was nothing seriously wrong with me and that I shouldn't be in a mental hospital. He said he'd often seen temporary breakdowns or depressions in Tehran and that many people recovered at home. If I got overly anxious, I could take a tranquilizer. So after I had been there for a month I was released. I took the tranquilizers on and off. But our relationship has been really strained ever since." A faint smile appeared on her face as she said, "The irony is that, as much as I feared the hospital, I felt a certain sense of freedom there, too. We said what we wanted. There was one woman my age who always took her clothes off and danced naked. We put on a play in the large reception room, when it was empty at night and no one stopped us. The nurses and orderlies left us alone."

My knees felt weak as we strolled, from all that Pari told me. We passed a sprawling building with a high wall around its courtyard. "That's where Mansour took me," Pari said.

"Pahlavi Sanitarium for Women" was written on a tile plaque on the wall next to the compound's wrought-iron gate. When the gate swung open and a guard let visitors out, I got a glimpse inside the courtyard. Patients wearing drab beige robes were sitting on benches, looking downward or staring into space. Some wandered around aimlessly.

The sun was beginning to set and the sky was full of streaks of red and purple. A pair of crows sat on a bare tree branch, and the muffled voice of the muezzin from a mosque reached us. We walked home in silence.

As I tried to sleep that night, my head whirred with Pari's disappointments and traumas. I was glad she had finally been with Majid, and seen him in the flesh, but now I saw Mansour in a different way. He appeared so kind and attentive to her, and yet he had committed her against her will and with no real cause. As a husband he had the power to commit his wife and no one would question him. I thought of him saying to me, "Your sister is cut off from reality." Now, after what Pari had revealed, his comment was upsetting.

In the morning, the roosters crowed from the coop Pari and Mansour kept in the courtyard. I heard Pari talking with Mansour in the dining room. My dark thoughts were blown away. Perhaps it was all exaggerated, I told myself. Her affair with Majid had to end, considering the circumstances. True, Mansour had committed her, but then he took her out when the doctor recommended he do so.

Howie was still asleep, so I joined Pari and Mansour for breakfast: flat bread and *sangag*, cooked on hot stones lining an oven, the kind of bread Maryam used to have delivered to our house, along with tea, feta cheese, eggs, honey, and jam. Pari and Mansour seemed like any couple together. I watched them as I ate and wondered if perhaps yesterday had been a dream.

Our trip was cut short by a sudden upheaval. Khomeini's son Mustapha, who like his father lived in Iraq, was found dead in his bed in the city of Najaf. Autopsy is against Islamic law and the cause of his death remains a mystery to this day, but many people suspected SAVAK of murdering him. Theological colleges in Qom closed in protest and demonstrations erupted everywhere. These protests were different from the demonstrations that took place in Iran earlier that year. In September there had been peaceful protests, mainly through letter-writing campaigns, by various segments of society, complaining about familiar and seemingly ever-present problems. They wanted improvements in their conditions. They criticized government officials for spending money on the wrong things and for hoarding it within their own circle. They criticized the Shah's twin sister, Princess Ashraf, who was extremely close to her brother, for her licentious lifestyle divided between Mecca and Monte Carlo casinos. A group of lawyers had banded together to criticize SAVAK torture and to monitor prison conditions. Dissident academics formed a group called the National Organization of University Teachers, and they joined students in demanding academic freedom.

All the open criticism seemed to signify that the Shah was giving people the freedom to express their views. But now the protests were loud and angry and sometimes violent, mainly organized by religious groups, with the secular segment joining in.

As Howie and I were returning to the house after a visit to a museum, we came across a crowd in a square.

"We have to weed out foreign vices. We have to put an end to nightclubs where foreign women in scanty clothes dance and where liquor flows like water." A huge crowd, mostly men but some women, too, in chadors, had gathered around the platform. "Yankee go home! English go home," they shouted.

Shopkeepers stood in their doorways, watching. The teahouses and restaurants had emptied. Coca-Cola and orange-soda bottles set on the outdoor tables in front of restaurants were untouched. Some boys had climbed up the tall cypress trees, looking down at the scene and yelling the same slogans.

"They steal our oil and give us nothing," the man on the platform said.

"Go home, oil eaters!" the people gathered around him shouted.

"Tehran has become a whore town. Women wander on streets wearing almost nothing." The voice of the man on the platform overwhelmed all the others. "Western whores calling themselves dancers perform almost naked in nightclubs where alcohol is served freely like water. Many of our people have to crowd into tiny huts or sleep on streets. They have only one set of clothes to wear day in and day out. They're forced to work as sweepers, garbage collectors, factory workers. And they're paid a starvation wage and given no benefits, while foreigners are stealing our money and insulting us. Do you know what our exploiters, the Americans and the English, call us? Camel culture. Bedouins."

Howie and I managed to find our way out of there and walked speedily toward Pari's house.

"This looks really bad," Howie said on an empty street.

"It's scary. Complaints are just piling up," I said. "Maybe it's even worse now than when I lived in Ahvaz."

On another street we came across a group of men wearing black clothes and holding black banners with slogans written on them in purple letters: "Weed out evil," "Death to America," "Death to English." They shouted, "We have suffered oppression for too long. We must unite, drive out exploiters."

"*Khanoon*, go cover up, please," a middle-aged bearded man said to me. I was wearing a blouse and skirt.

When we got home, Father, Mohtaram, and Pari were gathered around the television. When they saw us come in, they looked relieved.

"I heard in the courthouse that things are getting really bad for Americans and English in Iran," Father said. Father, who had so wanted us to come for the visit, encouraged us to leave the country as soon as possible.

, When Mansour returned from work a few hours later, he, too, said he had heard at work that things were getting bad for Americans and English.

The images of the protestors Howie and I had seen in the square flashed across the screen.

As we prepared dinner, I watched Pari and Mansour talking about all the tension in the country. But seeing them interact congenially made me reconsider what Pari had told me about Mansour. I tried to brush away my negative feelings toward him. In many ways, he seemed very tolerant of my sister. He hadn't divorced her in spite of knowing or at least suspecting that her heart was with another man, something that in the Iranian culture was so condemned. I remembered when I lived in Ahvaz reading about a woman being stoned to death by her husband and his relatives in Bandar Abbas. The husband didn't pay any penalty.

We crowded around the TV again when the news returned. They showed the same images of demonstrators in the square. The same scene appeared again and again on the streets of other cities, too, all over the country.

"The fact that a state-controlled TV station shows people's dissatisfactions is a sign that things are getting out of hand," Mansour said.

"The Shah opened the lid a little and people are encouraged," Father said.

I couldn't tell if he was approving or disapproving of the Shah; he was cautious, as usual, when talking about him. "It's so much the nature of our country, upheaval after upheaval," he added.

Thirty-five

Before we left for the airport, Pari took me to her bedroom and said, "I want to give you something." She went to her jewelry box on the bureau and took something out and handed it to me. It was a striking gold pendant with turquoise, amethyst, and rubies embedded in it.

"Are you sure you want to give it to me? It looks expensive and is so beautiful. Don't you want it for yourself?"

"It's a piece I managed to hide from Taheri. But I never wear it anymore." She hung it around my neck. "I like it better on you."

Father called to us to hurry up.

"I wish we had had more time to talk," Pari said, her voice tinged with sadness. "There are more things . . ."

"I'll come back again when things are calmer," I said.

Once we returned to New York, the rebellion in Iran only accelerated.

After being expelled from Iraq, Khomeini went to Paris, where he was more accessible to a large body of opposition forces. From his exile he preached that he would enforce traditional and religious values and redirect Iran's wealth from the Shah and from large industrialization schemes to the common people; he would make the country "democratic and Islamic."

Khomeini came from a religious family with an established clerical heritage that claimed descent from the Prophet Mohammad. He was born in 1901 in Khomein. He became an ayatollah in the 1920s and, following tradition, took the name of his birthplace. When Khomeini was only five months old, his father was murdered. Life in Khomein was miserable at that time because of three predatory khans who oppressed the population. Khomeini's father decided to do something about the situation and he went to Arak to ask the provincial governor for help. But the khans followed him to Arak and shot him while he was on horseback. He died instantly. Khomeini was a strong and energetic boy who excelled in sports. After his mother died, he left his birthplace and turbulent childhood behind and went to Arak and then to Qom for his education. Did the murder of his father create in him a spirit of revenge against its supposed instigators, the authorities?

As Khomeini gained popularity while in exile, religious groups, too, grew in number and status. Even intellectuals, more and more disillusioned with the Shah, began to back Khomeini. (They had become particularly unhappy with the Shah's formation of the Rastakhiz, which he made the only legal political party, banning all others, making the country a one-party state controlled by him.)

Then in January 1978, when a government-planted article in a leading newspaper ridiculed Khomeini as a medieval reactionary, the protest movement took a new turn. Senior clerics denounced the article, and seminary students took to the streets in Qom in larger numbers than ever before, clashing with police. Several students were killed. Anti-government demonstrations escalated, sweeping across dozens of towns and cities. Gradually all segments of the society, including women, united in protest.

In August more than four hundred people died in a fire at the Rex Cinema in Abadan. Many believed that SAVAK had set the fire so that religious fundamentalists could be blamed. In September more than one hundred thousand people took part in public prayers to mark the end of Ramadan, but the ceremony became an occasion for anti-government demonstrations that continued for two days, growing larger and more radical. The government declared martial law, and the next day troops fired into a crowd of demonstrators at Tehran's Jaleh Square. Hundreds of protestors were killed when tanks and helicopter gunships were called in. The shootings that day, which came to be known as Black Friday, made compromise with the regime, even by moderates, less likely. Any support the Shah still enjoyed was now gone. Khomeini sent messages to the rebels urging them to keep going until they overthrew the Shah. He called for a general strike across the country, precipitating even worse riots. Rich, poor, religious, secular, men and women, illiterate or highly educated, all stood behind the revolt.

In the fall of 1978, strikes against the oil industry, the post office, government factories, and banks demolished the economy. In November the Shah broadcast on television a promise not to repeat past mistakes, to make amends. He even had some prominent members of his own regime arrested. But his grip on people had weakened, and on December 10, 1978, eight million Iranians took to the streets to protest.

One-fifth of the protestors were from the government, forming a growing mass of opposition. The military was melting away; soldiers were no longer willing to fire into crowds. They accepted the flowers that demonstrators put into the muzzles of their rifles and joined in to support Khomeini. Public services were shut down, and revolutionaries seized government buildings, radio stations, and armories.

Khomeini openly called for the assassination of the Shah. People roamed the streets, shouting, "The Shah must leave," "Khomeini is our leader," "Arrest the murderer, the American king, punish him, kill him," "President Carter is the incarnation of Evil." In the crowds were women covered by chadors, male and female students in jeans, merchants in suits, mullahs in long black robes and turbans. They waved *tooman*s with the Shah's picture cut out of them. Some of the rebels invaded police stations and Tehran's main arms factory for weapons. On the Tehran University campus, they pulled down the statue of the Shah, one of hundreds that stood in public places, and broke it into pieces with sledgehammers. The British Embassy was set on fire.

Communication with my family in Iran was severed. No letters were going back and forth, no phone calls were possible. I had no idea if they were out on the streets protesting. I reached out to my brothers to find out if they knew anything about the family but they were just as cut off from them as I was. They both believed that the Shah had become even more tyrannical than when we lived in Ahvaz. A new government couldn't be worse than his, they said. Our conversations were always filled with anxiety about our loved ones back home and their total inaccessibility to us.

On January 16, 1979, after a year of nonstop public outcry, the Shah fled Iran, saying he was going on a "vacation." Carrying a small box of Iranian soil in his jacket pocket, he boarded his silver-and-blue Boeing 707 and flew to Egypt. He left the government in the hands of the regency council and Prime Minister Shahpur Bakhtiar, a former member of the National Front. In the following weeks, the Shah moved from country to country, seeking political asylum.

This time the Shah didn't have the support he had in 1953, when the CIA put him back on his throne. The Shah had become unpopular in much of the world, especially in the liberal West. Ironically these were his original backers and the ones who had the most to lose by his downfall. President Jimmy Carter, who at one time praised the Shah as a wise and valuable leader, now refused to intervene in the uprising against him. As a champion of human rights, he refused to allow the Shah to come to America.

In an Iranian specialty shop in New York, where I was a regular, the owner kept a shortwave radio tuned to an Iranian station. I tried to get the day-to-day news there. Things were barely functioning in Iran and I rarely got more than a few bits of information.

Then one day, as I listened, an announcer said, "This is the voice of the Iranian nation. The cruel, oppressive Pahlavi regime is finished and an Islamic government has been established under the leadership of Ayatollah Khomeini. We hope to receive a message from him now. Please keep listening," but then the radio went dead.

Khomeini returned to Iran on February 1, 1979. He denounced the materialism of the recent past and called for a climate in which social justice would prevail. On April 1, 1979, he declared an Islamic Republic that promised democracy. He was named the political and religious leader for life. Now the country was called the Islamic Republic of Iran, instead of Iran or Persia.

Alas, a reign of terror followed. Political vengeance was taken, culminating in the execution of hundreds of people who had worked with the Shah's regime. Khomeini condoned the assassinations of different people abroad and other terrorist acts. The small gains women had begun to make under the Shah were set back. Now all women were required to wear chadors. Women and men had to sit separately on buses, men in front and women in the back.

A cultural purge was unleashed against anything Western. Nightclubs and cinemas were burned or shut down. Pop singers like Googoosh were ordered to stop performing. Only a certain kind of music and Islamic propaganda programs were allowed on TV. Censorship of books was worse than ever—the publisher who kept Farrukhzad's poetry in print was forced to close down.

During those years many Iranians—minorities like Jews, Christians, Bahais, as well as more modernized citizens—escaped from Iran, legally or illegally, fearful of living under a fundamentalist Muslim government. My brothers urged Father to bring the whole family to America, but Father wouldn't hear of it. He was eighty-nine years old now and couldn't bear to leave Iran—his friends, his language and customs. He couldn't imagine, at this stage of life, starting out in a new country, and he had no intention of becoming dependent on his sons. He said, "I prefer to die in Iran."

I urged Pari and Mansour to leave Iran and come to America. Pari said that Mansour had the same attitude as Father: he wanted to stay in his own country.

And what about Bijan? Another hearing has been set up by my lawyer, Pari wrote in a letter.

❁

Then it was too late. The American government refused to grant visas to any Iranian not seeking asylum.

This, after President Carter allowed the Shah, who had lymphoma, into the United States to undergo medical treatment. The Shah had been traveling from country to country—Egypt, Morocco, the Bahamas, Mexico. Iranian students interpreted this gesture by President Carter as part of a ploy to restore the Shah to power, as the CIA had done in 1953. On November 4, 1979, the situation came to a head when students, numbering anywhere from three hundred to two thousand, and calling themselves the Imam's disciples, gathered at the American Embassy in Tehran. Finding a basement door open, they slipped inside and seized all the Americans in the building. The embassy staff quickly tried to destroy all the secret documents, but they were captured before they finished. Sixty-six were taken captive, including three who were found at the Iranian Foreign Ministry. After blindfolding the hostages and holding guns to their heads, the students marched them outside. With the secret documents in their hands, the students cried, "We have all we need from the nest of spies!" The crowd around them roared its approval. Other students spray-painted anti-American slogans on the walls of the embassy, in both English and Farsi: "Nest of Spies," "American Murderers." Then the students took the Americans back inside and locked them up. As a condition of the prisoners' release, they demanded the Shah's return to Iran to stand trial.

This was the Iran Hostage Crisis. The American government retaliated by applying economic and diplomatic sanctions against Iran. President Carter ceased importing Iranian oil and a number of Iranians living in the United States were expelled. He froze Iran's multibillion-dollar assets in America, further damaging the relationship between the two countries. Hatred of Iranians flooded the American news. Caricatures portraying Iranians as barbarians appeared on walls all over America. Some Iranians were evicted from their apartments by landlords. There were incidences of American high school students attacking Iranian classmates—in one case an Iranian student was reported to have died.

Winter turned into spring and the hostages were still kept in Iran. Frustrated and outraged, Americans urged Carter to take stronger action. Once the Shah's course of treatment was finished, Carter, eager to avoid further controversy, pressed the former monarch to leave the country. The Shah went back to Egypt and died soon after.

As the Iranians showed no signs of releasing the hostages, Carter finally decided to take a chance. On April 11, 1980, he approved a high-risk rescue operation called "Desert One." Though the odds were against its success, the president was devastated when the mission had to be aborted due to three malfunctioning helicopters. When another helicopter crashed into a transport plane during takeoff, eight servicemen were killed and three were injured. The next morning Iranians broadcast footage of the smoking remains of the rescue attempt, to them a stark symbol of American impotence.

In the United States, the yellow ribbons everywhere and constant media coverage provided a dispirited backdrop to the presidential election season. Throughout 1979–1980, the American public watched footage of Iran on a daily basis. News programs tallied the number of days Americans were held hostage. Nothing else seemed to matter to Americans, and America appeared to be a helpless giant.

During this period I found that my friends who had never been particularly political suddenly became patriots and attacked Iran. Even though their anger at the hostage takers was justified, they lumped all Iranians, myself included, with them. My husband tried his best to be fair, but I was sensitive to his remarks, and, to me, everything he said sounded slanted in favor of America. When I gave readings from my work, people with no interest in fiction came to ask questions about Iran and Iranians. One magazine, which had published several of my short stories as well as a condensed version of my first novel, rejected a story because it was "too sympathetic a portrait of Iranian characters."

My daughter came home from school one day looking sad; she asked me if she could change her name to Cindy. One of her classmates had asked her where she got her name, Leila. My daughter told her it was an Iranian name. Her friend made a face at the word "Iran." I didn't know how to distill the complex political situation into terms that a seven-year-old could understand.

Disasters for Iran were piling up. Saddam Hussein, capitalizing on the broken alliance between Iran and the United States, pressed Iran to relinquish its half of all rights to Shatt-Al-Arab. He wanted to reclaim the channel up to the Iranian shore. Iran insisted that the line running down the middle of the waterway, negotiated in 1975, was the official border. Saddam Hussein also perceived Iran's revolutionary Shia regime as a threat to Iraq's delicate Sunni-Shia balance. Khomeini, already bitter over his expulsion from Iraq in 1977, responded in anger. Saddam ordered the invasion of Iran in September 1980.

I thought how strange and ironic that the fetid Shatt-Al-Arab, which had caused so much heat and dampness in Ahvaz, was now a major focus of the dispute between the two countries, with much more terrible consequences than what we used to complain about.

I had only sporadic, indirect contact with my family in Iran. Someone would tell someone else and gradually the news would be relayed to me by a phone call from Great Neck or LA, where many Iranians had fled.

A man or woman would call the apartment and ask for me and say, "I must tell you . . . ," or, "It's sad news but I feel obligated to tell you . . ."

One afternoon I had a phone call from a woman in LA who introduced herself as Shaheen. She said she was an old friend of my family who knew not only my parents but Pari and Mansour. She had fled Iran just before Khomeini took over. We commiserated for a while over the state of things. Then she hesitated.

"I have bad news," she said finally.

My heart sank. What could be worse than all we had talked about? "Your father passed away. It's already a few months but I just heard it. May his soul rest in heaven. He died peacefully in his sleep." She elaborated that he had had pneumonia for a few days and then one morning Mohtaram woke and found him still and cold and his eyes wide open. Shaheen added, "He must have died of grief—over all the distance from his children, the devastation of the country."

I was overwhelmed by a rush of emotions. Father's caring reception when we visited had brushed away all my anger. He had had so much power over me, had forcibly changed the course of my life, but ultimately much of it had been for the good. I wished I had been able to have a real talk with him, and now it was too late.

Shaheen called a few months later to tell me my grandmother had died of "old age." She had had a fever for a few days and then died at home. I thought of her sweet wrinkled face the last time I saw her, years ago when she came to Ahvaz for a visit, and the youthful, loving face of her earlier years. She was the one who, so long ago, took me to Maryam.

I received a letter from Maryam, who had been lost to me for a long time, as she kept moving from place to place in towns with important shrines. She said because of the war between Iran and Iraq, Iranians had been expelled from Karbala. She had moved to Dubai, and Mohtaram, lonely and devastated after Father died, was joining her. Both Farzaneh and Farzin were married. Mohtaram had found a village man with limited education to marry Farzin. All her daughters were now married.

Thirty-six

Despite rumors that Carter might create an "October surprise" and free the hostages before the election, negotiations dragged on for months. Carter's all-night effort to bring the hostages home before the end of his term fell short. On January 21, 1981, the day of President Reagan's inauguration, the United States released almost $8 billion in Iranian assets, and the Iranians released the hostages. On that same day, now former President Carter went to Germany to meet the freed hostages on behalf of the new president. It was a difficult moment for him, fraught with emotion.

Not long after the hostages' release, I woke to a loud siren from an ambulance speeding to the emergency rooms of Mount Sinai or Lenox Hill hospital, an ominous and depressing sound I never got used to. I was alone in the apartment that night. Howie was in Boston, and Leila was staying with a friend. As the sirens receded, the phone began to ring. I picked it up and a woman said in Farsi, "Nahid, this is Azar."

"Oh, Azar, nice hearing from you. Is Pari with you?" Azar was the friend Pari had talked about in a letter, the one whose sister told Pari about Taheri's criminal past.

"I'm afraid not," she said, her voice trembling. "I'm sorry to be the bearer of bad news." There was a pause and then the sound of weeping. Her next words went through me like shards of glass. "I'm so sorry, Nahid, your dear sister, my dear friend, had a terrible accident. She lost her balance and tripped down the stairway of their house. It was too late by the time she reached the hospital."

I began choking on my own breath. I couldn't say a word.

"It happened a month ago—no, to be exact, five weeks ago, but it took this long for me to get your phone number from Mansour and then get through the international lines. Are you there? . . . Mansour was away for a few days. I was with her, so were Zohreh and another friend, Laleh. It took a long time for the ambulance to come." The line went dead.

The phone rang again and again, but each time as soon as I picked it up we got disconnected. After trying many times to reach information in Iran, I found there were more than a hundred Mirshahis listed. I didn't have Azar's address. I knew she had moved out of their house across from Pari's.

I had an impulse to call my husband but didn't. It was as if talking about it would make it all too real. Still the reality was there, and came to me in disturbing images. I saw two medics, both female, shrouded in black clothes, coming to Pari's aid as she lay at the bottom of the staircase. I imagined them listening to her pulse, her heartbeat, covering her with a sheet and carrying her to the ambulance waiting outside.

Lost her balance. Something ice-cold slipped into my crowded thoughts: the accident must have been intentional. Pari so closely identified with Furugh Farrukhzad, and she believed that the poet killed herself because she couldn't bear her situation in life. I'd seen Pari's perspective on her own life grow darker and darker. No hope. No escape. No passion. I could see her standing at the top of the steep stairs, looking down and telling herself, *Jump, and that will be the end of pain.*

I don't know how long I sat there, feeling broken into pieces. Neither do I recall how I got from the bed to the living room couch. I was filled with dread and doom. And then I remembered everything. Through the window I could see rain falling and thought, in a strange, hallucinatory way, that the rapid raindrops were my own tears. How was it possible that I would never see Pari again? At some level of my existence, in my fantasy, I had always hoped one day, somehow or other, she and I would live close to each other and resume our old intimacy. Now that dream was completely shattered.

I couldn't find Mansour's work number and I didn't know the name of his company. Mohtaram was still with Maryam in Dubai, and I had no address or phone number for either of them anymore, as they moved around a lot. My relatives in Tehran either had no phones or had changed numbers. I no longer had addresses for most of them. I talked about Pari's accident with Parviz and Cyrus; they were both shocked and grief-stricken, but how could we offer solace to one another or find answers to our questions about what really happened? I had no idea how to reach Manijeh. I suddenly had an urge to talk to her after all these years, partly to find out if she had been in contact with Pari in recent months.

In the days that followed I played and replayed in my mind my conversations with Pari when I had visited—the loss of Majid and of her acting ambitions, Mansour committing her to that sanitarium, and her dimming hope that she would ever gain any rights to Bijan or even see him.

For so much of my life I had found solace in writing. Maneuvering details into a coherent story had a calming effect. But I couldn't write about Pari's death. In fact I couldn't write about anything. It was as if a part of me had died with Pari. I thought, Pari, too, had always needed the world of the imagination, and she had, step-by-step and to an increasing degree, been deprived of that world. That deprivation cast a darker shadow on everything else in her life. She wasn't allowed to give her dissatisfactions and disappointments, her losses, shape and meaning and so she became their prisoner.

I must have looked strange to everyone around me. My daughter told me more than once, "Mom, you're so zonked out." How could I explain to this little girl, who had led a life so different from her mother's, what was pulling me inward? In fact she knew very little about my culture. She had never been to Iran, never met Pari, Maryam, or my parents, and didn't speak a word of Farsi. In my attempt to protect her from the harsh reality of my own culture, I hadn't introduced her even to the good things.

A friend, Julie, suggested I see a therapist. But how could a therapist help me change the facts of what had happened? Did I even want to stop grieving?

When Azar called again, I told her I would go to Iran to see her and Zohreh and Laleh, who had been with Pari at the time of the accident, and perhaps other people who had been with her close to the end. Then I could also go to Mansour's office and see him. I knew its location, as Pari had pointed it out to me on a walk. The only way I could cope with feelings of loss was to find out more about what had happened, to get closer to the truth of the accident. It quickly became an obsession.

❀

The Iran-Iraq war, which had started in1980, was still raging. It was a dangerous time to go to Iran but in the state of mind I was in, I was determined to go there no matter the risk. I called the Iranian Interest Section in the Pakistani Embassy in D.C., which now functioned as a go-between, since there was no Iranian consulate or embassy in the United States.

The official who answered the phone informed me that there was no problem with my going to Iran and returning, as long as I didn't show my American passport when arriving and leaving. I needed only to show my Iranian passport. I also had to follow the *hejab*—cover my hair and arms and legs. A head scarf and a raincoat would be sufficient, but I should make sure they were in dark colors. Bright colors on women were now officially condemned by Khomeini. He assured me that the war was being fought only in a small border area and that it would end soon.

I had to replace my Iranian passport because it now had to have a photograph of me following the *hejab*. The new passport also wouldn't have stamps used under the Shah on it. The old passport had to be sent to Iran instead of the Interest Section, and that would take a few months. The official cautioned me about certain things. If I took any books or magazines with me, I should make sure there were no photos in them of women with hair or skin showing. I also shouldn't wear makeup or nail polish.

As if he were a friend, he advised me to hide my American passport in the lining of my purse or raincoat so that it wouldn't be discovered easily. He also told me I had to go without my husband or daughter. My husband's being Jewish didn't matter as Khomeini, like the Shah, had declared Jews to be "People of the Book," but it did matter that he and my daughter, too, were American-born.

Almost all the Iran Air passengers were Iranians, and they were all somber. No alcohol was served on the plane, and the programs on the screens were in Farsi and were mostly Iranian propaganda newsreels.

As we began our descent into Mehrabad Airport, the flight attendant announced, "Please buckle your seat belts, we are landing. And cover up, please."

I put on my dark head scarf and my longer-than-usual dark raincoat, which I had bought for the trip. In the airport I was struck by how Khomeini's grim-faced photographs were displayed everywhere, replacing those of the Shah. Framed calligraphic quotations from the Koran—"In the Name of Allah, the Beneficent, the Merciful"—hung on several walls, some of them next to Khomeini's photograph. Armed, bearded guards in dark green fatigues stood in various spots.

I was relieved that nothing out of the ordinary happened as my passport was checked. The officer at the customs booth made me open my suitcase and purse. "Go ahead," he said. I felt a surge of relief again—he didn't notice my American passport hidden in the lining of my purse.

As I left the terminal building, I noticed signs on two entrance doors behind me, one saying, FOR MEN, and the other, FOR WOMEN. I got into a taxi and told the driver to take me to Esteghal Grand Hotel, the former Tehran Hilton Hotel, where my parents had stayed on my last visit. The driver, a bulky man with sad eyes and a sweet smile, complained about inflation and the rising prices of everything.

The atmosphere in the city, as I looked out the window, was as grim as Khomeini's photographs. Everything was black, brown, gray. Many of the street names had been changed to depressing ones: Martyr Square, Martyr Haj Ali Avenue, Imam Reza Alley, Execution Avenue. Slogans on walls read: "Women follow *hejab*," "Those who gave their lives to fight the evil Shah are now in Heaven," "Death to America."

When we reached the hotel, the driver helped me inside and, before leaving, said, "*Khanoon* be careful, a woman alone."

In the lobby were more photographs of Khomeini. With relief, I noticed two foreign-looking single women sitting in different spots. They were both wearing lightweight head scarves and raincoats, as I was. After checking in I followed the bellboy to my room.

It was a pleasant room with a handmade kilim on the floor and a quilt on the bed. A framed calligraphy print reading, "In the name of God," hung on the wall next to the door. Through the window I could see the mosaic on the mosque across the street and hear the water in the *joob* running along the street, gurgling gently.

I unpacked, took a shower, and sat in bed. I dialed our number at home to tell Howie and Leila that I had arrived safely but I couldn't get through— calls between Iran and America, never easy, had only gotten worse.

Thirty-seven

I n the morning, after a quick breakfast in the hotel dining room, I left for
Azar's house, where she was expecting me. I decided to walk.

I passed a street filled with houses belonging to Jews who had remained
in Iran after the revolution, then passed an enclave for Syrians. On another
street, a young boy was selling bouquets of geraniums from a bucket. "The
freshest and cheapest flowers in Tehran!" he shouted to everyone passing
by. I bought a bouquet to take to Azar. As I walked on, I realized that while
my mind was tied up in thoughts of Pari, I had been pulling the petals off
the flowers and they had scattered on the ground, leaving a trail behind me.

It had been a spring day, too, in Ahraz when Majid sent a flower to Pari
with an envelope tied to the stem. *Konar* flowers on the bushes lining the
path had been in bloom; it was near dusk and everything had an ethereal
quality. I could still hear the cooing of doves above the murmur of traffic
on Pahlavi Avenue.

Azar's building stood on a narrow street lined with two- and three-story
houses, divided into separate apartments, all with tall windows to allow
north light in. Some of the windows were covered by lace curtains. Azar's
apartment had been provided for her by the government after her husband
was killed on the streets during the upheaval leading to the revolution.

"I wish we were seeing each other on a happier occasion," Azar said as we embraced in the doorway.

As she hurried to the kitchen to make tea, I took off my raincoat and head scarf and sat on the sofa. The voice of a man singing a dreamy love song, accompanied by *santur* and *donbak,* blared out of a phonograph in the corner.

You came to me in the dark of the night . . . Your eyes bright stars . . .

It was the kind of song that the clergy would interpret as being about Prophet Mohammad revealing himself to someone, so it was acceptable. While I waited for Azar, I noticed jasmine flowers floating in a bowl on the coffee table. A rocking horse stood in the corner, and some toys lay in another corner.

Azar came back with the tea. She had taken off her head scarf, and her shimmering chestnut hair fell over her shoulders. She was dressed in black. "I've been wearing black for two years now, since Hassan was killed," she said when she noticed my questioning look. "If I didn't they would say I was disrespectful."

My eyes were drawn to a small painting on the wall behind her. It depicted a woman covered by a dark chador, holding a little boy on her lap, turning his face to her. The colors were somber—gray-blue, black.

"Pari gave that to me just recently. She found it at an art fair. It meant a lot to her but she didn't want it anymore. I'm not a soul mate with anyone as I was with Pari. At least my children have friends in the building. They're at school now." She stared at her hands folded on her lap. Then she said, "I've been bleeding heavily. Doctors can't find any cause for it, other than tension."

"I'm sorry," I said. "Life must be so hard with all the tragedies."

"It is so for everyone, and I had those extra traumas. My husband, my friend, dying."

"Azar, it's hard to believe Pari just fell down those stairs."

"We had gathered in her house because she wanted to tell us something, but then she fell." Tears collected in her eyes. "We were on the second floor. She went to another room to get something to show to us. When she didn't come back I went to look for her. Then I heard a moan and realized it was coming from the bottom of the stairs. I saw her lying there. I screamed and ran down the stairs. She was unconscious, Nahid, and the side of her face was bleeding. It's odd she didn't scream or anything as she was falling." Azar began sobbing.

I felt tears spring to my eyes, too.

"She could have hit her head and immediately become unconscious," Azar said after we had calmed ourselves. "Life was so abnormal for all of us. And she had all those issues. I don't want to allow myself to believe she did it intentionally. I hope it was only an accident."

The taxi crawled so slowly through the Tehran traffic that by the time I got to Mansour's office, it was closed. Back in my room at the hotel, I called home again but without success. I lay on the bed and closed my eyes. When I opened them it was dark outside. It was too late to go and see Mansour and I didn't want to just show up at his house, though I wanted to go there at some point, to see the steps, feel something about Pari in the air.

Laleh's house stood on a dead-end alley lined with large, expensive-looking houses, both modern and old-fashioned. A servant opened the iron gate and led me through a garden filled with apple and cherry trees. Zohreh and Azar were already waiting at the dining table, Laleh told me as she opened the door and led me inside.

All three women were well dressed and without head scarves inside the home. Laleh was older than the other two and had pale skin and light brown hair. Zohreh was dark-haired, had nearly black eyes, and wore a morose expression. A maid, Nane *joon,* brought in platters heaped with food— eggplant stew, a vegetable casserole, saffron rice, chopped salad. She was wearing a chador with the sides wrapped around her waist to free her hands to carry things.

"My two daughters have left their husbands and are back home," Laleh told me as we began to eat. "They both go to the university. Things are so ridiculous: boys and girls sit on separate sides, segregated as they are on buses and in many other public places. I taught sociology there. It was hard enough to teach that subject under the Shah, but it became worse after the revolution, so I quit."

"Did you and Pari join the crowds on the streets?" I asked the women.

"Yes, we all did," Azar said. "No one was sitting home."

"Now we all feel cheated. We gained nothing, and so many people were killed," Zohreh said.

"It's all so unfair," I said. "Pari couldn't have stayed on with that terrible husband, but then she had to pay such a high price for leaving him." I became aware of the bitterness in my voice and said nothing more.

"Yes, she had every reason to be depressed," Zohreh said.

"Do you think . . ."

"She once was so despairing after she came back from court that I was worried about her," Zohreh interrupted. "But I don't think she really wanted to end her life. She heard from someone who knew Taheri that her son had been trying to find her. She expected Bijan to come to her house any day."

"Pari never told me that," Azar said.

"She didn't tell me, either," Laleh said.

Zohreh shrugged.

There were sounds of footsteps and laughter, then two young girls walked in.

Laleh introduced her daughters. They both removed their head scarves and raincoats and emerged as stylish, attractive, nice girls. Soosan wore a pleated skirt and a T-shirt with a low neckline, and Nasrin a tailored blue dress, also with a low neckline. Laleh invited them to join us for lunch, but they had already eaten and went to their rooms.

"My daughters go against the rules as much as they can get away with," Laleh said to me. "That's the case with many young people; they take chances. Some of them are picked up by the moral police. If their 'crime' is wearing lipstick or nail polish or they aren't observing the *hejab* properly, they're flogged; if they're carrying any pamphlets or books that might sound anti-government, they're sent to jail. Everyone lives only in the privacy of their homes. You can get almost anything on the black market—American videos, liquor—but then of course there's always the dread of being caught. We live with fear and anxiety, the way it was under the Shah. My daughters wish so much to go to a university in America, but it's nearly impossible to get even student visas now. Why did it have to come to this?" She got up and went into the kitchen.

In a moment she came back carrying a silver-legged platter heaped with fruit. She set it in the middle of the table.

"Nahid," she said as she sat down. "Mansour committed Pari to a sanitarium. The doctors released her after a month."

"But wasn't that a few years ago?" I asked, feeling a painful squeeze in my heart.

"No, it was just before the accident. He put her in what used to be called Pahlavi Sanitarium."

"This was the second time he put her there," Azar said.

"Pari told me about the first time. I don't think there was enough justification for it," I said.

"I didn't think there was the second time, either," Azar said.

"One of Mansour's relatives told my husband that Mansour's brothers are already looking for a new wife for him. They all thought Pari was wrong for him, that she felt superior to him," Zohreh said.

We fell into silence. That Mansour would be substituting another woman for Pari made my heart ache. It was odd, I suddenly thought, that Mansour didn't try to reach me after the accident.

We talked awhile longer, sorrow casting a wider and wider shadow over us, but none of us reached any conclusions about the accident.

As I wandered aimlessly through different neighborhoods, my mind filled with images of Pari. I envisioned her funeral. Pari, who hated all the rituals of her wedding, would not have liked those rituals, either. Mansour would arrange that within twenty-four hours of her death her body would be washed by a woman in a mosque, on a stone slab, facing Mecca. After she was washed three times, she would be wrapped in a white sheet from head to toe, and then an *aghound* standing by her shoulder would say a prayer, reading the Koran's first *sureh,* starting with "God is Great." At the cemetery, Pari, still wrapped in the white cloth, would be put, without a coffin, into her grave, also facing Mecca. Then men, hired by Mansour for the occasion, would shovel dirt over her body. Then the *aghound* would say another prayer.

How unreal this all was. Pari, so full of life, was now out of reach. I wished I could believe what Maryam had told me on those long-ago days— that death was only a temporary state and the person will be brought back to life on the Day of Judgment and eventually reunited with loved ones.

After lunch I decided to get a haircut at the salon Pari had pointed out to me when I was last in Tehran. Pari said she went to the woman who ran the salon mainly in the hope of finding out things about Bijan; the woman heard about Bijan from her cousin who had a shop in Tehran where Taheri went periodically to purchase old rugs.

A sheet of paper pasted on a burlap curtain on the door read: "Haircut, blow-dry, thirty *toomans.*" Although it was Friday, the shop appeared to be open. I rang the bell. A plump woman with henna-red hair poking out from under her head scarf opened the door and looked at me blankly. I asked her if I could get a haircut without an appointment. She told me the shop was closed. I told her I was Pari's sister and wanted to talk to her.

"Oh," she said, her demeanor changing at once. "You must be Nahid. Pari talked about you a lot. She missed you. I'm so sorry about Pari *joon.* What a tragedy."

Farideh said she would give me a haircut and we could talk. I followed her through a courtyard and into a room. Photographs of women with different hairstyles decorated the walls.

She washed my hair, then asked me what kind of cut I wanted.

"Just shape it," I said. "One of Pari's friends told me that Bijan was supposed to visit. Is it true?"

"My cousin told me that Taheri was going to drop Bijan off at Pari's house on one of his trips to Tehran, that Bijan had been asking about his mother daily. He's fourteen years old now and understands everything."

"It's all so cruel."

"Pari and I were going to have lunch but that meeting never took place. Do you want me to color your hair?"

"I like to leave it natural."

"I put blond highlights in Pari's hair. She wanted to look good for her son."

"I wish I knew what was going on in her heart and mind before the accident."

"The same thought has been going around and around in my head, and some of the girls here who knew her wonder, too. We've all been very upset, of course. Everyone loved Pari."

"Go ahead, highlight my hair."

"If you want my honest opinion, I don't believe she just lost her balance. She was afraid that Taheri would never allow Bijan to see her, would make life hell for him if he did. Then, at the same time, Pari was afraid Bijan would be disappointed in her, or blame her for abandoning him, if he did see her. Her outlook was dark on that."

After Farideh was finished highlighting, she washed and blow-dried my hair. She held up a mirror for me to look at the outcome. "It's just like Pari's," she said.

As I was leaving I tried to pay her, but she refused the money.

"Please. I did it in honor of my dear friend."

Thirty-eight

The next day, in the lobby of Mogadessi National Oil Company, the receptionist, a woman covered from head to toe in a black chador, directed me to Mansour's office. As I walked along the corridor all the women I passed were also covered by black chadors. A door had been left ajar, and I saw that it was to a prayer room for women. Several women were standing in front of prayer rugs, bowing and rising.

Mansour opened the door. "Nahid *khanoon*, what a surprise," he said, giving a start.

He had lost weight, his hair was disheveled, his eyes bloodshot. His clothes, a brown blazer, beige pants, and a white shirt, all looked creased. I sat on a chair and he behind the desk and we looked at each other awkwardly.

He had a box of *gaz*, a Persian candy, on his desk, and he offered it to me. I shook my head. My throat felt constricted.

"You didn't even tell me about my dear sister's accident. I had to hear it in the middle of the night from a friend." I managed to speak after a moment of uncomfortable silence between us.

"I'm sorry, Nahid. I tried to call you but I couldn't get through, and then I couldn't bear trying again. I'm in shock myself." His voice grew tremulous.

"I was away for three days, visiting my ailing mother, and then that happened. Oh, I tried so hard to please Pari, to make her happy, but nothing worked. Sometimes she spent entire days in bed. She kept saying Taheri was following her around in a car. I never knew if she was imagining things or they really happened. She constantly talked about how meaningless her life was and how terrible she felt about Bijan. She kept saying she wished she were dead. I had to put her in a sanitarium. I was afraid for her." A touch of righteousness came into his voice as he said, "It was for her own sake but she felt I had betrayed her."

"Do you think she brought that on herself, the falling—"

"Nahid *joon*, I can't be sure. She didn't leave a note or anything. But she was giving her belongings away. I have to sort out what's left. I packed everything in boxes and put them in storage for now."

I thought of the pendant she gave to me and the painting she gave to Azar.

"I can't imagine life without her," Mansour sighed. "But she's finally at peace, a repose she didn't find living. I couldn't bear the house after what happened. I rented it and moved to an apartment. Why did God serve me so many blows? I lost both of my wives and my son."

I had intended to challenge Mansour but he seemed so grief-stricken.

"I wish I could be in the house again, see those steps," I said.

"It's hard with the renters. Besides, what's the point? Why bring back the horror?"

There was a knock on the door and Mansour opened it. A man in a suit whispered something to Mansour and left.

"I was just given an assignment that will take me out of Tehran for a few days," Mansour said, coming back to his seat. "How long are you going to be here?"

I told him I'd be in Iran for six more days, and I wanted to visit Pari's grave. He said it was in Behesht Zahra (Zahra's Heaven) cemetery, named after Prophet Mohammad's daughter, Martyr Fatemeh Zahra. He had had a tree planted next to her grave and he paid someone to attend to it. He wished he could go with me, but he didn't know how long his assignment would last. He advised me to wait a day or two before going to the cemetery; the computer system that identified graves was down temporarily. He himself would have trouble finding the grave without that guidance, the cemetery was so vast.

Outside, I felt so overwhelmed by helplessness and confusion that I wondered why I had come to Iran. Why was I tormenting myself? Was there something deeply damaged about me that had been scratched by Pari's death?

As if pulled by a magnet, I started toward the sanitarium. I recalled the exact location; it had penetrated my brain. I had a vague hope that a nurse or a doctor would remember Pari and tell me something about her. Maybe they could look up her records. I passed a row of bargain clothing stores, electronic stores, toy shops. On the wall of one store hung posters of John F. Kennedy next to posters of the dark-bearded Imam Ali, the first imam of the Shia Muslim faith. A group of boys in the red, green, and white shirts of the Iranian national soccer team rushed by.

I passed the British Embassy and entered Bobby Sands Street, named after an IRA figure who defied the British (the British still brought out anger in many Iranians). I passed a fruit market, the white-columned Parliament Building with its rose garden, then came across the American Embassy. Graffiti covered the walls. "The great Satan," "The archvillain." A plaque at the entrance door said, "Den of Spies."

Finally the sanitarium loomed. It was now called Aram Bag (Calm Garden). A muscular man with a curling black mustache was standing by the door.

After a few moments, I convinced him to let me in. The courtyard was empty, not like the last time I passed it with Pari. Judging by how quiet it was, this seemed to be the time when patients were kept indoors, perhaps to be given tests or medicine, or to be examined by doctors.

I entered the reception area, and after I explained to the receptionist why I was there, she led me to a nurse. Wearing a navy head scarf and a white uniform, the nurse was sitting next to a window, knitting. I introduced my-self, and she told me her name was Shirin.

"Of course I remember Pari," she said as I sat in a chair across from her. "We were friends. I took her out a few times for lunch. She was depressed but nothing serious. She was a delightful patient to have around. With her lively imagination she lifted us from the grayness of life."

"Yes, she had that capacity. Now she's dead."

Shirin gave a start. "She died? I'm so sorry to hear it. Of what?"

I told her about the accident.

"That's so sad, I can't believe it," Shirin said.

"Was she so depressed that she was suicidal?" I asked.

"I don't think she would have brought something like that on herself. She was full of life, in spite of everything."

"Her husband committed her here a few years ago, too. Do you think . . . I mean, was his bringing her here justified?"

"Her psychiatrist didn't think so, the last time anyway. That's why he let her go."

"They let her go quickly the first time, too. Is it possible for me to speak to her psychiatrist?"

"Doctors rotate. He isn't here now. But a young psychiatrist who saw Pari a few times is still here."

Shirin was self-educated, spent hours every day reading books, whatever she could find, and listened to an educational radio station that was taken off the air at times by the censors. She had turned down many suitors; she didn't like most men. She lived with a nephew in a luxury apartment build-ing in north Tehran. Her nephew was paralyzed in both legs from polio and his parents were dead. Before her death his mother had begged Shirin to take care of him. She put some money in Shirin's name and said she could live with her nephew in the luxury apartment, rent free. Shirin's life was better this way, as a nurse's salary was extremely low. And it was fulfilling to be of help to her nephew, whom she loved.

Just then a patient ran into the hall, screaming, "Water, water," and Shirin dashed out to help. When she came back, we resumed talking. I asked her more questions about Pari, and she asked me questions about life in America.

The silence in the hall was broken again by sounds of coughing, strange, harsh laughter, incomprehensible mumbles, and groans of misery. A middle-aged woman in a beige hospital gown shuffled down the hall. A red substance was smeared all over her face. She was saying to no one in particular, "Terrible, terrible."

Several nurses appeared. One of them took the woman's arm and led her away. Others passed by carrying thermometers, vials of blood, bottles of pills, and syringes.

When it became quiet again, Shirin said, "Was there any letter?"

"No, Pari didn't leave a suicide note or anything."

She shook her head and said nothing else.

Dr. Hejazi, Pari's psychiatrist, was young and sullen. His office was plain with no personal touches, and he didn't look at me as I sat across from him.

"If you know so much about medicine, why don't I give you my doctor's coat?" he said sharply.

"You talk to me like that because I'm a woman," I said, blood racing to my face. "You wouldn't say anything like that to a man."

"What I hate about Iranians living in America is that they pick up this kind of ridiculous jargon."

"You can at least tell me what medication she was on."

"Lithium, to calm her down."

"Isn't that given for a bipolar condition?"

"We give it for other problems, too. She wouldn't have been here if she didn't have problems," he said with a dismissive gesture of his hand.

I got up and left the room. The encounter felt unreal, as if it had been a nightmare. I remembered that as a child I once asked the pharmacist near

Maryam's house about some medicine I was picking up for Hamideh, one of our tenants. He turned to his partner and said with a derisive laugh, "Look at this girl, asking such questions!" I had felt hurt for days.

As I entered the courtyard, a patient sitting on a bench got up and came over to me. She gave me a folded piece of paper and walked away.

I unfolded the paper. *Please get me out of here.*

As I continued to the entrance, another patient came into the yard. "Get me out of this cage," she shouted. "What have I done to be punished like this? Get me out, get me out."

Another woman joined in. "I want to die, please let me."

Thirty-nine

At the cemetery entrance a giant pair of granite hands held a large red tulip. In the distance, through the smog, I could see the gold dome and minarets of a mosque. Vendors appeared, hawking bouquets or single flowers to people passing in cars or on foot. I stopped a little girl and bought a bouquet from her, then went to the booth next to the entrance and asked the man inside for directions. He went into a little room and came back in a few moments and told me exactly how to get to Pari's grave.

I walked down tree-lined paths, passing people sitting on blankets spread in the shade of trees. Trays of sweets and fruit wrapped in plastic and tied with black ribbons were set out for the memorials of their loved ones. A beggar in a dusty black chador, holding a sleeping child in one arm, the other hand outstretched, approached them one by one.

Finally I came across a row of marble headstones engraved with epitaphs like "Open the gates of heaven," and, "Your soul is already in heaven." I noticed two women kneeling by a grave and looking at photographs of a young man that were inside a plastic case fastened to a pole next to the stone.

"You're in heaven and at peace," one of the women said. "It's we mortals who are suffering."

A bearded cleric in a brown frock coat and a white shirt came over to the women and said, "He served his nation well, produced three sons and one daughter. He loved his country, religion, family."

I entered a plot of land with no tombstones; this was where people who had been executed by the new regime were buried. The sight of all the dead in this vast cemetery, some killed in the revolution, some by execution, others from usual causes, didn't make Pari's death ordinary or easier to bear.

Finally I came to the path where her grave was. The tree that Mansour had had planted shaded the grave. Two doves were engraved on the horizontal stone. Beneath the doves was carved:

Pari Mehramy: 1942–1981, beloved wife, mother, sister, daughter.

As I put the flowers on the stone, my mind denied that Pari was dead. "This is no place for you," I told Pari. "Come on out, I'm here to see you." Though I knew I had spoken the words, I was startled to hear my voice.

A teenage boy appeared and offered to wash the grave. As he performed his task he recited:

Oh, beautiful woman,
Your pure soul will be carried to heaven by two angels
Oh, the example of purity, you'll be soon in heaven
where a garlanded seat under cool shady trees is awaiting you.

I paid him well; he had asked for so little.

A man wearing a felt hat came over and asked if he could say a prayer for the dead. I nodded. He squatted by the grave and, closing his eyes, recited a *sureh* from the Koran.

As soon as he finished, a bird hopped on the grave and then flew away, going up and up until it was swallowed by the sunny sky. "That was her soul," the man said matter-of-factly. "If it's a bird it means she's in heaven; otherwise a fly would have appeared."

After the man left, I sank into a state of near-oblivion. Then I noticed a man who looked vaguely familiar staring at me. I was jolted out of my sunken state when I recognized Majid. Yes, Majid, the man who had been in Pari's heart for so long and then finally devastated her. He hadn't changed much since that time I met him in the park in Ahvaz, when he gave me a letter for Pari. Only a few strands of gray were strewn through his hair. His wide forehead was a little wrinkled, and his shoulders stooped slightly. He was wearing a casual woolen tweed jacket over jeans, the way American professors dressed.

He, too, recognized me and said, "Oh, Nahid *e aziz*, you're here."

You know, Nahid, what happened with Majid has weakened me.

"I come to her grave every time I'm in Tehran. I miss her so much. I'm not the same person without her." Majid's words brought me back to the present.

"Majid, she was devastated by some of the things you said and did," I said, and began walking away from him.

"Please, don't run away from me. I want to talk to you," he said, putting a bouquet of flowers he was holding on her grave and, in a few moments, catching up with me halfway to the gate. His face was damp with tears, his manner diffident. He was so different from the buoyant, self-confident man I remembered.

I tried to control my anger. I told myself I should talk to him, hear what he had to say.

"I'll take you to a teahouse where the 'moral police' aren't always on the lookout," he said.

We walked to his car, an old Chevrolet. As he began to drive through winding, narrow backstreets I tried to assess him from Pari's point of view. Here was the man who had brought her to such heights and depths.

At the teahouse, Majid led me to a quiet corner in the back. The walls were covered with posters of historical sights, a minaret in Isfahan, a garden in Shiraz. Copper lamps stood in the corners and the obligatory portrait of Khomeini hung on one wall. Two men were playing *kamanche* and *tar*. At other tables sat couples, single men, or groups of men, some smoking water pipes, some sipping tea.

"You were a shy, tense girl," Majid said. "You've turned into a confident young woman. America must have been good for you."

"When did you last see Pari?" I asked.

"I saw her once recently, at her request. She left a note for me with a friend saying that she wanted to tell me something. But when we met, she was reserved and we never got around to what she wanted to say. I wanted to start our relationship again but she told me bluntly that everything was dead between us. The sparks she had hoped to bring back by seeing me again were dead underneath the ashes. It was a sad meeting." He was whispering, being cautious the way people were under the Shah's regime. "It isn't easy for anyone here, women or men. We all fought for freedom, which got us caught in months and months of destruction, and what did we get for it?"

"There was that letter to your wife . . ." I fell into a strange daydream in which I was Pari, talking to Majid.

"That was very unfortunate. Someone had told Mahnaz, my wife, that I had been seeing Pari. I'm sure it was Pari's ex-husband. I don't know what he wanted from Pari; he had taken everything already."

"Remember that letter you gave to me on that picnic in Ahvaz? You encouraged her to leave her husband then."

"Yes," he said. "Why weren't we allowed to follow our deepest individual desires?"

"But, Majid, you didn't want to leave your wife," I said.

"I have children."

"So Pari was right about your disapproval that she had left her son behind?"

"She read all sorts of things into everything I said. It was for her own sake that I did and said certain things but now I wish I avoided those subjects. More than anything I wish years ago we had been able to go by our own desires. After I lost hope, I gave in to family pressure and married Mahnaz. I've been trying to do the best with my marriage."

"Pari said she wished she could shatter her life and put it back differently."

"I feel that way myself; it hasn't been easy for me."

A few men came in, looking around the room as if surveying the people. The women who had let their scarves or chadors slip to the middle of their heads quickly pulled them forward, and I made sure mine was in place.

"I thought they wouldn't show up here, but here they are," Majid whispered. "We'd better go, before they come over and ask how we're related."

We left quickly and he drove me to my hotel.

"We both are in mourning for Pari," he said.

At the entrance to the hotel, Majid said he hoped we could talk more. But we didn't make any plans to meet again. No words could erase things or make them different, I thought. And he seemed to be feeling the same way.

In the quiet of my room, I thought how both Majid and Mansour had done and said things that they thought were for Pari's own good.

One morning I went to Maryam's neighborhood, which was now closer in atmosphere to the rest of Tehran, which had more mosques everywhere, and all the women covered up. Construction was under way on Khanat Abad; Haj Abbas Alley was blocked off. I asked one of the construction workers when the job was going to be done. He said he wasn't sure. The residents had been forced to leave and stay away until the *joob* could be restored with good water running in it.

The memory of my last summer with Maryam came to me. Maryam had urged her sisters to take a vacation together. "I need to get away for a while, clear my head," I heard her say to her sister Khadijeh. The three sisters took us children for a three-week vacation to Farah Zar, a bucolic village two hours by car from Tehran. Khadijeh was a widow by then; Roghieh's husband was too busy to go with us but approved of his family taking a long-overdue vacation. The sisters hired someone to take us to Farah Zar in a truck. We filled the truck with bundles of clothing, bedding, towels, and cooking utensils. We sat on the canvas covering the cargo area and peeked out at the roads from between the slats. The aunts said prayers to make sure the journey was safe.

When we reached Farah Zar we had lunch at the main square's garden restaurant, then rented donkeys to carry our belongings. The roads were too narrow for a car or even a horse. In half an hour we reached the flat top of a hill where tents made of mosquito netting were set up for people to rent. Trees, redolent with fruit, covered much of the plateau. A stream wound through it, leading to a blue lake. Sheep and goats grazed in pastures at the bottom of the hill, and beyond the pastures were fields filled with shrubbery and wild yellow, lavender, orange, blue, and red flowers. We began to arrange our belongings in the tents. Aunt Khadijeh had one tent, her three sons shared another. Aunt Roghieh and her four daughters were in one large tent, and Maryam and I shared one. The aunts and my two oldest female cousins started on domestic tasks, while the two older male cousins went back to the square to buy ingredients for meals. The boys returned hours later. They said they had gone to a different vendor for every item: meat from the butcher, fresh herbs from a peasant who grew them in her garden and picked them right then and there, milk from another peasant (we drank it only after boiling it for sterilization), cheese from another.

In the evening my cousins and I walked on narrow paths lit by gas lamps. Numerous stars appeared so low in the sky that it seemed like we could reach and touch them. We walked to the square, which was teeming with people, and bought fresh pecans that the vendors plucked from a bucket of salt water and fresh corn roasted on charcoal and dipped in salt water. We ate them sitting on a bench and watched people go by, making up stories about them.

Zahra, who was my age, and I went off on our own some days, exploring hills, valleys, and orchards. Everything was enveloped in the sweet mystery of the village atmosphere. Through the open barn doors we could see women milking cows. In some shops women sat on the floor and knitted sweaters with colorful woolen yarn sheared from their own sheep and dyed. Behind gauzy curtains covering house windows we watched families carrying on—a man and a woman eating silently, a child climbing onto a stool to try to open a cabinet. On the way back we picked wildflowers.

Life was full of joy then, but looking back on that trip now, it seemed to me that Maryam had been anxious. She whispered to her sisters and stopped talking when I came upon them. On the last night of the vacation I woke to find her tossing and turning in bed.

"What's wrong?" I asked.

"Nothing," she said. "Go back to sleep, dear."

"Tell me, tell me what's wrong."

"Nothing, it's just being in a new place. Go back to sleep now. At night everything seems dark."

A few weeks later, Father came and took me away.

Forty

Just as I was leaving for the airport, the hotel clerk handed me a manila envelope. He said it had been dropped off for me by a man early in the morning.

I waited until I was in the taxi before opening it. It was filled with letters and photographs. There was also a note from Mansour, saying he thought I would like to have them.

I had no trouble leaving the country. Their main concern seemed to be that *hejab* was properly observed.

On the plane, I examined the contents of the envelope more closely. I found a postcard from Pari, addressed to me, one she for some reason never sent.

Dear Nahid, I hope all is well with you. . . . I may be going home soon. . . . A few days ago one of the nurses here took me out to lunch at Hotel Sahra. . . . It was a good day. . . .

I imagined her writing the postcard in the sanitarium. The Iranian woman next to me stared at me.

I couldn't bear examining the rest of what was in the envelope just then. I needed to be alone.

While waiting for my next plane in Amsterdam airport, I looked through the envelope again. I was startled to find a letter from Bijan to Pari.

Mother, I've been searching for you for a long time now. I'm hoping this letter will reach you. Many others I sent to you were returned. I may not have had the right address. . . . I want to see you at the first opportunity I have. It has been years since I saw you last but your expressions, your voice, everything about you are still with me. Mother, I never wanted to be separated from you, even when I was rude to you when you came to my school to see me. That was all due to my father's order and my own sadness that you left me. Now I understand perfectly that you had good reasons to leave. I'm glad that you managed to escape the confinement of the life my father imposed on you.

I know deep in my heart that I will be able to unite with you. Then I will never let anyone separate us. No one can stop me again from being your son. I have no recent photographs of you but a long time ago I stole one of us together from my father. You're holding me on your lap and looking lovingly at my face. Your lips are shaped as if you're talking to me, telling me stories. Your eyes, large and soft, your melodious voice, come to me from years ago. I can smell the scents of the cream and shampoo you used. Here in this faraway boarding school in Essex, where I have been for two years, I still feel your presence with me. My father sent me here hoping that I would pull myself together. I had dropped out of school and spent my time in a wayward way, took drugs. When I came here I had a hard time too and was about to be expelled when my father begged the school staff to give me another chance. I have finally pulled myself together. But I will never feel at ease with myself until I unite with you.

I'm not a child anymore but my need of you is that of a child. My fa-

ther never managed to destroy my love for you. It only went on growing, blossoming inside me. In the dawn of my life you were everything to me. Then there came the eclipse. But you are in my fantasies and dreams. In the last dream I had of you I was a child and you were holding my hand, taking me somewhere. We were walking inside a long, narrow tunnel which was brightly lit anyway. When I woke I was hopeful. I'm enclosing the most recent photograph of myself.

   Your loving son, Bijan

I looked for the photograph but instead found a note from Mansour. It said, "This came too late, after the accident."

I put the letter back in the envelope and pulled out a photograph of Pari. On the back she had written, "To my dear sister Nahid."

She was dressed in black and she had a melancholy, depressed expression on her face.

I pulled out a letter from Pari. It was only one line.

Nahid . . . I must talk to you . . . about pain . . . about misery. . . .

Back in New York I tried to push away my dark thoughts and feelings by immersing myself in the more stable, pleasurable aspects of my life—tending to my growing daughter's needs, teaching, going to movies and plays and concerts with my husband, and attempting to write. But the loss of Pari and not knowing what really happened remained like a dark hole in my existence.

I wanted to track down Bijan, to talk to him, invite him for a visit, or go and see him in England. I wrote Mansour at his office to find out if he had an address for Bijan. He wrote back that he hadn't been able to find the envelope that Bijan's letter came in and he apologized for not being more careful with it. He said he had been distraught going through Pari's belongings. He added that he had saved what was left of her clothes and jewelry and would give them to me the next time I was in Iran.

I tried to find Bijan through his boarding school in Essex but the principal told me he was no longer there and they had no forwarding address

for him. I asked about his father's address and was told they had been instructed to keep that information confidential.

Years went by and the war between Iran and Iraq continued to rage and
even escalate. The front lines shifted back and forth across Ahvaz and
Abadan, and I knew our house must have been demolished. My mind kept
going to Manijeh now. Had she and Javad left Abadan before the war
started? The conversation I had about her with Pari in Tehran kept going
through my mind. Pari had told me Manijeh was in some kind of trouble.

I began to write a novel about her called *Married to a Stranger*. I changed
her name to Minou.

> . . . Minou was going to be married the following day. Sparks of excitement
> leaped out of her as she thought of that. How could it be that she would be
> married to him, living with him forever, day after day, when he had been un-
> attainable, no more than a fantasy, a short while ago. Her future had been
> amorphous, a stretch of undefined days. In a matter of weeks everything had
> changed.

In the fictional account Minou's husband has an affair with a woman she
suspects he is in love with. One day she catches them in bed together and
leaves him. She goes to America to pursue her education.

Married to a Stranger was published in 1983. My happiness was diminished by the fact that Pari wasn't there to share the news with.

The war, which lasted for eight years, was one of the bloodiest of the twen-
tieth century. It was a devastating human tragedy. More than a million
people on each side were killed, and millions more were wounded and

made refugees. Both the secular Saddam Hussein and the theocrat Khomeini ruthlessly sacrificed their people, while America, along with other Western nations, provided weapons to both sides (for the sake of oil and military advantage in the Gulf). Iraq had more sophisticated weapons; to compensate, Iran sent boys as young as fifteen, unarmed, to fight on the front lines. Iraq bombed major Iranian cities, demolishing houses and buildings. Saddam Hussein's chemical weapons maimed hundreds of Iranians. There were food and medicine shortages. The government ordered rationing. There were not enough hospital beds because of the number of wounded and dying soldiers. There were blackouts everywhere.

Finally in August 1988 Iran and Iraq reached a cease-fire. After intense negotiations between the secretary-general and two foreign ministers, both countries accepted a UN resolution.

I decided to travel to Iran once again, this time to see Maryam, who had returned there. Despite all the political twists and turns, it was still relatively easy for an Iranian with dual citizenship to travel back and forth without trouble.

The plane was filled with Iranians returning home with hopes of uniting with or searching for their loved ones or finding jobs in reconstruction and rebuilding projects in the war-damaged areas. Some were going to their demolished homes in the hope of salvaging valuable family mementos in the rubble—jewelry, a box filled with old belongings.

From the window of the taxi taking me to Maryam's house, I could see the war damage. Shattered windows and partially wrecked buildings were everywhere. Some houses had black flags hanging above the front doors to designate that a member of the family had been killed in the war. In various spots soldiers sat on benches, crutches by their sides.

As I approached Khanat Abad, sweepers were cleaning the streets. It was a cool December morning and the beet seller was setting up his stall. Shopkeepers were washing the ground in front of their stores.

Maryam was squatting by the door to her house, wrapped in a chador, waiting for me, as she had when my grandmother brought me to her as an infant. She got up and we embraced tightly and kissed. Several years had passed since she visited Cambridge. Being back in that alley of my childhood, in Maryam's arms and enveloped in her scent of rose water, I felt as if no time had gone by since we had lived there together.

As we passed through the courtyard, I recalled how flowers were in bloom in every season. Now snapdragons crawled up a wall. The plum and cherry trees were still standing in their spots. The latticed window to the basement, the stained-glass panes, were intact. In the living room a samovar was giving out sparks. The comforting daily ritual of Maryam having tea with other women while my cousins and I played nearby came back to me. A tin can, perhaps the one I used to water the plants in the courtyard, stood next to the samovar. Perhaps it had been there all these years.

Maryam served tea and pastries and fruit and we talked. Mohtaram was in Ahvaz, which was one of the first cities to be reconstructed after the war ended because of the oil fields. She was there to see what could be rescued from our bombed-out house and to sell some properties she owned in the area. Manijeh's husband had died under mysterious circumstances, and she had married again and had two children, but Maryam didn't know where they lived. My other aunts and cousins had left for mountainous villages and hadn't returned to Tehran yet.

Maryam's life wasn't that different under the new regime, she told me, since her neighborhood had remained unchanged and because no bombs had been dropped on it. She had the same pattern of daily interaction with women, some from the neighborhood, and her new tenants. A young couple lived in the rooms that Ezat Sadaat had occupied. The husband had fought in the war, was wounded several times, and was finally sent home. He was a nice man, and assisted Maryam whenever she needed help with repairs and such things. Her other tenant was a widow who lived by herself. Maryam told me that Hamideh had died years ago, and Ezat Sadaat died of "shock and grief" when her nephew was executed during the Shah's regime.

It was easy enough, I thought, to attribute many things to "shock and grief," considering all the blows that had been dealt to people.

"How could that happen, she just fell down the stairs?" Maryam asked, confounded by Pari's accident. "She was a wonderful girl, and her fate was so terrible."

After a while I got up and walked from room to room. In my old room stood the crib that Maryam had kept in the basement after I outgrew it. It had a lace canopy and thick, protective cushions of a pale green silky material with a leafy pattern. A large rag doll, wearing a full-skirted blue satin dress and a blue ribbon in her hair, lay on one side. It was my doll from childhood. I held it in my arms and rocked it as I used to.

I woke every day to sparkling sunshine pouring into the room, to the sights of the trees and bushes in the courtyard, the murmur of Maryam saying her prayers, and felt utterly serene, as if I had no concerns in the world and was living moment by moment.

My serenity was shattered when I visited Pari's friends and her absence was all too real. They were preoccupied with their own problems and losses but Pari's name came up, followed by sighs and silences.

I couldn't find the hairdresser I had met on my previous visit. The house where she had her salon was now a religious school for children. I had hoped her cousin who knew Taheri could find out Bijan's whereabouts for me.

I wanted to see Mansour, partly to find out if he knew where Bijan was. But Zohreh told me Mansour had married and left Tehran, transferred by the company he worked for, but she didn't know where.

When I visited Pari's grave, I hoped that miraculously Majid might be there again but alas there was no such luck. I felt a loss, as if it were Pari who wanted to see him again one more time, give him another chance.

One morning I went to an office to leave my passport for "inspection." It would be returned to me at the airport when I was leaving Iran. This rule applied to all Iranians coming and going, part of the security during the Shah's time and continuing now.

It was siesta time when I returned to Maryam's house. In the alley I could smell saffron, turmeric, and dried lemon. A woman wrapped in a chador came out of a house in the middle of the alley and walked in my direction. She was deep in thought, seeming oblivious of her surroundings. When she saw me, she stopped suddenly.

"Oh, Nahid, I'm Batul. I knew you were visiting. My mother heard the news from Maryam." she said. "I was planning to come and see you."

Batul, my friend who had been with me in the school courtyard when Father came and took me away.

"It's amazing you recognized me," I said excitedly as we embraced and kissed.

"There are traces of the child Nahid in you."

"I see some of the child Batul in you, too." Her face was still round, her features soft, but now there was a touch of anguish in her expression and manner, as I saw on the faces of many people in Iran.

"We've had so many dark years, but thank God finally things are getting better. It must be hard for you to live so far away from home. I'd miss my family, this neighborhood, so much. Home is home, even with all its problems."

Forty-one

The next day I went to my old elementary school. I found it on the narrow, cobblestoned street lined with yellow-brick houses that looked new. The school was tucked between the stationery store that had always been there and a candy store. I stood in front of the school and stared into the courtyard. The large wooden door with bas-relief designs at the top was wide open. I could see students wandering around wearing head scarves and dark gray *rupushes*.

The day Father came and took me away rushed back to me all at once. I had been particularly happy that year, partly because I loved my teacher, Miss Modaresi. She was young, with long, lustrous brown hair and large dark brown eyes. Dimples appeared on her cheeks when she smiled. She read a poem or a few pages of a story to us every day. The themes were often nostalgic for what had been left behind or lost. Part of a poem floated forward from the recesses of my mind:

> *. . . a half-forgotten house, full of sunshine one moment and shadowy*
> *the next . . .*

A bell rang, interrupting the images of those long-ago days and brought me back to the present. The students rushed into classrooms, and then I could hear voices reciting lines from a text:

Roses come out every spring, nightingales begin to sing.

A gray-haired man came out of the school and started pruning the dried branches from trees on either side of the door. I told him I used to go to school there many years ago.

"You must miss home. Nothing is like home," he said.

How much happier I would be if it were possible to mesh my present life with the one from those faraway days, I thought. I wouldn't feel so fractured inside, so full of longing, envious of everyone who has easy access to their homes and loved ones. This was the price I was paying for the independence I had fought so fiercely for.

When I returned, Maryam gave me a bundle of letters she had saved, some were from me when I lived in Ahvaz, a few were from Mohtaram. As she prayed I read the letters.

A letter I wrote to her from Ahvaz said:

I miss home. I don't want to be here. Every day when I come back from school I expect to find you in the house. I'm waiting for you.

Another was from Mohtaram to Maryam:

I'm happy to give you one of my children. I know how sad you are that you don't have any of your own. I'm sending the ring along. . . . You know, my dear sister, that you should give it to her when she gets married.

When Maryam paused between her prayers I asked her about the ring.

"Look behind the curtain in that room," she said, pointing. "I found it there a few days ago and meant to take it out for you."

I sensed reluctance in her, as if there was something hidden in that ring.

She resumed praying and I went into the room. A curtain covered the alcove where Maryam used to keep bedding, pillows, sheets, and quilts. The curtain was dark blue with yellow daisies on it, probably fabric left over from a dress. I pulled the curtain aside. There was no bedding there now, just random items—a brass candlestick, a prayer rug, a rosary, a box. I opened the box, but it was filled with odds and ends, a tortoiseshell comb, several golden bobby pins, like the ones my grandmother wore, a yellow silk handkerchief. As I put the box back, my hand touched something. It was a blue velvet cloth tied at the top with a thin white ribbon. I untied the ribbon and found inside a gold cardboard box with a floral design on it. Inside the box was a gold ring with a cluster of tiny diamonds.

I put it on next to my wedding ring. It fit perfectly. When Maryam finished praying I showed her the ring on my finger.

I thought of the stories I had woven around Mohtaram having an affair with a jeweler.

At first, when they passed each other on the streets, she and the man exchanged glances.

Could it be true? It was such a taboo subject that I could never discuss it with Maryam or Mohtaram.

"I'm happy you have it now," Maryam said, but there was a touch of sorrow in her face. "I imagined you would live near me when you got married." Then she repeated what she had said when she visited me in Cambridge, "But it wasn't our destiny."

Epilogue

I began visiting Maryam regularly after that. When Khomeini died in 1989, things were not as strict as during his reign. Iran-America relationships have never been mended. President Bush, in his State of the Union address on January 29, 2002, named Iran, along with Iraq and North Korea, an "axis of evil." Now in 2006, there are huge tensions over nuclear weapons being made in Iran under the latest president there.

I know firsthand, though, that Iran's government hasn't gone from good to evil, but rather from bad to perhaps worse. Under the Shah's rule people didn't have most of their rights. I experienced firsthand my sister Pari automatically losing custody of her son when she left her abusive husband. During Mohammad Khatami's two terms as president (1997–2005), Iran went through a period of relative reform. Part of that was due to Khatami making the Internet accessible to a large number of Iranians. Women frequenting the hundreds of Internet cafés in large cities in Iran to go to chat rooms or look at blogs in Farsi and other languages have become aware of different ways of life. There are more women than men in universities now, and many girls hold jobs.

But then, rules in Iran are in constant flux and I have to assess the political climate every time I visit. At times I have had to hide my American passport in the lining of my clothes or I have left it with the American consulate in Istanbul; at other times I have been able to show it with no trouble. Sometimes I needed a letter of permission from my husband to go to Iran; at other times I didn't.

Typical of the meandering and unpredictable life my family and I have led, on one visit I found Maryam and Mohtaram living together. Maryam had rented out her house and moved in with Mohtaram and Farzin, who was divorced. They lived in an apartment on the top floor of a three-story building that Mohtaram purchased in Tehran. It was interesting how the apartment accommodated their individual needs, combining modern and old elements. It had a modern kitchen and bathroom but was set in a courtyard with high walls in the traditional Muslim fashion. From its balcony the turquoise dome of a mosque was visible. It was furnished with sofas, tables, chairs, and also thickly woven rugs on the floor and cushions to lean against. The building was on a quiet, tree-lined street but was within a few blocks of the bustling Vali Asr Avenue with shops carrying both traditional and modern merchandise. Maryam liked to spend time on the balcony facing the courtyard. "Sunlight soothes my aching knees," she told me.

I could see that Mohtaram and Maryam were closer to each other than to any of us children. In some ways we had let them down. I lived far away from Maryam, shattering her hopes that I would one day share my daily life with her. The idea of destiny became abstract to her at times when she was faced with reality. My brothers had no intention of returning home. Manijeh's blaming Mohtaram for her unhappiness in her first marriage, though in the form of a very mild protest, had hurt Mohtaram enough for her to comment on it. Farzaneh, married with two daughters, lived far away, out of the country. Farzin was "in her own world." And Pari, of course, was no longer alive.

"Pari, my dear firstborn daughter, was the focus of all my attention until Manijeh was born," Mohtaram told me. "Manijeh was weak and needed attention. I neglected Pari too much." She began to cry with fresh grief. "My wonderful Pari, I wasn't there for you when you needed me." Her grief and regret were deep and real.

Maryam even slept close to her sister, on a mattress in the ell of Mohtaram's bedroom. Mohtaram had adopted some of Maryam's values and now she prayed. This wasn't due to pressure from the regime—there was no way that the new ideology could be enforced in the privacy of homes. It was because Mohtaram wanted to be close to her sister.

The last time I visited, Mohtaram and Maryam both needed care. Maryam's arthritis had become more severe and she could walk only with the help of a cane. Mohtaram also could barely walk, although it was not clear what the underlying problem was—the doctors said it could be due to partial paralysis from a minor stroke.

Surprisingly Manijeh had moved into the second floor of Mohtaram's building. She was divorced from her second husband, and both her children were in America, living with their father's relatives. Manijeh devoted herself to taking care of Mohtaram, Farzin, and Maryam. She made sure that everything was running smoothly for all of them. She supervised their daily tasks and solved problems as they came up. She found a family, Nasrin and her husband and two children, to do the cooking, shopping, and cleaning, and to take care of the flower beds and the pool in the courtyard. In exchange, they lived rent free in the first-floor apartment and were paid a small salary. Our old servant, Ali, had moved out of our family's house years ago and now worked in an orchard belonging to his wife's family.

On Nasrin's day off, Manijeh did the shopping and cooking and helped my mother, aunt, and sister to take showers. She went out and returned with bags full of fresh produce, meat, bread, and pastries. She was happy to be of help to them. Of course, not everything about a person is in the open and explainable. Still, I had not expected Manijeh to be capable of so much tenderness and self-sacrifice.

Images from the past of Mohtaram's love for Manijeh kept coming to me: Mohtaram putting her arm around Manijeh and saying, "Isn't she an angel?" Mohtaram putting a flower in Manijeh's hair and saying, "She's like a flower herself." It is poetic justice, in some small way, that Manijeh is now Mohtaram's caretaker.

Once I had a chance to be alone with Manijeh. It was a pleasantly cool and sunny afternoon and I was sitting on the balcony.

I felt the old tightening in my chest as Manijeh came out and sat on a chair there, too. We had barely interacted during the visit.

"So much time has passed, so much has happened since those days at home," she said.

"Yes, it seems so far away and yet so near. I think of those days all the time."

"I wish I had behaved differently when you came home. I was so insecure and jealous. I haven't forgiven myself for accusing you of being the cause of Javad breaking our engagement," she said.

I was startled and shook my head vaguely.

"The truth is he was in love with another woman," Manijeh went on. "There's so much more to what happened." Her face, which had retained its beauty, became tinged with bitterness, making her look older for a moment. She sank into herself.

"I didn't see Pari for years," she said after she came out of herself. "I wish we had been able to reach out to each other."

"I wish she was here with us now."

"Yes, it's hard to believe what happened, how it happened. When she and I were both home at the same time, I could tell she was deeply unhappy. She used strong words. Once, after an argument with Father, before storming out of the room, she said, 'I'd rather jump off a bridge than stay with Taheri.' Another time she said, 'I wish I were dead.' But then at other times she seemed happy enough. She was excited about some projects she had taken on at the high school. And she kept up her hope that she would gain at least part-time custody of Bijan, which of course never happened. In a way we both lived in dreamworlds for a while, she hoping she would have her son back, that she could pursue acting. And me thinking I would win my husband's heart from that other woman."

The mountains had turned into a gray-blue curtain. Over the courtyard wall I could see streetlamps going on and children who had been playing on the sidewalks leaving to go home. Men rode by on bicycles, carrying loaves of bread, bags of pastry, and fruit.

"Time to get dinner ready," Manijeh said.

We got up and went inside. I was struck again by how the passage of time and all the new experiences had obliterated certain feelings and even perceptions. Those feelings we used to express by shouting, "I hate you," had simply melted away. We were now middle-aged women. We had lived with losses, traumas that, though of different natures, were so great in magnitude that they canceled out the long-ago grievances.

❋

It makes me happy when I think of Maryam and Mohtaram being so close to each other at this stage of their lives. Although I still view Maryam as my mother and it is her I address as "Mother," I have come to completely forgive Mohtaram and love her. I am grateful to her for being accommodating to Maryam. I am also more aware than ever of how difficult her life was— married at the age of nine to a grown man, starting at the age of fourteen to give birth to ten children and then losing so many of them. I imagine her and Father together in bed on their wedding night, he experienced with women, and she completely innocent, no breasts, no pubic hair. A child next to a grown man. I love Manijeh now, too, for devoting herself selflessly to Mohtaram, and Maryam and Farzin benefiting from it, too.

But the loss of Pari has left a hole in my existence, made deeper and darker by my uncertainty about what happened, how it happened. I have tried to track down her son but haven't succeeded yet after all these years. When I look at a photograph of Pari on my desk, with her hopeful bright smile, images rush back: how my loneliness disappeared the moment she entered our house in Ahvaz, she on the stage playing Laura, my dreams of writing a play for her, her telling me, as I read her a story, "You're so good." Then she is here with me, sitting next to me.

Yes, dearest Pari, it is to bring you back to life that I write this book.

READING GROUP GUIDE

By Nancy Ohlin

1. One theme in *Persian Girls* is that of belonging. Growing up, the author feels that she does not belong in Iran. But she feels likewise in the United States, and describes "the ambivalent feelings that had plagued me over the years in America, being neither here nor there" (page 202).

Why does she feel that she does not belong in Iran? Why does she feel that she does not belong in America? In your own life, do you have similar challenges of trying to bridge two cultures, two religions, or two other conflicting worlds?

2. Pari begs her father to help her divorce her first husband, Taheri, saying: "Aren't I entitled to some individual happiness?" Her father responds: "[Y]ou're under the influence of those American movies. Their idea of individual happiness is selfish and it has hurt their sense of family life. That's why so many Americans are miserable, lonely, killing themselves with drugs and alcohol. What we have is superior; each person should think of the happiness of the whole" (page 171).

What do you think of the father's statement? Does the pursuit of individual happiness—whether it's true love, education, pleasure, freedom from a bad marriage, or something else—ultimately detract from family, community, society? Can you name examples from your own life in which you chose individual happiness over the happiness of the whole, or vice versa?

3. Another theme in *Persian Girls* is destiny. When the author is a girl, her adoptive mother, Maryam, says to her: "It was your destiny to be my child. As soon as a baby comes into the world an angel writes its destiny on the baby's forehead" (page 25). Later, the author says: "I hadn't accepted that as a child, and now, too, I believed that it was my own sheer determination that had enabled me to come to America" (page 150).

Do you believe in destiny? Do you feel destiny played a role in the author's life? Do you feel that destiny has played a role in your life?

4. Throughout *Persian Girls*, Iranian women and girls are said to have to hide or downplay their beauty, and are even flogged for wearing lipstick or nail polish or for not observing the *hejab* properly (e.g., page 254). In contrast, the author discovers a serious beauty culture in the United States, at Lindengrove College. She recounts that before mixers with boys from other schools, "the bathrooms on my floor were filled with girls checking their makeup, spraying perfume on their necks and arms, fluffing up their hair, and examining their dresses one more time" (page 149).

What do you think of the two cultures' attitudes about women and beauty? Do you feel that both Iranians and Americans "judge a book by its cover" in similar albeit contrasting ways?

5. How do the women in *Persian Girls* support one another? How do they fail to support one another? How do men come between the women? What do you make of the scene in which Nahid and her friend Mahvash are temporarily estranged from each other because they desire the same man, the writer Ardavani (page 114)? How do you interpret the author's observation about her Lindengrove classmates: "If a student had plans with a female friend and then a boy called and asked her out at the same time, she would automatically accept the date and cancel plans with the girlfriend" (page 143)? Have you had similar experiences in your life?

6. The author's parents refuse to let Pari marry Majid, the man she loves. In reaction, the author says: "I wondered if Father and Mohtaram were evil. But my

grandmother, whom I loved so much, had done the same to her daughters, had forced them to marry men she and my grandfather chose. They themselves were victims of the oppressive system that dictated to people how they should feel and live their lives" (page 69).

How much did culture and religion shape the choices the author's parents made for their children? If her parents had been born in another time and place, would they have made different choices? For instance, would they have allowed the author to stay with her adoptive mother, instead of bringing her back to Ahvaz against her will? Would they have allowed their daughters to pursue their dreams and marry for love? In your own life, how much do you feel that culture and religion shape your choices? How much do you feel that culture and religion shaped your parents' choices for you?

7. After her father's death, the author says: "He had had so much power over me, had forcibly changed the course of my life, but ultimately much of it had been for the good" (page 242).

What do you think she means by this? Does she, in hindsight, agree with the choices he made for her? Do you think that she has regrets about defying some of her father's choices, by, for example, not returning to Iran after graduating from Lindengrove? Or is her statement simply a testament to the power of forgiveness? Did anything about the author's relationship with her father remind you of your own relationship with your father?

8. After the author's father forces her to return to Ahvaz, her biological mother, Mohtaram, is cold and distant to her. This goes on for many years. But then, the author overhears Mohtaram saying, "Nahid treats me like an enemy," and wonders: "Was it possible that I had started the pattern of coldness between us? Was it me who had rebuffed her that first day, years ago, when Father brought me home?" (pages 99–100). The author also worries about betraying her adoptive mother if she opens up to Mohtaram even a little. Later, before she leaves for Lindengrove, she accuses Mohtaram: "You gave me away." Mohtaram offers an explanation and then embraces her for the first time since she was a baby (page 136).

How do the author's relationships with Mohtaram and Maryam evolve over the course of the book? By the end of the book, has the author made peace with the fact that she has *two* mothers? Did anything about the author's relationship with either Mohtaram or Maryam remind you of your relationship with your mother?

9. The author repeatedly begs her father to let her go to an American college; he repeatedly says no. Then, one day, shortly after the Ayatollah Khomeini is arrested, he announces that he has changed his mind, and has even picked out a school for her.

Why do you think he changed his mind? Was he afraid that she would get into trouble in the increasingly repressive political climate—or was it something else?

10. In a note at the beginning of the book, the author says: "This is a book of my memories, as I recall them, and what I was told when I was old enough to understand. I haven't interviewed family members and friends to get their impressions of certain incidents in our lives."

In reading *Persian Girls*, did you ever find yourself wanting to know the other characters' points of view—the author's father, Mohtaram, Maryam, Pari, her other siblings, Pari's two husbands, Pari's lover Majid, and so on? Do you imagine that their accounts would be very different from the author's? In what way? In general, how can a writer achieve "fairness" or "completeness" in work of nonfiction that is told strictly from his or her point of view?

11. After Pari's death, the author becomes obsessed with finding out the truth of why she died. Do you feel that she accomplishes this? How do you interpret the events of Pari's life and death? In the end, the author says: "Yes, dearest Pari, it is to bring you back to life that I write this book" (page 288). Did she succeed in doing this for you as a reader?

12. After Pari reveals her love for Majid to her sister, the two promise each other that they will not succumb to arranged marriages. "We promised each other that we would marry only for love," the author relates. "Arranged marriage was a disaster, we decided. . . . We didn't want to be links in that long chain of tradition

that went back to our ancestors. Pari and I had to break the pattern" (page 66). Why do you think Pari eventually broke this promise and agreed to marry Taheri?

13. At Pari's wedding, the author overhears a conversation that suggests that some Iranians get into trouble with the law because they try to act "too Western." One man says: "It's all the Westoxication that creates turmoil." Another says that Iranians shouldn't envy or try to imitate Americans: "Our view of America isn't all realistic. If you examine the country closely you see serious problems there. All the suicide, murder, violence. There's no soul." A third man agrees: "[There's no] closeness between people there, no sense of family. They are a lonely crowd."

What do you think about these statements? Do you believe that the United States has a "Westoxicating" effect on other cultures? After the author and Pari see the movie *A Star Is Born,* Pari longs to be more American: "Those women can choose a career, marry a person they love. . . . We aren't given any options. Freedom is just a trophy the Shah dangles before us" (page 52). Do Pari and the author— before she comes to the United States—have a realistic view of this country?

14. When the author first comes to the United States, she gets various reactions to the fact that she is Iranian. The dean at Lindengrove insists that she wear her "native costume"—a chador—for Parents' Day, even though she did not wear it back in Iran (page 143). The father of her classmate Linda asks the author: "[H]ow do you like our country so far? Isn't it lucky you came here?" (page 153). Linda's mother tells her: "You're so much more refined than other foreigners" (page 154).

What do you think of these comments? Are they racist? In your life, how do you distinguish racist comments from nonracist ones, especially if they seem friendly or benign on the surface?

15. How much did you know about recent Iranian history before reading *Persian Girls*? How did your views about Iranian politics and culture change after reading the book? How did your views about American politics and culture change after reading the book?

© Maria Anderson

ABOUT THE AUTHOR

❋

Born in Iran, Nahid Rachlin has lived in the United States since college. Her works include four novels—*Jumping Over Fire, Foreigner, Married to a Stranger,* and *The Heart's Desire*—and a collection of short stories, *Veils.* As a student, she was awarded both a Doubleday-Columbia fellowship from Columbia University and a Wallace Stegner fellowship from Stanford University. Among her honors are the Bennett Cerf Award, a PEN Syndicated Fiction Project Award, and a grant from the National Endowment for the Arts. Rachlin currently teaches at the New School University and the Unterberg Poetry Center of the 92nd Street Y, and is an associate fellow at Yale University. For more about Nahid Rachlin, visit www.nahidrachlin.com.